JOAN

NEW YORK TIMES BESTSELLING AUTHOR

JOAN
LIFE BEYOND THE SCRIPT

JOAN LUNDEN
WITH TAMELA RICH

LASEGA
BOOKS

JOAN: Life Beyond the Script
Copyright © 2026 by Joan Lunden

All rights reserved. No part of this publication may be reproduced, stored in a retrieval system, or transmitted in any form by any means, electronic, mechanical, photocopy, recording, or otherwise, without the prior permission of the publisher, except as provided by USA copyright law.

No patent liability is assumed with respect to the use of the information contained herein. Although every precaution has been taken in the preparation of this book, the publisher and author assume no responsibility for errors or omissions. Neither is any liability assumed for damages resulting from the use of the information contained herein.

The QR codes in this book are provided for your convenience and link to videos on YouTube and other third-party sites. These sites aren't owned or controlled by the author or publisher, and availability may change over time.

Published by Lasega Books, an imprint of Forefront Books, Nashville, Tennessee.

Distributed by Simon & Schuster.

Library of Congress Control Number: 202592604

Print ISBN: 978-1-63763-492-9
E-book ISBN: 978-1-63763-493-6

Cover Design by Bruce Gore, Gore Studio, Inc.
Interior Design by Mary Susan Oleson, Blu Design Concepts

Printed in the United States of America
26 27 28 29 30 31 RR4 10 9 8 7 6 5 4 3 2 1

BEHIND EVERY SUCCESSFUL WOMAN IS . . .

As I contemplated what I wanted to express in this dedication, I was struck by something I read in a newsletter recently about women and aging: "As we age, the ache for connection gets louder, and more vital. The secret to joyful longevity isn't just green juice. It's community."

It made me think about my own personal connections and who was in my close community—those who I immediately want to call with any good news . . . or sad news . . . or often for advice.

I thought about all the aspects of my life that this book explores, which began in the 1960s, when women were still expected to limit their dreams to homemaking and childbearing. However, from an early age I learned that when I said yes to unexpected opportunities, more of them came my way. One by one, each experience brought me further than I could have imagined.

Looking back, I sometimes wonder how I pulled it all off.

But of course, I know the answer: It was only possible with the help of an amazing group of extraordinary women—intelligent,

DEDICATION: BEHIND EVERY SUCCESSFUL WOMAN IS . . .

loyal, and hard-working. And thus, this book's dedication became clear: **Behind every successful woman is a cadre of other strong, capable women who helped her get there.**

This ensemble of women doesn't consist of childhood friends or former college roommates—they are the women who worked by my side over the past five decades, colleagues who became family. They traveled the world with me, helped manage my career and, at times, my home life too. They made it possible for me to balance the demands of a national broadcast career with motherhood. Along the way, they became my confidantes, my closest girlfriends, and my lifeline. These women are still such an important part of my life and we get together for lunch regularly. There is no question, I could never have done it all without them.

Let me introduce them to you.

When I moved to New York City and then transitioned from local news to *GMA* cohost, the network paired me with TV veteran Chickie Silver to guide me as I learned to navigate my new role. She became like a second mother—advising me on everything from what tone to take in an interview to what I should wear. Chickie helped me hire Elise Silvestri—fresh out of college, just starting her career. It was her first job, my first national role, and I had a seven-week-old baby in tow. Neither of us knew exactly what we were doing, but we figured it out together. Elise went on to become a talk-show producer. She later worked with me on other programs, and after years of Elise helping me with *my* baby at work, I made sure that she was able to bring *her* baby to work. She stood beside me as a matron of honor at my wedding to my husband Jeff Konigsberg, and I've stood beside her through marriage, motherhood, divorce, and remarriage. Decades later, she still manages my speaking engagements. Our bond has never wavered.

DEDICATION: BEHIND EVERY SUCCESSFUL WOMAN IS . . .

Stepping into Elise's big shoes, Debbie Bierman ended up supporting me in a phase of my life neither of us anticipated: the tumult of a painfully public divorce. She not only had to manage my schedule and travel, as expected, but she also had to wrangle a relentless press, while helping me stay grounded enough to do my job. As with so many of the women who worked beside me, I celebrated her weddings and baby showers, just as she steadied me through storms.

Jill Seigerman came into my life when I was a single working mother with three young girls. We worked together for eight years, and what an eight years it turned out to be! She always described her role as "staying two steps ahead of Joan"—ensuring cars, flights, and hotels were booked and interviews all ran seamlessly, but she did so much more than that. Jill saw me through my last years at *GMA* and into the uncharted territory that followed as I took on daring exploits on *Behind Closed Doors* and went on to reinvent myself again and again. Along with Elise, she was a matron of honor in my wedding to Jeff.

When I started Joan Lunden Productions, my daughter Lindsay Weinberg presented me with a thoughtful business proposal for why she should helm operations. For over a decade, she ran my company as vice president, in charge of managing the staff as well as every other aspect of my career. A talented writer and producer, she was a tireless worker and a loyal protector of me and my Joan Lunden brand.

It's an amazing gift in life when one of your children joins you in your life passion, and in my case, two of them did. Lindsay's younger sister, Sarah Krauss, stepped in at one of my most vulnerable times—fighting breast cancer. Drawing on her talents and experience as a writer and producer, she documented and recorded my daily battle and developed a website, *Alive*, to help other women as

DEDICATION: BEHIND EVERY SUCCESSFUL WOMAN IS . . .

they struggled with the disease. Not only were Lindsay and Sarah the perfect people for their jobs, our work together connected us in ways none of us could have imagined.

When I was finishing this book, it was during one of many brainstorming sessions with my current partner-in-crime, Nicole O'Neill, that I got the idea for this dedication. We were discussing a list of things I needed for the book—copy that needed to be written and videos we needed to find. I couldn't help but be in awe and great appreciation for how she handled each request, saying calmly and confidently, "I got you. I'll work on this tonight when my daughter goes to sleep." It's what we women do. And it's what we women do for each other. It reminded me of what Margaret Thatcher said: "If you want something said, ask a man; if you want something done, ask a woman."

And finally, within my close circle of smart, capable female friends is one who would literally walk the plank for me, Laura Morton. She is in a category of her own. She has worked with me over the past three decades on videos and books, and I'm proud to say is now the publisher of this one. Laura and I met just after I divorced in 1993—another challenging point in my life and career. She was my wing-woman as I reentered the dating world, but thanks to her, I didn't have to face it alone. Once again, I had a fiercely loyal woman to stand by me, demonstrating the power of friendship and the power of the female connection.

This book is dedicated to all of them—to the women who have lifted me, steadied me, and stood beside me.

CONTENTS

An Interactive Memoir 11

Introduction 13

1. Come Fly with Me 17
2. Meet the Blundens 25
3. Missing 33
4. Picking Up the Pieces 41
5. Go Ahead—Underestimate Me. That'll Be Fun 47
6. Where in the World Is . . . Joni Blunden? 55
7. Coming Home to Change 63
8. Getting My Foot in the Door 73
9. Just Say Yes! 79
10. If I Can Make It There, I Can Make It Anywhere 85
11. Small-Town Girl on the Mean Streets of NYC 103
12. Accidental Anchor 117
13. Stepping Out in the Big Apple 125
14. The Fire Island Fiasco 131
15. The Glass Ceiling Won't Break Itself 137
16. Two-Timing 143
17. Ready in the Wings 149
18. I'll Have My People Call Your People 155
19. If Opportunity Doesn't Knock, Build a Door 165
20. An Exercise in Diplomacy 177
21. Two Phone Calls 183
22. Learning the Ropes 189

23. Good Morning, I'm Joan Lunden 195
24. Behind the Scenes at *GMA* 201
25. Perfecting the Balancing Act 211
26. Early Momfluencer 223
27. Changing of the Guard 231
28. Out of the Shadow 235
29. Life in a Fishbowl 245
30. Field of Land Mines 253
31. The Flying Inferno 261
32. He Had Me at Hello 271
33. Trouble on the Horizon 277
34. The Takeover and the Takedown 285
35. Head Up, Stay Strong, Smile, and Move On 293
36. Finding the Good in Goodbye 301
37. When a Door Closes 305
38. Becoming Brave and Bold 311
39. The Unexpected Weight of Opportunity 323
40. Reinvention Never Retires 329
41. Love, Motherhood, and the Freedom of Ageless Living 337
42. From Patient to Advocate 347
43. Then There Was One 357
44. Speaking of Legacy 365
45. Surfacing with Intention 375

FOR YOUR VIEWING PLEASURE 381
ACKNOWLEDGMENTS 385

AN INTERACTIVE MEMOIR

I've worked in television for most of my adult life, and so much of my story exists on video, from the news segments I anchored to the commercials, campaigns, and live events I took part in. So when it came time to write this book, I realized I had a unique opportunity: I could not only tell you my story but show it to you.

Throughout these pages, you'll find QR codes that look like the one at the bottom of this page. Each one links directly to a video connected to the story you're reading—whether it's a pivotal moment in my career or a behind-the-scenes glimpse into my personal life. To use the codes, open the camera on your smartphone and hold it over the image. A small prompt or link will pop up on your screen—usually near the top or the bottom. Be sure to tap that prompt; it's what actually takes you to the video. Just seeing the QR code in your camera isn't enough.

I hope this interactive experience brings the story to life in a whole new way.

GMA's final tribute to Joan, 1997

INTRODUCTION

I've come to realize that I have spent my entire life in a full sprint—always chasing, always pushing forward, always revving the engine to its highest gear.

The running started early. By elementary school, I was placed in a grade-up program, surrounded by older kids, where I was expected to keep pace. I raced through the years, skipped a grade in high school, started college at sixteen, and launched into a career that was anything but slow. My life wasn't something that unfolded naturally—it was a high-performance roller-coaster ride, looping through five presidential inaugurations, five Olympics, and three royal weddings. I've reported from twenty-eight countries, jumped with the Golden Knights, trained with SEAL Team 6, and, yes, even bungee-jumped off a bridge in New Zealand.

And yet, looking back now, I sometimes wonder: *Did I even have time to absorb it all?*

There are moments—big, important moments—that I should have treasured forever, but I find myself turning to Google and YouTube just to remind myself that they even occurred. That's what happens when life moves at warp speed: you don't get to slow down long enough to truly take it all in.

I've met the most incredible people along the way—big dreamers, big thinkers, big doers—who dared to aim high, and

INTRODUCTION

in doing so changed the world. I've met computer geniuses who quite literally altered the way we live our lives. I've met doctors and researchers who have spearheaded groundbreaking discoveries. I've met busy, everyday moms who have marched on Capitol Hill to demand social change, and twentysomethings who have created international organizations to serve the needs of the less fortunate in countries around the world. These people lived their purpose.

It made me wonder how I defined my purpose. Was it in the power of the interviews and world events I covered? Or was my purpose to use the platform I'd built to spotlight important medical breakthroughs and advocate for social change?

Exploring that question is one of the reasons I'm writing this book.

The other? To answer the question people love to ask someone who has been in the public eye: *How did you move on?*

WHAT HAPPENS AFTER THE SPOTLIGHT SHIFTS?

When I left *Good Morning America* after twenty years, a reporter asked me, "After being in a role like this, do you think you'll ever be able to top it?"

Rude, right? But also . . . a fair question.

Twenty-five years later, I guess the answer is *no*.

Not that I needed to top it—or even wanted to.

The truth is, I didn't chase the next big TV gig in earnest. Instead, my career morphed, evolved, and expanded in ways I never expected. And maybe that's the real story here: reinvention, resilience, and what happens when you step off a fast track and into the unknown.

INTRODUCTION

Of course, constantly pushing forward is what landed me at so many crossroads in my life. In my twenties, I found myself at one such crossroad: breaking into the male world of media. In my thirties, I found myself at yet another crossroad: staying on the job and in the public eye throughout my pregnancy and negotiating a network contract that would allow me to bring my baby to work. In my forties, I faced the crossroads of midlife, when I didn't recognize myself or my body, took charge of both, and transformed my health. In my fifties, I married a man ten years younger than I was and dared to have two sets of twins—with the help of a surrogate. In my sixties, challenged by social stereotypes about aging, I pivoted from interviewing change-makers to championing medical and social causes myself. And now, in my seventies, I'm daring to live my new "younger-older life," refusing to be a prisoner to the age on my driver's license.

We've all been at crossroads; we've felt the ground beneath us shifting. Perhaps you've had to reinvent yourself—and maybe you weren't ready to. If so, we have more in common than you might think.

Here's what I've learned: No matter how successful you are, life will knock you down from time to time. The question is, how do you get back up?

You might be reading this book because:

- You're going through a tough time, and you need a kick in the ass to keep going.

- You're trying to balance career and family, and you feel like you're failing at both.

INTRODUCTION

- You're watching your industry push you out in favor of someone younger, cheaper, or shinier—and you don't know what's next.

- You've lost someone you love, and you're wondering why you still feel that ache years later.

I've been there. I've experienced all of it, and I promise you that even when you don't know what's coming, you can always bet on yourself.

YOUR ROAD MAP FOR REINVENTION

If you're buying this book for yourself, I hope it gives you solace to know that you're not alone.

If you're buying this book for your daughter, I hope she sees it as a blueprint, a road map for what's coming.

While I was the first woman to do a lot of things, the truth is that reinvention isn't just for the ambitious—it's for all of us.

And if there's one thing I want you to take from this book, it's this: No one gets to tell you when your best days are behind you. *You* decide that.

I've learned that you don't have to chase the next *big* thing to keep growing. Sometimes reinvention doesn't look like topping what came before; sometimes it's about embracing what *is* and being open to whatever comes next.

That's where I am now.

Still dreaming. Still doing. Just with a little more perspective.

Chapter 1

COME FLY WITH ME

May your dreams defy the laws of gravity.
—H. Jackson Brown Jr.

An alarm blared inside the cockpit.

Colonel Buda blurted out, "Oh shit." Not the words one wants to hear from a U-2 pilot when approaching the Armstrong Limit, where exposure to the atmosphere can kill you in sixty to ninety seconds.

This wasn't how today was supposed to go.

For nearly two decades, I had been the host of *Good Morning America*, delivering breaking news and stories that took viewers around the world. They had seen me go on plenty of adventures, but this was different. My prime-time series, *Behind Closed Doors*, took my reporting to another level, granting me access to places the public never saw—from training with Navy SEALs to learning spy techniques with the Central Intelligence Agency.

This day had started like any other high-adrenaline *Behind Closed Doors* shoot—except this time, I would be strapped inside a U-2 spy plane, heading for the edge of space. The U-2 wasn't just a plane, it was a Cold War relic, a spy aircraft designed to fly undetected at the highest altitudes. No civilian had ever been granted permission to fly in one before.

I was encased in a pressurized suit like those worn by the first space shuttle astronauts, which caused even the simple act of breathing to drain my strength. As I stepped out of the transport van and shuffled toward the flight line, where the massive U-2 reconnaissance aircraft waited, I felt as agile as the Stay Puft Marshmallow Man of *Ghostbusters* fame. Air Force Squadron Commander Colonel Mario Buda was already several paces ahead, moving effortlessly despite the weight of the oxygen tank strapped to him. By contrast, I was struggling with the ten steps leading into the cockpit.

Once I was aboard, two crew members snapped, strapped, and secured me into the tight space behind Buda (most U-2s have only one seat). I wasn't a passive joyrider that day—I had undergone an extensive Air Force training program that taught me how to read my dauntingly complex instrument panel and how to escape into near space if, heaven forbid, a disaster occurred.

The moment the canopy closed over my head, the claustrophobia that had been creeping in since they sealed me into the space suit intensified. I reassured myself by briefly reaching my right hand down along the edge of my seat to locate the ejection handle, just as I'd practiced during flight simulation the day before.

I tried to refocus, shifting my thoughts away from disaster response to our upcoming flight sequence. At one point, Buda would briefly turn the controls over to me so I could pilot the aircraft while cruising at 150 knots. I rehearsed my opening lines for the show several times, committing them to memory:

Flying at sixty thousand feet above the earth, at the edge of the atmosphere in a U-2 reconnaissance plane, I'm Joan Lunden, and this is

Behind Closed Doors . . .

Before we taxied, I had my first official duty: calling the control tower. "Pinion seventy-one, taxi with Lima." (True confession: I was pretty proud of myself, and we hadn't even taken off yet.)

Our request to taxi onto the runway came back affirmative.

The moment was surreal, yet somewhat familiar. I was practically born in the cockpit of a plane—albeit not one that could fly into near space like the U-2. My father was an avid private pilot—so avid that he wouldn't marry my mother until she qualified for a pilot's license. He said he wanted her to be a copilot in the air as well as in his life.

As we accelerated down the runway, a blue Camaro driven by Major Brandon King sped alongside us for a final visual check. "Aircraft is good," he assured us through our helmets' comms system. "No leaks. All flight controls in position. You're clear."

Buda's voice crackled through my helmet. "Watch your knees. Here we go."

In seconds, we were climbing in what felt like a vertical trajectory.

Our three-hour flight plan from Beale Air Force Base called for us to travel along California's northern coast, where I grew up, and onward to Washington State before heading south again. Since my eighty-two-year-old mom still lived nearby in Sacramento, the producers let me bring her along. "Glitzy Glady," as everyone called her, was undoubtedly flirting with the generals in the control tower now that I was out of sight.

I looked to my left and marveled at Mount Shasta's peak below, haloed by piles of cumulus clouds. (I've been a TV weathergirl, so I know my cumulus from my cirrus.) Just as I was taking it all in, Buda slid the sunscreen from the canopy. What an experience it was, zooming between earth and space in Technicolor contrast between aquamarine skies below and deep cobalt space above. I never wanted this moment to end.

Since the mid-1950s, the Air Force and the CIA have used Lockheed's U-2 for gathering vital security information without being detected by ground-based radar or reached by enemy fighters and missiles. We have this aircraft to thank for, among other findings, photos of Soviet missiles aimed from Cuba at the United States during the Cold War. What blows my mind is that the U-2 doesn't have the same landing gear other planes have, with one wheel in the front and two in the back. Instead, the U-2 relies on only two wheels in alignment, like a bicycle, making it the most difficult airplane in the entire Air Force fleet to land. One of the crew described the landing process to me as "trying to drive a semi down a tightrope."

After Buda checked the atmospheric conditions, he determined that it was safe for me to take the plane's yoke in my hands. "We don't wanna go below about 130 or above about 160," he reminded me. As I learned in my training, if you fly the plane 10 knots too fast at altitude, it will literally rip apart and disintegrate, and if you fly 10 knots too slow, you can stall the craft and take it into a spin. *No pressure, Joan.*

"Am I doing okay?"

"You're doing great. Ready to climb again?"

Buda took the yoke back and we climbed to more than sixty thousand feet, where we admired the curvature of the earth. I had never expected to see this except in those gorgeous NASA pictures.

The show's executive producer and director, Eric Schotz, broke into my reverie and told me to record the show's open. "Flying at sixty thousand feet above the earth, at the edge of the atmosphere in a U-2 reconnaissance plane, I'm Joan Lunden—"

An alarm blared inside the cockpit.

Buda blurted, "Oh shit." Not the words one wants to hear from a U-2 pilot when approaching the Armstrong Limit, where exposure to the atmosphere can kill you in sixty to ninety seconds.

My heart was beating in my throat. "What?"

"We just lost the AC."

I took a long breath and thought, "No big deal. I'm in a pressurized suit. Who cares about air-conditioning?" But then Buda clarified that *AC* didn't mean air-conditioning in this instance.

"It's our alternating current, Joan. We're at risk of fire!"

My hand reflexively shot to the ejection handle, and I reminded myself that if given the command—*egress, egress, egress*—I would pull it and the mechanism would thrust me out of the aircraft, strapped to my seat. At an altitude of three miles, the parachute would automatically open, and I'd have to simultaneously manage the pressure in my space suit and guide myself to a safe landing with the straps. No biggie. I'd dreamed the whole sequence last night and had a perfect landing.

My positive self-talk was interrupted when Buda opened his mic and made what could only be called a holy-shit announcement: "This is Colonel Mario Buda calling in an emergency aboard a U-2 reconnaissance aircraft. We are currently headed to Beale Air Force Base; we have a full load of fuel and two souls aboard."

Two. Souls.

Beale went on high alert, mobilizing rescue crews. Just as the airfield came into view, Buda spoke again, his voice controlled but firm. "Joan, I'm sorry to say we have another problem. I'm trying to put our landing gear down, and my instruments say it isn't responding."

It isn't responding?

As I listened, I still didn't feel a sense of panic—although, in retrospect, I probably should have been more scared. But I'd flown in many planes for this show, and we'd never had a story go sideways when covering the armed forces. Ever.

"I need you to look in the lower left corner of your instrument panel," Buda instructed. "Tell me if the gear is up or down."

I checked. "Still up."

All hell then broke loose in the control tower. We would need to do a low flyover so the ground crew could visually confirm whether the landing gear was truly stuck or if it was just a faulty reading.

As we flew ten feet above the runway, I glimpsed the emergency vehicles—bright lime green, lined up in formation. Alongside them were firefighters in silver Teflon suits, braced for the worst. Forget that this unusual aircraft has only two wheels; we would need to land on the plane's belly—no wheels at all—if that landing gear really was still up inside the plane.

Buda's voice remained steady. "Joan, I want to go over emergency procedures, just in case the plane catches fire. Are you with me?"

With him? I was hanging on his every word.

Meanwhile, Eric had realized my mother was in the control tower. She hadn't caught the gravity of the situation—too busy flirting with an Air Force colonel, thank God. Eric discreetly signaled the officer and whispered to him, "Please get her out of the tower now. Her husband was killed in a plane crash." The officer whisked her away under the guise of a base tour.

The moment of truth came as Buda flew the huge aircraft over the runway for a visual inspection from the ground. We were so low that I could now actually see the firefighters' faces through their helmets. At the speed we were traveling, it all happened in the blink of an eye, but we could hear the cheers in the control room through our helmet comms as it was reported that our landing gear was firmly down.

After all that, we circled around and came in for a normal landing after a flight that was anything but normal.

As we taxied in, my mind drifted to my father—his excitement over his shiny new twin-engine plane, the bigger, more powerful aircraft that had worried my mom. The one that had taken his life.

And here I was, pushing limits, staring down fate, flying at the edge of space.

I guess I truly am my father's daughter.

 *An emergency aboard Joan's U-2 flight*

Chapter 2

MEET THE BLUNDENS

Encourage and support your kids, because children are apt to live up to what you believe of them.

—Lady Bird Johnson
Former first lady of the United States

Let me tell you about my family, the Blundens. (Yes, that's my real last name, as I'll explain later.)

My father, Dr. Erle Murray Blunden, was born to Seventh-Day Adventist missionaries in New South Wales, Australia, in 1912. His mother, Nellie, was an English teacher; his father, Harold, was a pastor who later became a global church leader. Dad was raised *proper*—pageboy haircut, short pants with knee socks, ramrod posture, and afternoon tea.

In 1914, Harold and Nellie set sail for China with their three young children to further their missionary work. Twelve years later they moved to the US and settled in Southern California. This is where the Adventists had established the College of Medical

Evangelists, which later became Loma Linda University School of Medicine and was where Dad earned his medical degree in 1937.

He wasted no time in setting up a practice in Fair Oaks, a Sacramento suburb, taking over from a doctor who had passed away. But medicine wasn't his only love; his fascination with aviation soared alongside his career. He joined the Fair Oaks Flying Club, and before long, he and a group of fellow enthusiasts purchased 150 acres to create a private airport called Phoenix Field.

Around this time, Dad's world expanded in another life-changing way: He met my vivacious mother.

Mom, Gladyce Lorraine Somerville, was born in 1919 in Chaseley, North Dakota, experiencing an upbringing quite different from my father's. She grew up doing farm chores and attending a one-room schoolhouse. When she moved to California as a young woman, she landed a well-paying job in Shell Oil's accounting office. She told me she felt like the luckiest girl in the world when she met my father—handsome, wholesome, respected. Dad, for his part, was drawn to the fiery redhead who spoke her mind, including her declaration that she was *not* willing to become an Adventist. Dad didn't drink, smoke, or eat meat; Mom loved her filet mignon with béarnaise sauce—oh, and the martini with an olive that goes perfectly with that.

Theirs was a classic case of opposites attracting. And yet, despite their differences, they shared one deep longing: to have a family of their own. After multiple miscarriages, Mom and Dad decided to adopt the newborn son of an unmarried hospital nurse. Dad was in the delivery room when Jeff was born, and Mom was over the moon when they brought him home. Her girlfriends threw her a baby shower, but she spent most of it in the bathroom throwing up—turns out she was pregnant with me. Seven months and twenty-nine days after Jeff's birth, I arrived. We were raised like twins, and were often dressed alike.

While Dad was setting bones and saving lives, Mom carved out her own domain. She was a force in the Women's Auxiliary for doctors' wives, serving as president and chairing fundraisers. The secret to being a good 1950s wife and mother, according to her? "After a day of shopping and lunching with the girls, come home and immediately throw some onions in hot oil. As the aroma fills the house, everyone thinks you've been cooking all day."

I can't resist sharing one of her tricks with bacon. I often did my homework in the kitchen while she made her favorite sauce, always starting with diced onions sautéed in bacon grease. One day, it hit me: *Dad doesn't eat bacon.*

"Is there a difference between eating bacon slices and using bacon drippings in a recipe?" I asked.

Mom's mischievous smile told me she'd been caught. "A little bacon adds so much flavor," she said smoothly. "Daddy doesn't *know* it's in there—he just knows he likes my cooking."

At seven, I accepted this logic without question. Was it an ethical dilemma? Maybe. But did I ever rat her out? Nope. Not even when Dad complimented the meal. Still, I must have felt a little guilty, since I remember it so vividly decades later.

Ironically, today's health-conscious world praises plant-based diets, proving Dad and the Adventists to have been ahead of their time. But Dad's passion for health went far beyond our dinner table; it followed him into the operating room and extended to every patient he cared for.

At the end of the day, when other doctors headed home, Dad went back to the hospital for rounds, checking in on patients after their surgeries. If I was lucky, I got to tag along—the aspiring Dr. Joan

Blunden at Dad's side. I always selected a pretty dress with a bouncy crinoline skirt underneath and buckled-up black patent leather Mary Janes, worn with white ankle socks trimmed in frilly lace.

On the drive to the hospital, Dad would tell me about the patients we would visit and what to expect in their rooms. Mercy General had a distinctive "hospital smell," likely from the cleaning solvent used to make sure everything was purified. Even as a little girl, I never found the smell off-putting because I knew it kept the patients safe. Daddy told me so.

In each patient's room, Dad proudly presented me to his patients. "This is my daughter, Joan. She wants to be a doctor one day."

The patients always talked to me as Dad lifted their wrists to check their pulse, counting the beats for thirty seconds, according to the time on his gleaming silver watch. Sometimes he asked me to do a pirouette to show off my dance skills, which I'd learned at the Shari Lou Casey Dance Studio, along with acrobatics, tap, and baton twirling.

In later years, my dance studio marched in every parade within a ten-mile radius. Shari Lou and her husband, Jim, plucked me from the majorette formation to perform acrobatics on my mom's two-toned Ford Fairlane 500. Classic car fans know it's technically a hardtop, but at the push of a button, the top folded into the trunk. Jim Casey built a large wooden platform (painted gold, of course) that rested atop that open space, leaving a small cutout for himself at the wheel. I wore a gold sequined costume and gold ballet shoes as I performed handstands, headstands, cartwheels, and splits atop the moving car.

Enough 1950s nostalgia; I mention some of these memories only to emphasize the deeper meaning of such experiences. Little boys have always had coaches who encouraged them to test their mettle and win trophies and accolades. While little girls also get that encouragement today, it's been a long time coming. Thanks to the Caseys, I got a chance to stand out too. It's hard to overestimate how these opportunities benefitted my self-confidence, which would serve me well later in life.

By 1959, Dad's vision for a "fly-in ranch" on our five acres at Phoenix Field was taking shape. Our home was built around an airplane hangar. There was no garage, much to Mom's dismay, but when Dad said, "Let's fly to Reno for dinner," he won the day. We'd walk down the hall past our bedrooms, and he'd slide open the massive hangar doors, pull the plane onto the tarmac, fire up the engine, and taxi out to the runway.

Several of Dad's medical colleagues were flying enthusiasts, and it wasn't unusual for them to land at the airport and taxi right up to our house—like pulling into a driveway—for weekend brunch. Mom put on quite a spread, but Dad had one request: "Glady, they're pilots! Dial back the screwdrivers and mimosas."

Dad was a quiet giant in cancer surgery who often flew to other cities for conferences or to assist on complex surgeries, and sometimes we went along. On one trip to San Francisco, Mom took Jeff and me shopping while Dad gave a lecture. Later, we went to the hotel where Dad was speaking. As Mom led us into a grand ballroom, we saw hundreds of doctors listening to Dad talk. Another man stood beside him on stage, nodding along. Near the end, Dad introduced this man as his patient and asked him to remove his shirt.

I gasped, grabbing Mom's hand. Sections of the man's body—from his shoulder to his waist—were gone.

Mom squeezed my hand and whispered, "For some patients, removing the sick part means they can live a long and happy life. Your dad says scientists are working on new ways to treat cancer patients."

We weren't supposed to see or hear any of that, but we did. And I never forgot it. Moments like that made me see my father not just as *my* dad but as someone who was larger than life—someone who saved people. Someone who always seemed invincible.

Maybe that's why it was so easy to believe nothing bad could ever happen to us. Life was full of adventure, and in the winters it meant heading to Squaw Valley, known these days as Palisades Tahoe. My parents bought a home there just before the 1960 Winter Olympics, and some of our happiest memories were made on the slopes in the company of the Klein family. Dr. Marvin Klein was a gynecologist and close friend and colleague of my dad's. He and his wife, Helen, were raising two children, Richard and Barbie, who were the same ages as my brother and me.

Dr. and Mrs. Klein and my dad, who were all excellent skiers, would hire an instructor to spend the day with us kids so they could enjoy the more advanced slopes at their own pace while we advanced our skiing skills under supervision. What about Glitzy Glady? Mom never learned to ski, but she always dressed to look the part in the very latest ski attire. And she'd complement her outfit with an oversize pair of tortoiseshell cat-eye sunglasses—never ski goggles, as they would mess up her weekly shampoo and set.

January was "Birthday Month" in our family, and if there was snow in Squaw Valley, that's usually where we celebrated Mom on the fifteenth and Jeff on the twentieth. On Friday morning, January 17, 1964, Mom was scrambling eggs and frying her famous hash brown potatoes when we heard on the morning TV news that the entire state of California was expecting stormy weather, and Lake Tahoe was in for heavy snowfall. Jeff and I were super excited at the prospect of skiing on fresh powder.

MEET THE BLUNDENS

That weather report may have been a source of concern for my mom, since we were driving there, and also because Dad would be flying in from an American Cancer Society conference in Los Angeles in his new twin-engine plane, a Cessna 310. This was a big step up from the single-engine planes he'd always flown.

Mom was against that plane. "It's way more powerful and, therefore, way more dangerous." But Dad's confidence was unshakable, and as much as Mom worried, she eventually relented.

By the time we arrived at our destination, the morning sun was shining so brilliantly that it made us squint. Sure enough, as the day progressed, a light snow started to fall. I will always remember that magical scene as we schussed back and forth across the slopes, our tongues catching snowflakes. Jeff and I squeezed every possible moment out of that day, quitting only after the snow started driving sideways, our visibility too impaired to continue. We had to call it a day. A fabulous day.

After dinner and a mind-numbing episode of *The Flintstones*, the phone still hadn't rung. As conditions outside worsened, Mom would pick up the receiver every once in a while to be sure we hadn't lost service. While my brother and I were excited to hear from Dad about his first flight in the new plane, we were so exhausted that we didn't complain when Mom said it was time for us to go to bed.

Of course, that left Mom waiting alone, worrying. She knew Dad had taken off from Los Angeles because he'd called to say it was stormy, so he had to file a VFR flight plan with the LAX tower, which was customary when flying in inclement weather.[1]

As an obedient child, I went to bed as asked, but my last

---

[1] A Visual Flight Rules (VFR) flight plan outlines a pilot's intended route and departure and arrival times, and it allows pilots to fly under both VFR and Instrument Flight Rules (IFR) during the same flight.

thought before falling asleep was, *I sure hope nothing has gone wrong in that big shiny new airplane.*

I dozed off and dreamed about flying with Dad. Not in the new Cessna—I'd never even seen the inside of it. No, we were in our red-and-white Beechcraft Bonanza, and Dad was guiding us back toward Phoenix Field. As was his usual custom, he spoke a little ditty into his headset: "Little flower in the tower, tell me the runway and the hour." This was his signature way of asking the controller what runway to land on and at what time. Mom always told him it was way too corny, but sometimes I heard the air traffic controllers chuckling.

I invite you on a photo journey—from the 1950s to the present, my life has been full of twists, turns, and tremendous joy. Come walk with me through the years that shaped who I am.

MY CHILDHOOD

Flying was such a big part of our family life that our 1959 holiday card featured Mom, Dad, my brother, Jeff, and me in an airplane.

With Dad and his nurses in 1954. We'd just returned from a Christmas vacation in Honolulu, where he brought each of them a fresh Hawaiian lei.

Me at age six with Mom—"Glitzy Glady" to her friends. When I'd ask what I could be when I grew up, she always said, "Anything you want—just hitch your wagon to a star."

LEARNING STAGE PRESENCE

Left: At nine years old, I performed the hula at a local Polynesian restaurant—one of my first chances to feel brave in front of an audience. Moments like that were my earliest confidence builders. Right: At ten, my dance instructor plucked me from the majorette unit to perform acrobatics atop my mom's convertible in local parades. Baton twirling and dance competitions weren't frivolous to me; they were lessons in confidence, stage presence, and the thrill of competing to win.

The summer of 1967, after high school graduation, Mom suggested I enter a local beauty contest—"Miss Fair Oaks." I was blonde, but Mom said, "Only brunettes win beauty pageants." So we dyed my hair brown. I won. Second place was a blonde. Moms are always right.

A TURNING POINT FROM MEDICINE

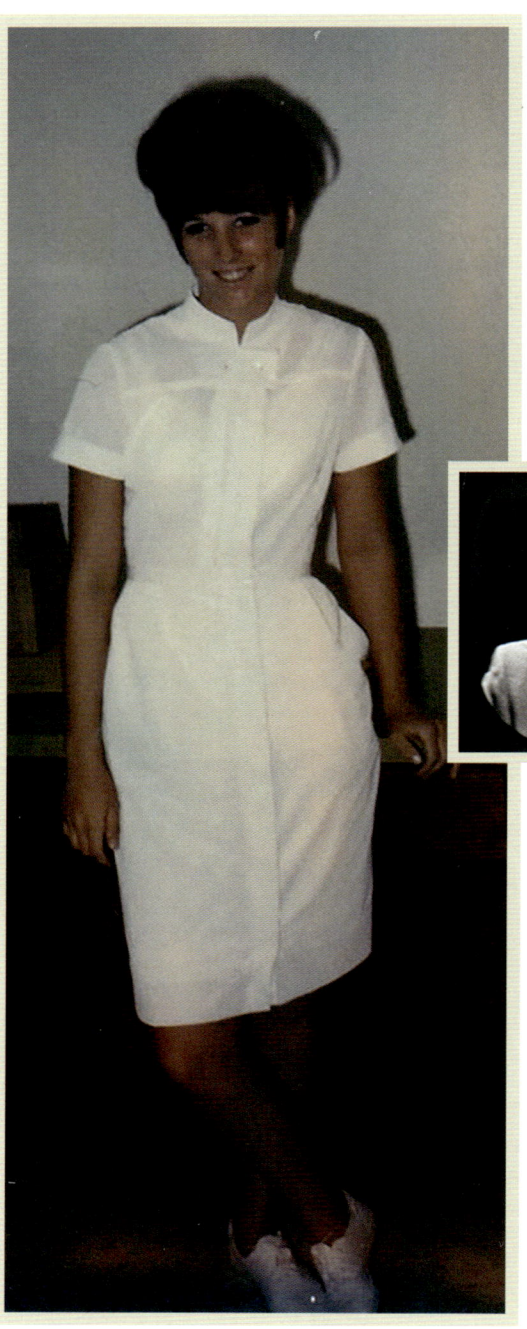

Still in my "Miss Fair Oaks" brown hair and still dreaming of becoming a doctor like Dad, I took my first job after high school in 1967 as an assistant to the X-ray techs at the hospital he had helped found. That's also where I learned that stitches and scalpels weren't for me.

My Dad on KCRA-TV in the early 60s talking about the latest advances in cancer surgery. Little did he know that years later, I'd launch my television career on that same station.

. . . TO JOURNALISM

I'd only begun my news career in 1973 but I moved to NYC in 1975 to take a job as a street reporter for WABC *Eyewitness News*. This is my first press photo.

GOOD MORNING... AMERICA

On August 28, 1980, I took my seat next to David Hartman on the set of *Good Morning America*, the beginning of the most incredible adventure of my life.

Right: No one predicted that this photo—holding my seven-week-old daughter Jamie on my first day as a *GMA* host—would make headlines nationwide. What ABC meant to keep quiet, that I'd been allowed to bring my baby to work, became *the story*.

BRINGING BABY TO WORK

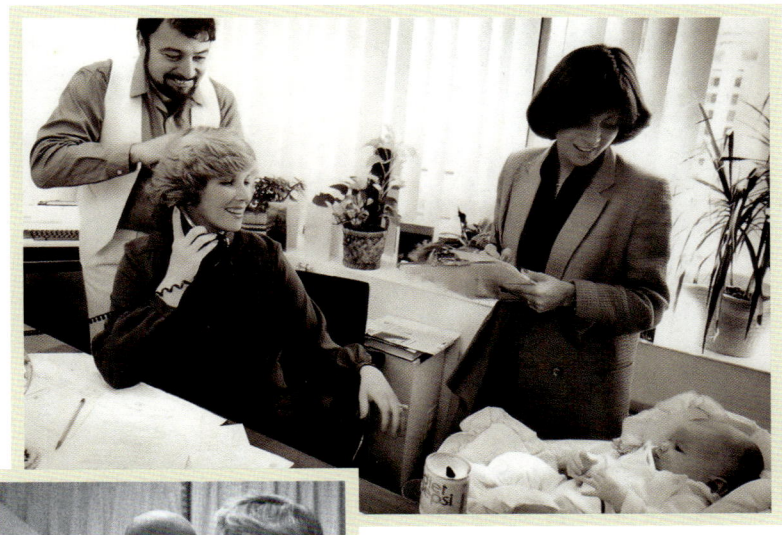

We were all grateful that baby Jamie was content and cooing as I got ready for a press interview. When she fussed, my first *GMA* assistant and lifelong best friend, Elise Silvestri, walked her around the office like our little *GMA* mascot.

Left: ABC turned the dressing room next to mine into a nursery for Jamie. She had a crib in my office too. I used to joke that Jamie had more beds than Conrad Hilton.

As my daughters grew older, they loved coming to work with me on the days they could play with and bottle-feed baby snow leopards.

LIFE ON THE SET . . .

On the *GMA* set with Charlie Gibson, Joel Siegel, and Julia Child in 1989. Left: Sylvester Stallone drops by to discuss his 1982 releases *Rocky III* and *First Blood*.

In 1988, I was so excited when I got to interview Audrey Hepburn, one of my all-time favorite actresses. She wasn't there to discuss her films but rather her humanitarian mission.

Whenever Billy Crystal was a guest, we knew it would be fun!

We were a tight supportive team, Charlie, meteorologist Spencer Christian, and me. After breaking my shoulder in 1992 from a horseback-jumping accident, I spent months with my arm in a sling. Fans sweetened the ordeal by sending me hand-painted slings of their own.

Diane Sawyer, Barbara Walters, and me—three women making our way in morning television.

Left: At the piano with the amazing Stevie Wonder (1995).

LIFE ON THE ROAD

In 1985, I flew to Morocco to cover Michael Douglas, Danny DeVito, and Kathleen Turner as they filmed *Jewel of the Nile*.

Left: When several of our scheduled global trips were sidelined by political unrest in the Middle East, we launched our series of bus tours across America.

The *GMA* trio in DC for yet another presidential inauguration.

In 1994 when we took the show to Alaska, Charlie and I got a helicopter tour of the glaciers. We set down on the Mendenhall Glacier to get this shot. The glacier behind us almost looks like a painting, but it's real, and it's moving—slowly making its way down the gorge.

Right: In 1994, we set sail on Chesapeake Bay to talk with four-time America's Cup winner Dennis Conner. Conner let me take a turn at the wheel of *Silver Heels*—does it look like I know what I'm doing?

Left: Mush! Taking the reins of a dog sledding run at the Krabloonik resort at Snowmass Village in Aspen, Colorado (1996).

In 1991, we greeted America from the stage of the Grand Ole Opry. We were all smart enough not to try to sing that morning.

Nashville, 1991—on our Southland Bus Tour. Naturally, I volunteered to take the giant trike for a spin.

In 1995, we did the show from Bigfork, Montana, and I tried my hand at roping.

At the 1995 Superbowl, as usual I was volunteered to compete in the NFL Experience, thus the outfit, LOL.

Right: In 1994—live from a ridge of the Grand Canyon with Charlie. The standing rule that day was: "Don't look down!"

In 1994, we took the show to China, broadcasting live from Hong Kong. It was a time of uncertainty and unease as the city awaited the 1997 handover from the British government to the People's Republic of China.

MY FINAL *GMA* SHOW

Charlie and I traveled the world with Spencer. They were like family to me. No matter what was going on, we could always make one another laugh.

Just as I was there for Celine Dion during her first *GMA* appearance—when she was nervous and still learning English—she was there for me at that last show offering strength when I needed it most.

As Celine Dion sang to me during that teary finale show, I was surrounded by my family; my mom, my daughters Jamie, Lindsay, Sarah; and of course, Jeff. As you can see from our faces, it was a beautiful but bittersweet tribute. I think the look on Mom's face says "How dare you take my fabulous Joni off this show." You tell them, Mom!

THEN AND NOW

THEN: On this morning in 1996 we unveiled our new *GMA* set to America. ABC News had taken over the reins of the show and replaced our set with this duplex loft design. Little did we know at the time that we, too, would soon be replaced.

NOW: In the summer of 2024, Charlie asked me to join him on stage with the Cape Cod Theater Group in Falmouth, Massachusetts, to perform in A.R. Gurney's acclaimed play *Love Letters*. It tells the story of a lifelong friendship told through letters exchanged from childhood to adulthood. Charlie had seen the play forty years earlier, soon after joining me on *GMA*, and had always dreamed of performing it with me.

LOOKING INTO THE FUTURE

This is what I look like after a full night's sleep—
time to relax, renew, and get ready to reinvent.

Chapter 3

MISSING

There are moments which mark your life.
Moments when you realize
nothing will ever be the same
and time is divided in two parts:
before this, and after this.

—John Hobbes in *Fallen*
(screenplay by Nicholas Kazan, 1998)

I awoke to a hand on my shoulder and a whisper in the dark. "Joni, wake up."

Jeff's voice pulled me from a deep sleep, the edges of my dreams still clinging to me. His grip on my shoulder was firm. Not a nudge—a grip. "Come on," he said, his voice tight. "Mom needs us downstairs."

Mom needs us?

When we reached the living room, I saw them—two uniformed officers standing just inside the front door, their hats in their hands. The taller officer cleared his throat. "Mrs. Blunden, they've lost contact with your husband's plane."

Mom sat on the couch, gripping the armrest as their words hit the air like a thunderclap. I felt Jeff stiffen beside me.

Lost contact. Not crashed. Not dead. Just . . . lost.

Mom faced us, a steeliness in her voice. "We don't know anything for sure yet."

There had been heavy rain and a lightning storm in LA when Dad had taken off, and the weather was still so bad that they had been unable to send out search planes.

When the officers left, Mom took a deep breath and squared her shoulders, trying to put on a good face. After clearing her throat, she said, "Let's not jump to conclusions. We still don't know what happened, kids. Let's start packing up our things so that we can leave as soon as it's light out and get back home as quickly as possible."

I turned toward the stairs, my legs heavy beneath me. *Missing.* The word sat like a weight on my chest. What if we got home and there was no news? What if we got home and the news was worse?

Outside, the wind howled against the windows, snow piling up in thick drifts.

By morning, the officers were back, and a snowplow was clearing a path to the main highway. The officers explained that Dad's plane was presumed down somewhere between Los Angeles and San Francisco. *Presumed down.* It wasn't the same as *gone*, but it wasn't far off either.

Then came the excruciatingly slow drive home to Sacramento. We sat in an unnatural, uncomfortable silence, afraid to say anything. And what could we say? Despite our entire lives being shaken to the core, I think Jeff and I were afraid to ask questions; we knew there were no answers—not yet, anyway. Besides, Mom had her eyes glued to the snow-packed road, determined to get us back home safely, where hopefully we'd get word about Dad's whereabouts.

MISSING

I kept my forehead against the cold glass window, watching the trees blur past, my thoughts drifting to Dad. Dr. Erle Blunden, cancer surgeon. The kind of doctor people trusted with their lives.

It seemed like we couldn't go anywhere without someone stopping him—the grocery store, a restaurant, the gas station.

"Dr. Blunden, you saved my mother's life."

"Because of you, my husband lived to see his grandchildren."

"You operated on me seven years ago, and I've been healthy ever since."

I had been so proud to walk beside him as his little shadow, knowing that *my* dad was the one everyone looked up to. It was an extraordinary life. A *secure* life.

Until now.

By the time we arrived home, the house was full—doctors' wives were bustling in the kitchen, murmuring in hushed tones. Despite the crowd, I didn't hear a thing.

At sunrise the next day, the search resumed. By midday, the news arrived. As we started hearing details of the morning search and the discovery of the crash site, with no survivors, it was difficult watching Mom's normally smiling, exuberant face melt into agonizing sadness and despair. I felt as if there was absolutely nothing I could do to help. My mother could organize a fundraiser, manage a household, and keep a social calendar running like a well-oiled machine. But this?

There was no script for this.

The wreckage of Dad's new airplane, or what was left of it, was found strewn over the side of a mountain in Malibu Canyon less than half an hour's drive from the LA airport. No one could figure out what had caused the crash. It would never be known.

The house didn't feel normal—not only because Dad wasn't there but also because so many ladies were helping Mom plan the funeral and coordinate meals. I didn't know where to put myself, and in a strange way, I almost felt like an onlooker. While the adults were scurrying around, "handling everything," my brother and I were lying on the carpet in the living room in front of the television. Nothing seemed real, and it was too scary to try to make sense of what had happened or what effect it would have on our lives. When you're young and your existence depends on your parents, it's hard to imagine how your life will go on in such circumstances.

I overheard one of the women say that it would be a closed casket, and then Mom asked if she could just take a look at him before the service. I had to control my gasp when I heard the answer: "Oh dear Glady; the plane hit the side of the mountain at full speed, so there really isn't a body left for you to see."

One of the ladies who was there comforting Mom had gone through the same thing herself a year earlier. Her physician-husband had been one of my dad's close colleagues and also one of his flying buddies. Like Dad, her husband had crashed along with another doctor as his passenger. It was my dad who had gone to her house to tell her the horrible news. I heard her say under her breath, "Those men and their damn airplanes."

In fact, the Bonanza aircraft that Dad and so many of his colleagues had flown for years had once been dubbed by the aircraft industry as "the doctor killer."

In the midst of the turmoil that was playing out in our house, I think the adults sometimes forgot that young ears were nearby, and while we may not have looked like we were paying attention, we were curious and listening. One of the doctors' wives said to my mom, "Joni was such a daddy's girl; I imagine this will be harder on her." She was right. I was very much a daddy's girl. He was always telling me how I could be anything I wanted to be when I grew up. My dad's constant words of encouragement ring in my ears to this very day. They are, quite often, my inspiration to rise above the roadblocks of life, to succeed as a parent, a spouse, a worker, and a friend, and to be the best I can be.

Decades later, I received a social media message from the wife of an LA County deputy:

> Joan, with a lump in my throat I heard you speak of your father's death. My husband was one of the deputies who retrieved your father's body and that of his passenger. He came home that night extremely upset. Please know we never forgot about that awful accident.

It was only a paragraph, but it was a paragraph connected to my dad's final moments. The only other connection I'd had to the crash had been a grainy black-and-white photograph from a newspaper that I found in my mom's mementos after her passing. With this stranger's remembrance of Dad's crash, I suddenly felt like I could create a mental image of the crash site and what those final moments must have been like for Dad. As much as I didn't want to think about it, I couldn't help myself. I read it again, and again, with tears streaming down my face.

The FAA authorities said there hadn't been enough left of the plane to determine the actual cause of the crash, but they speculated that the plane might have had electrical problems—and perhaps they were unable to trust their instruments. Apparently, Dad had experienced some electrical issues with the plane on the trip down to Los Angeles and put it into service to be worked on at LAX while he was at the conference. They had deemed it good to go; however, after Dad had taken off, there was no radio communication with the plane.

Another theory was that Dad might have had a heart attack. As we received more details, we were surprised to learn that Dad wasn't alone in the plane. He had offered to fly Dr. Byron Hall, a cancer researcher, home to San Francisco on his way to us in Lake Tahoe. Dr. Hall was also an avid private pilot and was likely excited to have a chance to fly in the new plane. From accounts given by people who lived in the area, it appeared that the plane had gone down into the canyon and then back up before plummeting into the mountainous area, seemingly at full speed.

If Dad did have a heart attack, he would have slumped forward, pushing the yoke forward as well and causing the plane to descend rapidly. Since Dr. Hall was also a pilot, he may have pulled my dad back into his seat and yanked hard on the yoke to stop the descent, but as the plane headed upward in a steep incline, that could have caused the engine to stall and they would have plunged back down again.

While Dad was only fifty-one, he was a hardworking, driven man. A heart attack wasn't out of the question, even though he had just had a complete physical, which was required for him to receive the certification to fly the new twin-engine aircraft. That medical report had deemed him healthy and in good condition.

None of us would ever know exactly what had happened in those final moments. There were only theories. Guesses. And grief.

* * * *

MISSING

A long black limousine. A church too small for the crowd. People standing outside in the drizzle, listening over a speaker. These are my recollections of the funeral. When the service ended, my brother and I sat in the limo overhearing people as they passed by.

"So many people in that church are alive today because of Dr. Blunden."

"I don't think there's ever been a funeral this big in Sacramento."

"Oh, those poor children, losing their father so young."

Hearing Dad spoken about in the past tense made my stomach churn.

Inside the church, the pews had been packed with doctors, nurses, and former patients. The sound of crying had filled the air. Even men cried. People had approached Jeff and me to say how much they had loved and respected Dad, and how devastated they were. They were well-meaning comments, but a burden on our young hearts.

Even with the overflowing crowd at the funeral, I don't think I fully grasped how much my dad meant to the world. I had always been his little shadow, walking beside him in hospitals, in restaurants, in grocery store aisles. He was larger than life, a man people depended on. And now he was gone. The world felt emptier without him. Smaller.

Chapter 4

PICKING UP THE PIECES

*Don't pray for life to be easy.
Pray for yourself to be strong.*

—Reverend Phillips Brooks

Anyone who has lost a loved one knows that once the funeral is over, people tend to go back to their normal lives. The family is left to grieve and to figure out how to go on. My father's death was sudden and unexpected. While it changed our family structure, Mom was determined not to let it change our lives entirely. She now had to take over as both mother and father to raise my brother and me. At fourteen and thirteen years of age, my brother and I were just getting to know our dad as young adults. There was so much unfinished business—so much we still needed to learn from him and say to him.

My mom was a strong woman, and while nothing could ever have prepared her for this, she rose to the challenge. "It's the three of us now. We're a team, and we will be okay."

Mom's first order of business was to find a doctor to take over Dad's medical practice. She knew how important my dad's patients were to him, so she desperately wanted to find a doctor who had the personality and background to make them feel comfortable. Without a moment's hesitation she reached out to Loma Linda University to find a Seventh-Day Adventist physician. They recommended a Norwegian surgeon, Dr. Trygve Opsahl, who was cut from the same cloth as Dad—he was serious, soft-spoken, and service oriented. Most of Dad's patients stayed with the practice because of Dr. Opsahl.

Mom also had to figure out how to handle both the family finances and the finances of the multiple business projects Dad had had in the works. He'd launched quite a few endeavors in recent years. While he was a sought-after surgeon, he also had a big dream: to build a much-needed hospital in our community. In 1962, he had helped bring a group of investors together to begin construction on that dream, which would become the American River Hospital.

He had also partnered with his friend, colleague, and skiing partner Dr. Marvin Klein to build their own medical building, the Country Club Medical Center. At about the same time, they bought a plastic surgery hospital out of bankruptcy court in the Los Angeles area. They planned to bring the Bel Air Hospital back to life as a general hospital. Dad was realizing his life's mission: to bring quality health care to more people in need, and to open new medical institutions that would help patients regardless of race, religion, status, or ability to pay.

Mom understood that it was critical for her to dig down deep and find the strength and courage to keep our lives as normal and upbeat as possible. But even our longtime resident gardener, Mr. Dillard, who'd idolized my dad and had always been so loyal, and whom we thought would remain with us and continue to maintain the property that they had worked so hard to cultivate, came to Mom shortly after the funeral. "I'm so sorry, Mrs. B, but I'm afraid I have to leave. I know you're a wonderful person, but I just can't work for a woman."

Putting on a happy face could not have been easy, especially since a lawsuit was filed against my father's estate by the grown children of Dr. Byron Hall, who had perished in the crash with my dad. It was a lawsuit they could never win. It claimed willful negligence, meaning that my dad crashed the plane on purpose with no regard for his passenger. While they would never be able to prove such a thing about Dad—the missionary and doctor who saved lives—it tied up his estate and his life insurance, as well as every business project he'd left behind, as it dragged on through the courts.

Mom had to deal with the attorneys, insurance companies, and bankers while trying to support us. I honestly don't remember being aware of just how difficult that time was for her, but I do remember constantly hearing her on the phone pleading with the bankers to give her more time, until the estate could get settled.

In fact, a few times I remember Mom stopping the car as we were pulling into the driveway, jumping out, and ripping a legal notice off a tree near the gated entrance, hoping we wouldn't ask questions. She was defiant in how she ripped those notices down, but I also think she had to have been embarrassed—in fact, mortified, not to mention frightened—about what these creditors could actually do to us. She eventually told me they were foreclosure notices from dispassionate banks that did not give grace to a widow trying to untangle an estate that was complicated by a lawsuit.

I was too wrapped up in the dramas of my own teenage world to understand the magnitude of what she was dealing with. Then again, maybe my mom did such an amazing job at keeping life normal for my brother and me that I didn't have to. When the estate was finally settled, we were able to stay in our home and life continued, but those few years were really trying for my mom.

Mom's story is not unlike the stories of many other women, who, after enjoying a nice lifestyle, suddenly had to reenter the workforce due to a death or divorce. My vivacious and tenacious mother ultimately decided to go into real estate sales, since, as the wife of a prominent doctor, she knew a lot of people in our town, assuring her a built-in clientele.

Meanwhile, construction on the medical center was almost complete, and those twenty medical offices needed tenants. Since Dr. Klein was a partner in that business and his wife, Helen, was a real estate agent too, she joined forces with Mom. It was a crash course in business for Mom—contract negotiations, leases, financing, and so on.

Mom and Helen also had to get the Bel Air Hospital staffed and ready to reopen as a general hospital. It was an overwhelming task, but in a surprising twist, it also provided an unexpected adventure for Helen's daughter, Barbie, and me. At the end of the school year, the four of us packed up and headed for Bel Air.

Most hospitals in that era were like the ones Dad took me to when I accompanied him on his rounds in my crinoline dresses and Mary Jane shoes, but this one was a contemporary round building perched on a hilltop overlooking opulent mansions. Each patient room had spectacular views of Los Angeles, and Barbie and I were told we could sleep in a different room every night if we wished—and we did.

Our moms gave us an easy task: counting leftover inventory from when the hospital specialized in plastic surgery, like saline breast implants. Barbie and I laughed hysterically as we counted out five hundred right boobies and five hundred left boobies. (There were safety issues concerning rupture and gel exposure with those first-generation saline breast implants, and they were eventually outlawed.) On some days, to entertain us, or perhaps to get us out of their hair as they worked, our moms dropped us at Huntington Beach to spend the day sunning (and, I should add, scheming ways to be noticed by the surfer boys—as if they would ever give two glances to a couple of girls fresh out of middle school).

While it may have been giggles and sunscreen for us that summer, I can only imagine how Mom and Helen must have been feeling at the prospect of it all—interviewing hundreds of people in order to hire nurses, chefs, maintenance staff, secretaries, and a hospital administrator to run the place. With Mom's overwhelming desire to fulfill my dad's dream, each hire and each order for medical and kitchen supplies must have filled her with such relief and satisfaction. In just a few short months, a staff was in place and the kitchen was up and running, ready to serve patients. The hospital was poised for its grand opening. When I think about it now, it was an astonishing accomplishment.

I suspect that the enormity of the tasks before Mom distracted her from her grief and let her begin to heal. In fact, I think that summer away from our family home—the home where Dad's absence was so glaring—served as a healing respite for us all.

I don't think it ever really occurred to me just how young my mom was when she lost my dad, until I turned forty-one and was newly divorced and asking myself some of the same questions she must have been asking: *How do I go forward and create a new life for myself? How will I care for my young children by myself? Will I ever find love again?*

JOAN: LIFE BEYOND THE SCRIPT

I was watching Mom transform herself into a businesswoman, meeting the challenges of the moment while maintaining a calm and positive home life for her children. I now understand that watching her in those years following my father's death, as she remained strong and determined in the face of adversity, provided me a master class in resiliency and reinvention.

Chapter 5

GO AHEAD— UNDERESTIMATE ME. THAT'LL BE FUN.

*Life isn't about finding yourself.
Life is about creating yourself.*

—George Bernard Shaw

That sun-filled summer in Los Angeles with my good friend Barbie felt like a turning point. Finally, I could just be a teenage girl again, tuning out the tragedy and feeling almost normal. As an adult, I recognize that it would have taken more than a summer in Bel Air to lift Mom from her own personal hell, but at fourteen, I was more focused on how to dress and act as a freshman at Bella Vista High. I would be starting school solo, since Mom had enrolled my brother at Menlo, a private prep school for boys in Atherton, California. She hoped he'd benefit from the male influence there, now that Dad was gone.

Like most kids, I was nervous on my first day—everything was new. I had no idea where my locker, classes, or the gym were, and Bella Vista was huge—nearly two thousand students were enrolled there. As usual, I was one of the youngest on campus, mixing it up with the older kids. But I was used to that.

As mentioned earlier, it had started when I began elementary school. The principal's solution to overcrowding was to create overflow classrooms, blending younger, advanced students in with kids in the next grade up. I'd tested above my first-grade level and landed in a second-grade class while still answering to a first-grade roll call. Skipping grades wasn't an option at the time, and with my September birthday, I was already younger than my normal classmates, let alone the second graders. This continued throughout my years in grammar school.

One perk of being in the advanced class? I could take Spanish, which thrilled my dad. He loved flying to Mexico with Mom in our plane, he loved practicing the language with me, and he loved the idea of my following in his footsteps as a doctor. Over breakfast, he'd grin and speak to me in Spanish, delighted that I was absorbing it so easily. "Joni, imagine when you're a doctor and you have Spanish-speaking patients. You'll be able to connect with them in a way most doctors can't." I would smile back, because at that point, I believed I would become a doctor too. But while Dad saw my future so clearly, I was still trying to figure out my place in the present.

In the fall of my fifth grade year, two new faces appeared in my classroom at Earl Le Gette Elementary—fraternal twins, Jed and Jay Johnson. Jay had curly blond hair and a mischievous streak, while Jed was quieter, more preppy. It didn't take long for them to become part of our world. In fact, over time, Jed became like another sibling, and Mom became a second mother to him.

GO AHEAD—UNDERESTIMATE ME. THAT'LL BE FUN.

By 1961, I had completed the sixth-grade coursework, even though I was technically still in fifth grade. When my classmates—including Jed and Jay—moved on to middle school, I was left behind with a group of kids I barely knew.

Rather than letting me advance to middle school, the administration at Earl Le Gette kept me in the same grade, repeating the curriculum while acting as a teacher's assistant. At the time it felt like a wasted year, but looking back, I can see that stepping into that leadership role shaped me in ways I didn't yet understand.

The following year, I reunited with my friends at Kingswood Middle School, where childhood friendships started shifting into what adults called *puppy love*. Jed and I decided we were a "couple"—whatever that meant at eleven years old. We might have held hands or said sweet things to each other, but none of us smoked, drank, or experimented with anything beyond innocent romance.

Over time, our puppy love deepened into a lifelong friendship that lasted until his passing in 1996, as you'll see in later chapters.

At the end of seventh grade, history repeated itself: My friends moved on to high school, and I was left behind once more. I swore to myself, *Never. Again.*

That summer, I strategized. A new middle school—Andrew Carnegie—was under construction, much closer to my home. I had watched it being built, biking past the chain-link fences and dreaming about walking through its gleaming hallways. I didn't actually live within that school district, but I hatched a plan. A few weeks before the school year began, I put on my cutest sundress and sandals, marched into the brand-new office, and pretended I belonged.

"Hello, I'm Joan Blunden," I announced with practiced confidence. "I'm an eighth grader living nearby, and I need to enroll in this beautiful new school."

The office ladies, charmed by my enthusiasm, handed me the enrollment forms, no questions asked. "Just get your parents to sign them," they said.

I couldn't wait to tell Mom that I'd enrolled myself at Andrew Carnegie. She was so proud of what I'd pulled off on my own that she couldn't be mad—although she now needed to register my brother at the school too.

I was barely thirteen and had just pulled one over on the school district! It was my first experience with a truth I would carry into adulthood: *If you want something, don't wait for permission—act like you belong, and people will believe you do.* Simply make your plan and confidently pursue it. Believe in yourself and your ability to make it happen.

That same hunger to push forward, to take charge of my own future, didn't fade once I got to high school. If anything, it only grew stronger.

While my fellow freshmen were worried about football games and high school dances, I was strategizing my early graduation. I wanted to complete high school in just three years, and Mom was on board. I signed up for correspondence courses from UC Berkeley. Between those, summer school, and night classes, my plan got underway.

One afternoon, Mom called me into the kitchen. "Joni, come here and look at this ad for the Hawaii Holiday Summer School." Eight weeks in Honolulu, taking two required classes while living near Waikiki Beach? I jumped at it.

That summer wasn't just about schoolwork—it was about reinvention. It was my first time truly living on my own, staying in a dorm on a hill overlooking the University of Hawaii. Each morning, we attended classes at Punahou (yes, the same school Barack Obama would later attend). By noon, we were on a bus to Waikiki, free for the rest of the day.

Surfing. Sailing. Scuba diving. Or, if you were a teenage girl, suntanning and flirting with surfer boys.

Something about living on that college campus changed me. It felt like I belonged there. If I just kept up the hustle, I would be on a real college campus soon enough.

When I came home, I wasn't the same girl who had left. My confidence had skyrocketed. My wardrobe had transformed—hip-hugging bell-bottoms and crop tops, because come on, it was the sixties. Now I was ready to mix it up with the older, cooler kids.

The true test of my early-graduation plan came when it was time to make my junior year my senior year. Mom and I scheduled a meeting with Mr. Johnson, the principal. I laid out my case—how I had already completed my junior-year coursework and how I would meet all the graduation requirements by the end of the school year.

Instead of cheering me on, he frowned.

"How do I know if I make you a senior that you'll actually complete the correspondence courses and night school classes? Why would I want to take that chance on you?"

I was stunned. Hadn't I already proven I could handle the work? Hadn't I already taken control of my own education? Why was Mr. Johnson staring me down like I was some kid who was in over her head?

Mom, never one to back down, made it clear how ridiculous this was. For the first time, I felt insulted—really insulted—that this man had underestimated me.

We pushed back—hard.

Eventually, he caved.

If we're keeping score, and I know I am, it's Joan 1, Mr. Johnson 0.

I aced all my courses, met the graduation requirements, and proudly walked with the Class of '67. But because one final grade hadn't arrived by gown-ordering day, Mr. Johnson refused to let me wear a white robe and stand with the top 5 percent of my class—even though I had earned it.

No pat on the back. No "Good for you." Just a final jab from a man who had underestimated me.

To this day, I still wonder why my determination wasn't rewarded. Was it because I bent the rules to achieve my goals? Because I was a girl? Would he have treated me differently if I'd been a guy? Maybe a star athlete?

It was 1967. Women couldn't buy homes or have credit cards in their own names. Girls had to wear knee-length skirts to school. But not taking charge of my own destiny wasn't an option. It never even occurred to me that anyone would dissuade me from doing so.

Graduating early was my launchpad into college, but before I took that next step, I wanted to prove something to myself. I had worked so hard to accelerate my education, but what was it all for? Was I really cut out for a career in medicine like Dad? That summer, I decided to find out the only way I knew how: by stepping into his world.

One of Dad's colleagues helped me get a summer job in the radiology department at the American River Hospital, even though at sixteen I was legally too young to work there. Mom and I found a uniform store where I tried on a few different styles. They were all dresses back then, unless you'd qualified to wear scrubs, and I wasn't going to be going anywhere near an operating room.

As I buttoned up my white uniform, I pictured Dad's face—how proud he would have been to see me working at the hospital he had helped to build. I imagined us crossing paths in the halls, his voice calling out, "Lunch in the commissary today?" But that was just a dream. I took a lap around the place to see the plaque on the wall in dedication to him and peeked into the Erle Blunden Library, which housed all his medical books—the ones I used to watch him read in his big easy chair. The halls that should have been filled with his presence only echoed his absence.

Every morning, I loved parking my silver 1967 Ford Mustang in the hospital employee lot and showing my credentials at the employee entrance. I wasn't directly involved with patients; technicians handled that. My job was to collect the X-ray plates from the pass-through door to be processed in the lab. A small role, but in my mind, I was part of something bigger. The ER was next door, but I didn't need to be inside to feel the intensity. Alarms blaring, gurneys rushing in, doctors and nurses making life-and-death decisions. And me? I was just outside, realizing for the first time that this world might not be mine after all.

When I returned home in the evenings, I'd often be so exhausted that I would lie down on the sofa to wait for Mom to finish making dinner and instantly fall into a deep sleep. I was finding that going to school was nothing like adult life in a hospital where you're on your feet for eight to ten hours a day. Mom told me that sometimes she'd just cover me up with a blanket and let me rest for as long as I needed to, with a huge smile on her face, knowing how proud my dad would have been. It was a wonderful exhaustion; I never minded it. And yet I came to understand that it takes a certain personality to work in the medical profession, to remain calm and clear-headed when treating sick or injured people. The enormity of providing care to them humbled me. I didn't have that personality. The blood, the needles, the pressure—it unsettled me in a way I couldn't ignore. For the first time, I had to ask myself, *Am I really meant to be a doctor? And if not, then what?*

If Dad were there, what would he have said? Would he have reassured me, told me that not everyone was meant for the operating room? Or would he have urged me to push through, believing that, with time, I'd get over it? I'd never know. And that was the hardest part.

Letting go of the dream was disorienting. I had spent my whole life thinking I would follow in my father's footsteps, but now that path had vanished. On a deeper level, I couldn't shake the fear that letting go of the dream of being like Dad was also a way of letting go of him. Without that shared path, was I quietly removing myself from his life, and therefore from him?

I felt unmoored, drifting without the anchor of the future I'd once imagined. But while I was still questioning who I was without that connection to my father, Mom was already steering the ship. It was time for college, but you might remember that the summer of 1967 was called the Summer of Love . . . and it featured Woodstock, pot, and protests, in addition to free love. So regardless of the fact that I'd been accepted at UCLA and Stanford, she was not about to let me be exposed to that environment. Nope, not happening.

Instead, Mom had seen a tiny ad for a college called World Campus Afloat (today it's called Semester at Sea), where students studied while sailing around the world. Unbeknownst to me, she had sent my high school transcript and the essay I'd written for the other colleges to World Campus Afloat, and I'd been accepted. That was how I would be spending my first semester in college: traveling the globe!

Chapter 6

WHERE IN THE WORLD IS... JONI BLUNDEN?

The biggest adventure you can ever take is to live the life of your dreams.

—Oprah Winfrey,
The Oprah Winfrey Show, 1997

While other freshmen were hanging posters in dorm rooms and navigating campus maps, I was boarding a cruise ship in New York Harbor—sixteen, solo, and headed for fifteen countries. My college experience didn't begin with a lecture hall; it began with a passport.

Mom shipped my trunk to the SS *Ryndam*, a fifteen-thousand-ton ocean liner transformed into a traveling university. I would be reunited with my belongings when I boarded the ship in New York City.

Landing at JFK, I felt the first real stirrings of independence; I was about to embark on the adventure of a lifetime. A kind man sitting next to me on the plane had suggested I look for a sign outside the airport that read "Bus to NYC," as the Manhattan bus station was a quick walk from the Hotel Pennsylvania, where all the students were to meet up.

After checking in, I made my way to my room, and could already hear music and laughter from students gathering together. As I passed an open door, a cute boy sitting on the floor looked up at me and said, "Hey, go put your bag in your room and come back here." I didn't hesitate—I hightailed it down the hall, dumped my suitcase in my room, and went right back to him. We connected instantly and were inseparable for the rest of the semester. Finding a boyfriend early turned out to be a stroke of luck, considering the student body had a three-to-one ratio of females to males.

That boy was a twenty-one-year-old junior from the University of Arizona, and his friends were also juniors and seniors. They were experienced travelers with American Express cards, vehicles waiting at every port, and reservations at the best hotels. I was sixteen, so I simply followed their lead and evaded questions about my birthdate.

We held classes at sea and took field trips when in port. I enrolled in sociology and world religions, eager to study the cultures I was encountering firsthand. My youth wasn't a hindrance; on a ship traveling from country to country, we were all in the same boat—literally. There wasn't the same rigid grade structure found on a traditional American college campus.

From Portugal to Morocco, Kenya to Japan, I saw a world that challenged everything I thought I knew. In South Africa, apartheid was evident everywhere we went, with signs that read "Whites Only." Apartheid wasn't just an injustice in a textbook—it was a cold, undeniable reality staring me in the face. My classmates and I exchanged uneasy glances. What made this beautiful place so deeply divided? Some of our classmates of color decided to stay aboard the ship rather than face segregation, but it never occurred to me, as a teenager, to stand with them by joining their boycott.

In India, I saw poverty that stunned me—people lying in the streets, dead bodies collected in carts at dawn. In Mombasa, we rented black-and-white zebra-striped vans to explore the Serengeti, only to be stopped at a Tanzanian border crossing at night, where soldiers wielding badass submachine guns made it clear we weren't welcome. These weren't typical college experiences, but they were shaping me in ways I was only beginning to understand.

After a whirlwind semester at sea, the idea of settling into a "normal" college routine back in the US felt suffocating. So, when a classmate from the ship told me about Universidad de las Americas in Mexico City, I didn't hesitate. Another adventure? I was in, and I'm sure my mother was relieved to have me away from hippie college culture for a while longer.

My mom flew with me from Sacramento to Los Angeles, where I was to meet up with my shipmate. Once again, she would kiss me goodbye as I headed off to further exploits—this time at an international college, although now, at least, I had turned seventeen. When we got to LA, we found out at the last minute that the other girl had backed out. I would take the international flight by myself. But I had no intention of missing out on this experience. There was no turning back. This was a go, even if I was making the journey alone.

When I landed in Mexico City, I took a cab to the home where I was to live with a Mexican family. The father had passed away, and the mother took in American college girls to help with the household costs and with raising her three young daughters. None of them spoke any English. Not a word. There were three other American girls living there too, although they were all twenty or twenty-one and on their junior year abroad.

I ended up rooming with a super fun girl from Coos Bay, Oregon, named Diane Chandler. She had studied outside the US since her longtime boyfriend had gone off to Vietnam. She also wasn't looking for the "college drinking and dating experience." Diane and I instantly hit it off; all the awkwardness I felt entering the house melted away. We stumbled and giggled our way through meals, using our best Spanish to ask for fried or scrambled eggs. We thought it was funny at the time, but as I look back now, I'm not sure how the family felt about it.

The college taught its classes in English. When selecting my courses, I was intrigued by one called cultural anthropology. It would cover many of the countries I had recently visited with World Campus Afloat. It was an upper-level class, though, and because I hadn't taken the prerequisite introductory course, I figured I'd go to the professor and talk my way in. After telling him about my round-the-world voyage to fifteen countries and the field trips I took in each one, he actually seemed excited to have me be a part of the class. He felt that I'd have a great deal to add to the discussions. Negotiation . . . successful.

When that spring semester ended, I had no desire to return to the US, and neither did my roommate and new best friend Diane. We did, however, decide that we'd had enough of the college's immersive language experience; it was time to leave the Mexican family we were living with and find an apartment. We teamed up with three other girls and moved into a furnished place. It was nothing fancy, but it had a kitchen—not that any of us knew much about cooking. When the school year ended, the other girls left to go back to the US.

WHERE IN THE WORLD IS . . . JONI BLUNDEN?

What had started as a single semester abroad for me stretched into years. With each passing season, Mexico became more like home.

Diane and I had fallen in love with Mexico City, and we were double-dating guys who were best friends, so why would we want to leave? We both convinced our moms that we would be fine living on our own. It was perfectly safe. Neither mom thought to question us, since we were very sure of ourselves. We found a furnished apartment in a brand-new building in a nice residential area close to the vibrant Zona Rosa, where all the big hotels, chic shops, restaurants, and nightclubs were. When we saw it, we could hardly believe it—the place was decorated in a very contemporary style, complete with a red carpet in the living room. If Diane and I had been party girls—which we were not—we'd have just found the most incredible party house you could want.

At eighteen, I was learning the ins and outs of paying monthly rent and electricity bills. Few apartments had phones, but downtown hotels had centers where we could make collect calls home, so I spoke with my mom only once a month. It may sound odd, but I don't remember receiving letters from her, or sending them either. It seems strange now that I tell it, but I was still a teenager, after all. In retrospect, I can see that we didn't have the typical mother/daughter relationship. I had no need to call and ask, "What should I wear on my date tonight?" I was completely on my own. There was no helicopter parent figuring things out for me—ever. And I loved every minute of that freedom.

Very few apartments had televisions either, so for the entire three years I lived in Mexico I didn't get much news about what was happening back home. And a lot was happening. I couldn't even tell you where I was when Martin Luther King was assassinated in 1968, because I didn't hear about it until much later.

I do remember hearing that an American astronaut was going to walk on the moon, so on July 21, 1969, a few of us went to someone's house to watch the coverage on a small, grainy black-and-white TV. It was quite a moment as Apollo 11 astronaut, Neil Armstrong, stepped out of the *Eagle* lunar module onto the moon's surface and said, "That's one small step for man, one giant leap for mankind." I imagine that, had I been on an American college campus, there probably would have been thunderous applause and cheering. Mexico City had none of that—but I had seen it happen in real time.

At one point, Diane's longtime boyfriend, who'd been in Vietnam for several years, was scheduled to return home and wanted her to come back to the US to be with him, which she did. I still had no desire to go to an American college or to live in a dorm. By now, I felt comfortable living on my own in a foreign country.

I got the bug to work again so I could be more financially independent (it's hard to curtail ambition). I found a part-time job as a model for a chic clothing store that held fashion shows at fancy restaurants in the posh shopping area of Mexico City. As I walked among the diners, showing off the latest designs, I could answer questions in Spanish such as, "*¿En que colores viene?*" (What colors does it come in?). While I wasn't fluent by any means, I didn't let that detail slow me down. I learned the words necessary for each presentation, and most patrons never knew the difference. A few times when I didn't understand what someone was asking, I'd say, "*Lo siento, pero yo no hablo español*," which means "I'm sorry, but I don't speak Spanish." Naturally, I'd get a bewildered look, but I would then quickly move on to the next table.

I heard about an exclusive private college for women and enrolled there to help me learn the language faster. No one spoke English at the school, so of course I learned Spanish rather quickly.

WHERE IN THE WORLD IS . . . JONI BLUNDEN?

As it happened, I didn't need to speak Spanish for my next adventure: my short-lived film career, which began and ended with a bit part in an American movie that was being shot in Mexico. It all started aboard a return flight from a visit to my mother in Sacramento. The man in the seat next to me was doing public relations work for a movie called *Macho Callahan*. It starred David Janssen, Jean Seberg, and Lee J. Cobb and was filming on location outside Mexico City. He told me they needed some extras, and that I looked enough like Jean Seberg (this was a man with a vivid imagination) that it might even be possible for me to sit in for her in some scenes, since she'd been out with dysentery. A few days later, he contacted me and said that the cast and crew were coming to town from their desert location in Durango to shoot some scenes at Churubusco Film Studios. If I was still interested, he said I should report to the movie set.

I played a saloon girl in several scenes, wearing a costume with a corset-like top, fishnet stockings, and spike heels. I could be seen hanging around the poker tables in the saloon and walking through the dirt streets of the make-believe Western town. Although I appeared on screen for only about a minute and a half without speaking, it was my first taste of show business. I didn't see the movie until years later when my mother and I were driving through Reno, Nevada, and saw a marquee advertising *Macho Callahan*. We pulled over, parked, and went into the theater. You had to be quick to catch me, but of course my mother could spot her little girl with no problem.

In 1968, Mexico City was gearing up for the Summer Olympics, but by this time there was growing unrest among college students there, just as there was around the world in Italy, France, Germany, and Japan. If you're old enough, you may remember news reports about army tanks rolling onto the campus of Mexico's

National University ten days before the opening events of the Games and military troops shooting into crowds of unarmed students, killing an untold number.

After the tragic massacre, my sense of security as a young student living in Mexico eroded. There seemed to be huge social changes happening during 1970 and into 1971 as Luis Echeverría Álvarez took over as president. That's when I made plans to return to the US.

I lived in Mexico from 1968 to 1971. While I was busy traveling the world and living in a foreign country, young Americans back home were being sent to Vietnam, and thousands were dying there. Students were protesting on college campuses. The sexual revolution was in full swing. Bras and draft cards were being burned.

In Mexico, the Vietnam War and the domestic problems of the US received very little attention in the press; the women's rights movement was totally ignored, and the sexual liberation movement was virtually unknown south of the border. I had missed a lot.

Although I had no way of knowing it yet, when I returned to the States, the overachiever in me was going to suffer from a severe case of arrested social development.

I have never returned to Mexico City since I lived there. Maybe it's part of my personality that once I've closed a door and moved on, I don't look back.

Chapter 7

COMING HOME TO CHANGE

Don't be like the rest of them, darling.
—Coco Chanel

I passed through customs at the San Francisco International Airport in 1971, scanning the baggage area for Mom. But it was overrun by thirty or so saffron-robed dancers who chanted, clapped tambourines, and wove through the crowd with white daisies and pamphlets. The chaos reminded me of temples I'd visited abroad, though I had no idea at the time that these were Hare Krishnas, or that their movement was sweeping through California.

Most of them looked American despite their robes. Some of the men had shaved heads except for a single long ponytail, while others wore their hair past their shoulders. The women floated through the terminal, smiling serenely and passing out flowers in exchange for donations. I edged toward the back of the crowd, trying to keep both the luggage carousel and the arrival doors in view. I was confused—and captivated.

I had spent five years traveling the world, immersed in unfamiliar cultures, and yet this scene, in my own country, felt as foreign as anything I'd encountered overseas. But as I processed what was going on around me, I realized how accustomed I had become to stepping into the unfamiliar. It dawned on me how far I'd come from the girl who first boarded the SS *Ryndam*.

As I searched for my mother, I wondered what kind of twenty-one-year-old I might have been if Dad hadn't died when I was so young. Would he have let me sail off at sixteen the way Mom had? While he valued exploration, he'd been raised by Seventh-Day Adventist missionaries whose ideas about risk and propriety were stricter. Maybe he would've steered me toward a calm, reputable college. Maybe even medicine. Who knows? Maybe I would have learned to handle blood, needles, and scalpels in time.

After I returned home, I enrolled at California State University, Sacramento, and quickly realized how out of place I was. While some classmates wore denim overalls, headbands, and hippie jewelry, I wore the dresses and pantsuits that I'd adopted during my more adult life in Mexico City. One student even asked if I was heading to a job interview after class.

That sense of not belonging spurred my next bold move. I didn't have a clear goal; just the conviction that I wanted to be in charge of something. Then I saw an ad for a modeling school. I didn't need modeling lessons, but I wanted to understand the business. I signed up, and within a month I was planning my own competing school.

In early 1972, I opened the Joni Lisa Charm and Modeling School—borrowing part of my name, Joan Elise, for the business. I advertised in the local paper and soon had a mix of eager teenagers dreaming of magazine covers and thirtysomethings looking for an escape from unhappy marriages.

COMING HOME TO CHANGE

One of the first people to walk through my door was Michele Dillingham, a talented fashion artist. I was creating my curriculum, and she offered to illustrate it. It was kismet! We became instant friends and remain close to this day.

While I was helping teenage girls stand up straight and smile (why was this so difficult?) and booking older students into local restaurant fashion shows, I realized I was spending more time counseling my students than advancing my own career. Mom, who was always direct, put it bluntly over lunch one day: "If you spent half the time on yourself that you spend on those perfect strangers, you'd be a star in no time." How is it that mothers always know best?

Then fate, or tenacity, or a combination of the two, took control of my life. One afternoon, I was taking an hour off from work to finish writing a paper for one of my college classes when a man walked in. He introduced himself as Bill DeBlonk and said he was an ad salesman from the local NBC station, KCRA-TV. He wanted to book a model for a commercial his client—a local ski shop—was shooting. As I began to show him photos of my models, he said, "I think you should do it."

Taking that job led to several other commercials and a friendship with Bill, who joined my mom and me for dinner at our home one evening. At one point, Bill leaned forward, setting down his fork. "You should come down to KCRA and talk to our news director about working on the news."

I blinked. "The news? Doing what? What's a woman going to do on the news?"

Bill smiled. "Things are starting to change. They need women. You've got the education and the looks, and you've been all over the world. You'd be great."

Unbeknownst to me, two years earlier the FCC had introduced

rules requiring broadcasters to include women on their programs. They strengthened the rules a year later, requiring licensees to actively recruit and promote women and minorities and to report their employment practices.

I wanted to dismiss the idea immediately. I wasn't studying journalism; I had no experience in broadcasting. And yet . . . a small spark of curiosity flared.

It wasn't until later that night, as I lay in bed, that Bill's words really sank in. I stared at the ceiling, my mind racing. There were hardly any women on the news—other than Barbara Walters. Did that mean the door was closed? Or was it just beginning to open?

I could have ignored Bill's encouragement and let it pass as just another conversation. But something inside me wouldn't let it go. Could I really just . . . call up the news director and say I wanted to work on TV?

A nervous thrill ran through me. Why not? Nothing ventured, nothing gained. Shouldn't I be open to anything that might hold potential for the future?

That night I kept thinking about Bill's seemingly wild suggestion. It left me with a bunch of questions, and now I wanted to know the answers. Bill had written the name and number of the news director on a piece of paper before leaving the house, so maybe I should call him. But what would I ask him? I grabbed a pen and a legal pad and decided to make a list. How would I prepare for a job on the news? Should I take certain college classes or go to one of those broadcasting schools I'd seen advertised on TV? How would the industry be changing, and what types of jobs would women be filling in TV news? As I looked down at my list of questions, I made my decision: I would call that news director the next day to find out more about this intriguing career idea.

COMING HOME TO CHANGE

The next morning, I found the piece of paper Bill had left with the number of the station and the name of the news director: Paul Thompson. I had only to call and ask for an appointment. What could it hurt? The number Bill had given me was a direct line to the newsroom, and whoever answered the phone yelled out, "Paul, it's for you." When he picked up, I said, "Mr. Thompson, my name is Joan Blunden. Bill DeBlonk suggested that I call you to discuss working for your newscast." A very pleasant voice answered, "Bill told me you might be calling and that if I was smart, I'd give you an appointment to come in. So what are you doing this afternoon, about two o'clock?"

Wow! I don't know what I'd expected, but I hadn't expected that response. I quickly collected myself and said, "I'll be coming in to see you, thank you."

"Okay, see you then."

I went back to my room and reviewed my list of questions. What exactly was I hoping to get out of this meeting? I wasn't sure, but I knew I had to at least explore the possibilities. Now I just needed to find something "reporter-like" to wear.

That afternoon, I drove to the television station in downtown Sacramento. I'd been there once before to shoot that commercial for the ski shop, but I didn't know where in the building the news programs were produced. I announced myself to the receptionist in the lobby. "I see you on the schedule, Miss Blunden." She waved her hand. "Just go straight to the newsroom. It's on the second floor."

As I walked up the stairs with no idea what to expect, I entered what I'd describe as a giant bullpen with rows and rows of metal desks and people sitting at typewriters frantically typing away. I would learn that they were all reporters working on stories under a deadline for that evening's broadcast.

As I stood there taking it all in, a tall, distinguished gray-haired man walked out of the only private office and motioned for me to come in. As news director, Paul Thompson was at the helm of this busy newsroom, but he instantly put me at ease. He told me that he'd been a bit skeptical when Bill suggested he take this meeting because I had no experience, but Bill had said with assurance, "Just wait till you meet her; you'll see what I mean." With that, Paul gave me a huge smile that said, *Now I see what Bill meant*.

He asked me to tell him about myself. "Well, I'm currently studying psychology at Cal State University and running a small business, but I spent my first semester of college traveling around the world aboard a ship, visiting fifteen countries. After that I lived in Mexico City for a few years, attending college there." His eyes got big, and he said, "Wow, you've had some amazing life experiences . . . and do you speak Spanish?" I liked the way this was going. "I wouldn't say I'm fluent, but I get by."

"So what do you want to know about the news business?" he asked. I went over my list of questions: what kind of training was needed to become a reporter, what was the potential in news, how was the industry responding to the pressure to hire more women, how would women be incorporated into their broadcasts. That last question seemed to spark his interest—perhaps due to the edict from the FCC to add women to news broadcasts. He sat up straight, leaned forward, and said, "Well, clearly you know how to construct an interview, and you seem to have a lot of confidence and good presence, despite having never been on TV. I'd like to take you into the studio, if you've got the time, and have you audition. Let's see how you do."

As we walked into the studio, a young man approached us and handed me some papers. "Here ya go, some copy for you to read to the camera. Take a seat on the set and we'll be ready for you in a couple of minutes." It all seemed so surreal, settling into one of the anchor chairs on the actual KCRA news set I'd seen so many times on the TV in my living room.

As I took a moment to look over what I was supposed to read, a man came in and pulled a big TV camera over, positioning it right in front of me. He popped his head out from behind the camera at one point and said, "Hi, I'm Stan, and I'm the cameraman. You look great." It was such a kind thing for him to say, to try to ease my obvious nerves. He added, "They're ready in the control room, so just start by introducing yourself. I'll count you down. Here we go: five . . . four . . . three . . . two . . . one."

I took a deep breath, trying to steady my voice. The lights were blinding, the camera's red light flicked on, and suddenly it was real. I had memorized the first sentence of the story, so I looked directly into the camera and said, "I'm Joan Blunden, and tonight's top story is . . ." To make the situation even more difficult, it was 1973, and the top story almost every night was about the Vietnam War. That day was no different, but I did my best not to butcher the Vietnamese names in the story.

It was the first time I'd ever done anything like that, but I guess I made a good impression, because when the audition was over, Paul came into the studio with a big smile. "I see why Bill told me to take the meeting; you really do have a terrific presence." While he was very encouraging, he didn't offer me a job—not that I had gone in expecting one, as I'd only been on a fact-finding mission. Then he added, "Let's keep in touch, because we're going to begin a new, early five p.m. news program in four or five months, and I want to include some consumer reports and, uh . . . you might just be perfect for that."

"I'd love to have the opportunity to do that," I said with newfound confidence. The area of consumer reporting on local TV news was as new and untested as I was at that time. There was no talk of hours or salaries or benefits or any of the things that are so important to discuss in job interviews today. Of course, I hadn't approached today as a job interview. Nevertheless, I left the station with the unmistakable feeling that an opportunity may have just been put in place—a chance to work for a television station.

As I was leaving, I felt like someone was following me. I turned around and immediately recognized KCRA's weatherman, Harry Geise, who had been an institution in Sacramento for as long as I could remember. At fifty-odd years old, Harry was a jolly fellow even when the weather forecast was grim. When I think of him now, I see that he actually resembled Gene Hackman.

He introduced himself and said, "I saw you auditioning and heard Paul talking about a job in the news department. A few stations around the country have introduced 'weather girls,' and I'd love to make you Sacramento's first weather girl."

To be perfectly honest, a job reporting the weather didn't sound the least bit interesting or enticing, as I didn't know a thing about meteorology. But then a little voice said, *This might lead to something bigger*. Maybe I could learn about the weather and the TV news business at the same time. Mom had taught this girl to recognize an opportunity. "That sounds terrific."

"Great. Be here tomorrow morning at five and we'll get started."

Did he just say five, as in five a.m.? The next morning, I woke up at an ungodly hour to get my first taste of early-morning TV life. Little did I know that it was just the beginning. What mattered was that I had just cracked open a door into a world I had never imagined for myself. A world that until this moment had seemed like it belonged to other people—mostly men, and in one rare case, Barbara Walters. Could it belong to me too?

Harry warned me that this would not be a regular paying job—and he was right. I was considered a trainee at the station, and trainees made thirty dollars a week. Thankfully, salary wasn't an issue, since I was still living at home with my mom.

I had no idea where this road would lead, but I knew one thing for sure: by saying yes, I had just taken the first step.

Chapter 8

GETTING MY FOOT IN THE DOOR

A sign on the door of opportunity reads "Push."
—Ace Antonio Hall,
American author and motivational speaker

I was at the TV station at 4:55 a.m. to begin my apprenticeship with Harry the weatherman. Along one side of the newsroom, in addition to the office of the news director, was a room for the wire service machines. In those days, reports from the AP, Reuters, and the National Weather Service came across huge teletype machines that continuously printed updates on rolls of paper that editors and journalists relied on to prepare for broadcasts. When you opened the door to the news wire room, a staccato of *rat-a-tat-tat*s assaulted your ears as the machines churned out stories round the clock. Reporters ripped these stories from the teletype machines and took them to their desks to edit and retype on color-coded triplicate forms, with copies being distributed to directors, producers, and technical directors. This was how the world worked before computers!

Harry was already at his big metal desk poring over a stack of reports that had just come in over those big teletype machines. By five a.m. I heard Harry delivering weather forecasts for radio stations up and down California's Central Valley. "We're looking at heavy rains today for your area . . ."

I quickly figured out why these early-morning weather reports were so critical to his listeners; many were farmers in one of America's leading agricultural regions. In fact, a lot of those farmers were Harry's private clients, since he was one of the first weather professionals to use computers to analyze data. With this knowledge, he helped them plant and harvest crops accordingly. Harry was running what today we would call a "side hustle," and he was making serious money with it.

I've always been a fast learner, and in a short time I could locate the high- and low-pressure systems on the map and find the slides that matched cirrus and cumulus clouds for Harry's forecast. In those days there were no computer-generated weather maps; they were heavy plastic boards with colorful views of the Sacramento area, the state, and the nation. With a thick black marker I would draw fronts, temperatures, and storm systems on those boards. Once a program was over, it was my job to wipe the boards clean with paint remover for the next show's forecast. I was always up to my elbows in marker ink by the end of day.

Harry was excited to be molding me into the first weather girl in Sacramento. Unbeknownst to me, after six months of training, he began urging management to let me handle the live weather report on the noon newscast. Unfortunately, management wasn't buying it. Apparently, it was still too soon to have a female weatherperson.

One morning, though, a few minutes after I arrived at the station, the phone rang at the weather desk. It was Harry. "I'm calling to let you know that I just called in sick, and there's no one else to sub for me today, so you're doing the weather on the noon broadcast."

"Are you kidding, Harry?" I asked.

"No, I'm not kidding," he said emphatically. I also heard a bit of mischievousness in his voice.

I took a deep breath and told myself, *Come on, you can do this. If you believed in Santa Claus for five years, you can believe in yourself for five minutes.*

To this day, I don't know if Harry was really sick; I tend to doubt it. But it was one way of getting me on the air, whether the station management was ready or not.

I'll never forget how I felt as the morning progressed after Harry's call. I'd describe it as a mixture of pure panic and total exhilaration. As usual, I ripped the weather reports off the wire-service machines, summarized the current weather, wrote the forecast, and selected the slides that best matched the predicted weather for the day.

At 12:20 p.m. I made my live television debut.

Since I hadn't planned for that first appearance, I wasn't exactly dressed appropriately. It was December, and I'd intended to meet my mom for lunch and do some holiday shopping, so I wasn't wearing an on-air outfit. I was wearing . . . wait for it . . . white leather hot pants with a matching white leather jacket trimmed in rabbit fur at the collar and sleeves. Before you fall down laughing, you should know that hot pants were very trendy at that time. I may have gone a little overboard when I paired the outfit with white leather boots that tied up the front.

Nevertheless, there I was, getting black marker on my white ensemble. As the nerves kicked in, my vocal cords constricted, making my voice rise a few octaves. I must have sounded like a tape being played at the wrong speed.

In the 1970s there were no teleprompters—those marvelous inventions that roll the script right in front of the news anchors' eyes—so the anchors had to read from paper scripts. But when you're doing the weather, you can't have a paper script in your hand; you need to have your spiel *in your head*.

But come on, how hard could this be, really?

In working with Harry I had learned that when I wanted a map to appear, I had to click a button on a small device I held in my hand. That click lit up a red light bulb behind the set. When the stagehand saw the bulb light up, he would physically slide the next big plastic map into an opening on the "weather wall" so it looked to viewers as if it had just magically appeared.

I practiced what I'd be saying on air, knowing that I would have to do it all from memory. *There will be thundershowers in Montana* (or, wait, was it Wyoming?) *and unusual hail in Florida* (no, that can't be right; was it Georgia?). My knowledge of basic geography has never been strong, and now with nerves kicking in, I was trying hard not to let it elude me completely in the heat of the moment.

My fast-paced delivery didn't serve me well, because I finished everything I had to say in about two minutes and still had another minute of airtime. No one ever really thinks about how long a minute is. Try looking at your watch right now . . . for a minute. Then imagine having to fill that time with something meaningful to say . . . to a million people. The only thing I could do was repeat what I'd already said. Worst of all, I must have said that we weren't going to have a white Christmas in Sacramento three times. Well, of course we weren't; up to that time, it hadn't snowed more than four times in the city's history.

GETTING MY FOOT IN THE DOOR

When the longest three minutes of my life ended, I couldn't go back upstairs to the newsroom because I just knew everyone would be rolling in the aisles. I wiped off my weather boards, packed up my black markers, and left the building. That was my initiation—my baptism by fire on live television—and I can still feel the anxiety build up today just thinking about it.

The next day I tried to be as quiet as possible as I ascended the linoleum stairs to the second-floor newsroom. I hoped to enter unnoticed. Surprisingly, nobody fell down laughing at the sight of me, so I figured I'd done all right, although I probably asked Harry ten times if I'd blown my big chance. As it turned out, I hadn't. Now he was able to occasionally schedule me on that noon show.

KCRA's popular anchorman, Bob Whitten, who had been at the helm of the news show for years, took me aside after my second appearance and said, "You sounded like a little toy that's been wound too tightly. It's because you're speaking so fast that your vocal cords are constricting. Let me give you four words of advice: think L-O-W and S-L-O-W." I was like a sponge at that stage of my life, and his helpful advice still comes to mind today whenever I'm walking onto a stage or entering a meeting or even a party (especially if I don't know many of the guests). It sounds so simple, doesn't it? Yet it's one of those gems you can call upon to make you feel calm and confident even if you feel just the opposite.

In today's world, that advice would likely be translated to "breathe in and breathe out." However you remember it, the next time you're filled with nerves before giving a report or getting up in front of a PTA meeting, just pause, take a deep breath, and then exhale, allowing your muscles to relax. Put a smile on your face (a confident smile) and think "L-O-W and S-L-O-W." I guarantee this will help you feel—and look—relaxed and self-assured.

I don't really know why Harry Geise took a chance on me the way he did after such a short time working with him. I asked him once, and he said, "I knew you could do it; you were a great student, and you had enough self-confidence that I never had a second thought as to whether you could pull it off." Harry wanted to pioneer a woman weatherperson, and I happened to be there at the right time.

Well, actually, I didn't just *happen* to be there at the right time.

I was there because I'd acted on a suggestion that others might have scoffed at or ignored. Looking back, it was a gutsy, brash move to call the KCRA news director. If I hadn't made that call, I wouldn't have been in the studio, and Harry Geise would never have seen my audition.

Of course, once you get your foot in the door, that's just the beginning. Over the years I saw again and again that the more experience I got on the air, the more comfortable I became. Success didn't appear overnight—it came as I got a little better every day. It added up.

It wasn't long before I was called back into the news director's office.

Chapter 9

JUST SAY YES!

*You don't have to see the whole staircase.
Just take the first step.*

—Martin Luther King Jr.

When you get called into your boss's office, it can feel like a visit to the principal's office—although I can neither confirm nor deny whether that ever happened to me.

Paul Thompson could see that I was nervous as I took a seat on the other side of his desk, so he quickly put me at ease by reminding me that when we first met, he'd mentioned the station was adding an early 5:00 p.m. news broadcast to the lineup, and he thought I could be their new consumer reporter. He was clearly relishing his role as mentor, saying, "It's time to take the next step in becoming a news reporter, and maybe an anchor."

Looking back on that moment, I could have easily said, "But I don't know how to find stories and produce them. How will I ever pull that off?"

Instead, I thought, *Maybe I could do it if I just tried.*

Research has always come naturally to me. Since Sacramento is the state capital, I went to the Department of Consumer Affairs the next day to ask what viewers should know when buying products. The people I met with were excited to hear that we wanted to focus on issues like product recalls. My next stop was the Department of Agriculture, where I asked what consumers should know about food prices and food safety. Lastly, I went to the California State Capitol to ask about pending consumer legislation.

I got tremendous cooperation from everyone, along with a mountain of information, since the people I'd spoken with had been laboring for years to get media attention. I couldn't wait to tell Paul Thompson that I could do a nightly consumer report! But believe me, I was convincing myself as much as I was convincing him. I started with a two-minute consumer spot each week, which grew and, in many ways, launched my career as a journalist. I was getting great experience, and Paul Thompson saw my increasing capability. A few times I was even allowed to sit in for an anchor when they were out sick. My self-confidence was on the rise, despite the jibes of local television critics, notably one man named Chris Wise, who wrote a column for the *Sacramento Union* newspaper. He used to make mincemeat out of me at least once a month.

Admittedly, there was plenty to criticize. I was once told that I spoke "California slang," which translates to "gonna," "shoulda," "comin'," and "goin'." I also was made aware, through his critiques, that I would say "pitcher" for "picture," "nu-cu-lur" for "nuclear," and "re-la-tor" for "realtor," among other verbal typos. His criticism was justified, if a little vicious, and I still have his newspaper columns in a file to remind myself of those early days.

I never met Chris Wise, so I don't know how I might have reacted to him in person. My mother did, though, and she said it was all she could do to keep herself from kicking him in the shins.

I was also learning about some of the technical aspects of being on the air. One common production technique resulted in some hearty laughter at my expense. A process known as chroma key allows a person—let's say, a weather reporter—to stand in front of a green or blue screen with an image projected behind them—say, a weather map or a video of a stormy day. The camera cuts out anything that's the same color as the screen being used (green or blue), creating the illusion that the reporter is standing in the midst of the storm.

This is a very basic technique, but of course I wasn't aware of it. Consequently, during my report on food prices, I didn't realize that every time I looked down at my script, my blue eye shadow basically functioned like a blue screen. When the control room rolled my film of fruits and vegetables, viewers saw bananas, apples, and lettuce coming out of my eye sockets. (Please, no critiques about wearing blue eye shadow; it was the seventies.)

I later learned that people in the newsroom practically peed their pants every time it happened. These laughs at my expense were not uncommon when I started out, because many of my colleagues were wondering why this blonde, who seemed to have just walked in off the street, was getting all this airtime. Most of the reporters were men who had been in the news business for years, working their way up from newspapers to radio stations to smaller TV stations and finally to KCRA, where they felt they deserved the opportunities for advancement that were now coming my way. I totally get it. They weren't wrong; it wasn't fair. It was for TV ratings. And, might I add, I was rising to the occasion and pulling it off.

I had even learned to edit my own film using a hot splicer. After viewing what my cameraman had shot, I'd choose pieces of that film, connect the ends of those pieces together on the splicer, apply the hot glue, then press down on the splicer so the pieces became one continuous strip of film. Then I'd cross my fingers, hoping that I'd been successful and that my splices would hold together when the control room techs ran the film during the newscast that night.

The fact that my appearances on the news programs were now being tracked and evaluated, and viewers were responding positively, meant that it wasn't long before the news director called me into his office again. This time he asked, "How would you like to take a shot as an anchor on the noon news?"

"YES!" (It's in caps because I said it with that much enthusiasm!)

Wow! Was this really happening? So what if I'd never anchored before; I would learn.

Paul Thompson's belief in me and my ability to learn quickly was encouraging. "You'll make mistakes," he warned me, "but I know you can handle the job, and I think you have the kind of image that will increase our audience at the noon hour, when there are a lot of women watching."

A few days later I became the anchor for the noon newscast, and my new life motto became *Whenever someone asks if you can do something, just say yes, then go figure out how to do it.*

As I learned my craft in front of the viewing audience, every mistake I made was reported in the media—and I made some stupid ones, such as pronouncing the Russian newspaper *Pravda* as "Pra-va-da." (Come on, I'd never heard of the paper before—and I still think the writers purposely misspelled it on my copy so that it would trip me up, which it did.) These kinds of errors only added fuel to the fire for my detractors. But sometimes you must be willing to risk not being great to have the opportunity to learn how to be great as you pursue what you want. I could see that television was a fertile field for a woman, and that if I learned quickly enough, there would be the potential to move up—even more quickly than a man. So, I jumped at every opportunity to learn a new skill.

My job as anchor led to the opportunity to write and produce the noon news program. This was the best thing that could have happened, since I learned how to use the news wires, write and edit copy, and construct a news program in a way that kept the audience engaged. I was learning and mastering new skills every day, and I was beginning to think there was a future for me in TV news.

The television business is like any other business, in that when a person gets just barely enough experience to handle a particular job, he or she starts thinking about the job one step farther up the ladder. So, what was the next rung after anchoring and producing the noon news? Perhaps anchoring the 5:00 p.m. early news? Or even the 6:00 p.m. nightly news?

As it turned out, the success of our noon news program caught the attention of other local stations in Sacramento. And, well, I couldn't have dreamed what happened after that.

 *Joan on KCRA in Sacramento, 1974*

Chapter 10

IF I CAN MAKE IT THERE, I CAN MAKE IT ANYWHERE

The reinvention of daily life means marching off the edge of our maps.

—Bob Black, The Abolition of Work (1985)

I was descending into JFK when I saw the Statue of Liberty, followed by the Twin Towers. That's when it hit me: I might actually be about to land a job at the number one station in the country—and I hadn't even applied.

I'd been perfectly happy anchoring the local news in Sacramento for the past ten months. I was twenty-five years old and had been in the chair for only a short time. I was pleased with my progress, and so was my boss; our noon news broadcast had the highest ratings in town. That's when something strange happened: Tapes of my broadcasts started circulating around the country. Not because I sent them out but because other people did. What was going on?

It's a truism that when one station achieves dominance in a market, the other stations try to figure out why their competition is ahead and how to emulate the features that made the other station's programming a success. To find out what the competition is doing right, a station will often bring in an expensive consulting firm that specializes in conducting audience polls and making recommendations. They use several methods for rating programs and the people on them, essentially asking respondents what they watch and why, which on-air personalities they like and don't like, and why they feel that way. One of these scoring methods is called the Q Score.

The Q Score is a rating that television personalities often live and die by. It works like this: A questionnaire is sent out to several thousand people who represent a random sample of the population. The questionnaire contains a list of about three hundred people from every area of television—news, sports, entertainment, etc. Next to each personality's name is a brief identification. Those completing the questionnaire are asked to answer two questions about each person on the list. The first is "Do you recognize this person?" The second asks the recipient to rate the personalities they recognize as follows: That person is (1) One of my favorites; (2) Very good; (3) Good; (4) Fair; or (5) Poor. A personality can turn out to be very well-known but not at all liked. The rating, or Q Score, is a ratio of familiarity to likability; an excellent score is 50 percent, and not many personalities reach that level.

Two things happen next, which I learned about only after the fact. One of them is legitimate, while the other is something that might be called a dirty trick in any other industry.

Once the news consultants deliver their performance reports to the trailing station, they suggest what the station should change;

sometimes it's the set or the show's opening, but usually it's bringing in a personality who can help them compete and hopefully eclipse the ratings success of the other top stations. They may even try to hire someone away from the other local station or look for talent outside the city who can possibly compete.

In other instances, consultants will go so far as to send completely unsolicited videotapes of the anchor who's garnering audience attention and high ratings to other stations around the country who might be looking for someone new. In other words, they try to get rid of the competition by finding them a job in some other town.

In this case, I was the one to benefit from this tactic. The consultants began sending videotapes of me to news directors in places like Detroit, Atlanta, and Minneapolis, hoping I'd get a job offer from some other city, which would effectively remove me from the Sacramento television market.

Since I didn't have a clue this was happening, I was floored when I got my first call and potential job offer: "Hi, I'm the news director at the NBC affiliate in Detroit. We have your tape here and we'd like to talk to you about an opening in our news department. We're interested in hiring a female anchor." I was completely taken aback. I hadn't sent out any tapes. Even though I had no idea what was on the tape he'd seen, I tried to play it cool and said, "I'm glad you like it. I'd love to talk to you, but I'm on a deadline right now. I'll have to get back to you."

Over the course of the next two days I got more calls, so I went to Bill DeBlonk, who had led me to KCRA in the first place. "Bill, something strange is happening," I said. "I'm getting calls from television stations in big markets like Detroit and Chicago. They say they have my tape and want to talk to me about an anchor job with them. But I didn't send a tape to anyone. In fact, I don't even have a tape of me anchoring. Any idea what's going on?"

It didn't take Bill long to figure out what was happening, but he also advised me to think seriously about accepting one of the offers. "Even if you think you're ready," he said, "in this business, like any other, the grass isn't always greener in the next town." Of course, as an ad salesman for KCRA, he wasn't keen on the idea of my leaving the broadcast with the high ratings.

Bill was probably right. After all, I was perfectly happy anchoring in Sacramento. I had just bought a little house, I was dating a nice guy, and my family and friends were all living close by. The last thing I was thinking about was leaving my small pond, where I was becoming something of a big fish.

I had also learned enough about the competitiveness in the television business to have doubts about my ability to handle jobs in a bigger city. I knew deep down that after less than two years, I was not an experienced newscaster by any stretch of the imagination. Still, when you get calls from news directors in big cities like Detroit who want you to anchor their news programs, you start to wonder whether you should be thinking bigger than Sacramento.

My tapes were obviously traveling fast, because in the next few days I got two more calls. So, let me be honest here: My ego was beginning to grow.

I went back to my buddy Bill, and this time he said, "If you're getting these offers, maybe you do need to think about them seriously. I know someone who can give you good advice about which stations you should actually consider."

Bill put in a call to Phil Boyer, who had previously been head of sales at KCRA and was now in New York City, where he was vice president of programming for the ABC-owned stations. Bill handed

IF I CAN MAKE IT THERE, I CAN MAKE IT ANYWHERE

the phone to me, and I recounted the offers I'd received. Boyer listened and then said, "There aren't that many women anchoring on local news programs, so stations are really on the hunt, but if you're getting all these calls, I'd like you to send me your tape, since we have an opening at our local station here in New York City."

"I don't have a tape of my own," I said.

Bill said he'd get one of the station's editors to put a tape together and send it to Boyer as quickly as possible. With the help of a tape editor at KCRA, we pieced together a five-minute demo and sent it off to New York the next day.

Less than a week later I got a call from Phil Nye, the news director at WABC-TV in New York. When Boyer had received my tape, he handed it right over to Nye, knowing that he was looking for a female reporter who could also anchor on weekends. Nye asked me to fly to New York ASAP for an interview and an audition. Now it was starting to feel real. I needed to let my station know what was happening. Harry Geise, the weatherman who'd given me my first break, advised me to go for it. Of course he did—good old Harry always mentored, supported, and encouraged me. May he rest in peace.

I knew it was time to tell my boss, Paul Thompson, that I'd been asked to go to New York to audition as an anchor there. I was nervous and felt a bit guilty, since Paul had been such a supportive ally. "Paul, I need to let you know what's been going on," I said. "I've gotten calls from news directors in a number of cities about anchoring, and now there's an opportunity for me to go to WABC-TV in New York City, and I think I have to at least give it a try."

"I know that it's flattering," he said, "but the fact is, while you're learning incredibly fast, you still have had very little experience. I won't tell you not to move on it, but I must tell you that I don't feel you're quite ready. Besides, I'd hate to lose you."

"To be clear," I said, "I wasn't looking for a job elsewhere. These calls just came to me out of the blue. But I do think I owe it to myself to at least pursue this possibility in New York City."

"Well, if you're comfortable acting on it," he answered, "you've got to go for it. You'll never forgive yourself if you don't try. Just remember, if things don't work out, you still have a job here as far as I'm concerned."

That was all I needed to hear. It was a go.

In a few days, I had gone from not even knowing a job was available to wanting it very badly. Besides, I was learning the importance of being open to opportunities when they came along, and, just as important, acting on them.

My colleagues in the KCRA newsroom almost laughed out loud when they learned about my trip to New York and that I was dumb enough to think I could get a job there. As a prank going-away present, one of them even put a newly released book on my desk called *We're Going to Make You a Star* by Sally Quinn. Quinn had been a society reporter for *The Washington Post* and had become notorious around DC for her tough interviews. But without any previous TV experience, she was plucked from obscurity to become an anchor on *CBS Morning News*. She was thrust into stardom so quickly; she failed almost as quickly.

In her book, she relayed a conversation she'd had with her agent, Richard Leibner, in which she asked him about her chances at CBS. Leibner said, "Sweetheart, before I say anything, I want you to know something. If you're half as good as they think you are, if they use all the potential they have to make this a great show, if they spend the amount of money they'll have to spend to make it any good, if they get the best producer and staff in the business . . . then your chances are one in ten you'll last out the year."

My upcoming audition in New York also precipitated a confrontation with the owner of KCRA, Jon Kelly—a confrontation that gave me another reason for wanting to get the New York job.

(Side note: Jon Kelly had previously asked me out on a date, and when I said no, he'd gone straight to Paul Thompson and told him to fire me. Paul, ever my mentor, was furious that Kelly would expect him to give me the boot simply because I'd refused to date the station owner. He told Kelly that if he insisted on firing me, he would have to fire him too. The demand for retribution was rescinded, and life went on.)

Kelly had learned that I was going for the audition in New York. He viewed my audacity to go after another job as an insult to KCRA, which had molded me into the anchor that I'd become. Okay—there was some truth to that. The day before I was to fly to New York, my mother came to meet me at the station so we could go for a celebratory lunch. As we were heading out the door, we ran into Kelly in the hall. He half blocked the way and said, "I hear you're going to New York."

Uh-oh . . .

"I am," I said. "I'm leaving in the morning, but it's only an audition."

"You'll never make it, you know," he said. "And even if you do get the job, you'll be back here in six months, begging on your knees for your old job back."

It was a cruel thing to say to me, but doing so in front of my mother was a compound felony. All I could manage was, "Thanks for the good wishes, Jon." When we got outside, my mom let out her rage. "How dare he be so insulting—especially in front of your mother."

As I was getting ready for my trip, I wanted to know what the weather would be like, so Harry (the weatherman) suggested we call a colleague of his back east, Gordon Barnes, who was the weatherman for WUSA-TV in Washington, DC.

Harry phoned Barnes, who gave me a complete rundown on East Coast weather, and during the conversation I told him the reason for my visit.

"It sounds like a great opportunity," he said. "Who's your agent in New York?"

"My what?"

"You mean you're going to talk to the news director at WABC-TV about a job and you don't have an agent?" he said.

"We don't have agents in Sacramento," I said. "I only make two hundred forty dollars a week."

"Well, when you begin talking about starting salaries at sixty to eighty thousand a year, you're going to need an agent," he said. "Why don't you call my guy, Richard Leibner?" And with that, he gave me Richard's phone number.

I called Mr. Leibner and had a short and direct conversation with him. He said he'd represent me—and why not, since I already had a good shot at the job. He ended the call by saying we'd be in touch when I got to New York.

On the flight across the country, as I sat reading Sally Quinn's book, I kept seeing the name Richard Leibner. It didn't penetrate my consciousness at first. It took me until Missouri to realize that the same Richard Leibner who had represented Sally Quinn and thrust her into a hot seat—a job that was too big for her to handle—was going to be representing me in New York City. Was there a parallel here? I surely hoped not.

Upon landing in New York, I made my way through the crowded airport, picked up my bag, and headed for the sidewalk to catch a cab to the city. The cab pulled up in front of the Park Lane Hotel, a towering modern building in midtown Manhattan, where WABC-TV had made reservations for me. After I checked in, a bellboy took my two small bags in hand, led me to my room on the fortieth floor, and drew the drapes to reveal a panoramic view of Central Park. When I opened the window, the sounds of an outdoor concert in the park filled the room. It felt like a scene from a movie.

I called Richard Leibner and told him where I was staying, and he said he'd come by to pick me up at nine thirty the following day. "We can walk from the hotel over to WABC," he said. "It's not far, and it will give us some time to talk."

At exactly 9:30 the next morning, Richard called from the lobby. "I'm downstairs. Are you ready?"

I'd been up for hours and had been dressed since 7:30. In fact, I'd slept only fitfully at best, and was glad to see the light coming through the window at about six because that meant I could get up instead of lying there with my eyes wide open, thinking disastrous thoughts. During those hours of half sleep, I tried to tell myself that I was perfectly capable of anchoring the news and that the worst thing that could happen would be that they didn't like me.

Of course, that actually *was* the worst thing that could happen.

Richard was waiting for me in the lobby, and as we left the hotel, he took my arm and steered us toward the *Eyewitness News* studio on Columbus Avenue and Sixty-Sixth Street. I had put Quinn's book in my purse, and Richard noticed it. He said, "Hey, don't believe everything you read in that book. I'm innocent." That, coupled with the fact that he seemed like a nice guy, helped to calm my nerves.

As we walked the few blocks, Richard told me what to do and

what not to do. "Basically, be yourself," he said. "They won't ask you anything technical, so don't worry about that; they just want to get a sense of what you're like as a talent."

All I could think was that at KCRA, they didn't call us "talent."

He went on: "If they start to talk about salary or contracts or anything negotiable, just tell them they have to speak to your agent about that. Don't get drawn into a money conversation. If they say the starting salary would be fifty thousand dollars, don't say, 'Great, I'll take it.'"

I wanted to say, *Fifty thousand dollars? You must be kidding! I'm making two hundred forty dollars a week in Sacramento. I was afraid that if they offered me anything like that, I'd say, "Where do I sign?"*

But I kept my mouth shut.

Richard added, "Again, try to be yourself. Only you can do that. They don't know that much about you, but they're obviously looking for someone with your image, so sell *your* image and not that of someone else."

When we got to the corner of Sixty-Sixth and Columbus, just outside WABC-TV, Richard said, "Good luck, and give me a call this afternoon." I walked toward the door with my heart in my mouth, and as I opened it, I got cold all over—not from the air-conditioning but from my nervousness. As I approached the receptionist, I said, "Hi, my name is Joan Blunden. I have an appointment with Mr. Nye."

I was ushered into Phil Nye's office, where he and several other WABC executives were waiting. He introduced me to everyone, and we sat down to talk. Nye was very pleasant, and I liked him immediately. After a few minutes of casual talk, he and Don Dunphy Jr., the assistant news director, took me down the block to a huge studio where they did the local news show.

I was wide-eyed. It was so much more professional-looking than our news studio in Sacramento. I had never seen so many lighting grids, cameras, and pieces of furniture on a set before. I would later learn that a lot of the furniture was for *Good Morning America*, which also broadcast from the same studio in the early morning; *Eyewitness News* used the other side of the studio in the evening.

Nye said they would wait in the control room while I went upstairs to get ready for my audition. I was too embarrassed to ask him why I was going upstairs. As it turned out, they were sending me to a room where a makeup artist was standing by to get me ready for my on-camera audition. This was also a first for me. In Sacramento we put on our own makeup and did our own hair in the ladies' room. Here, a nice, reassuring woman named Sylvia did both of those things for me. She was very complimentary about my skin and hair, and that was a boost, because I was plenty worried about going in front of the camera.

When I went back downstairs to the studio, I was met by a stage manager who handed me some news copy, and I made my way onto the set. The stage manager pointed to the camera, and when the red light went on, I took a calming breath. I said to myself *L-O-W and S-L-O-W*, and then I read the copy for about five minutes.

Just before I began reading the story, I suddenly remembered what Sally Quinn had written about her debut on network television. She said they put her in a chair on the set and gave her a script and that was it. When they said, "You're on the air," she didn't even know that the camera with the red light was the one she was supposed to face when she talked. Okay—I was way ahead of her on that score, at least.

When I finished the audition, Nye and Dunphy took me to lunch at La Scala, a chic Italian restaurant, and they both praised my performance. Whew! I wanted to ask them questions about working at WABC, but I was reticent because I didn't want them to think I was too pushy or uninformed. And though I thought that I would need training if I got the job, it didn't feel right to ask that. It would seem as if I were admitting I really didn't know what I was doing. I played it quiet and answered their questions instead of asking my own.

What they were offering was a reporting job with the promise of anchoring the weekend news at some unspecified time in the future. It wasn't exactly what I had expected, and it was a little frightening because I had no experience in street reporting. I voiced my concerns—that I'd primarily been an anchor—but Nye and Dunphy didn't seem to be worried. Looking back on it now, I can't imagine why they thought being a reporter in New York City was such a piece of cake, because it certainly wasn't.

After lunch we shook hands on the sidewalk in front of the restaurant and went our separate ways. That was it. I called Richard from a telephone booth on the street (remember those?) and told him about what had gone on, specifying that we hadn't talked about money at all and that I had given them his name as my agent.

I was a little numb. I walked slowly back to the hotel, changed clothes, and spent the rest of the afternoon wandering into and out of little shops on Madison Avenue. That night I went out to dinner with my childhood friend Jed Johnson, whom I'd reached out to when my New York City trip was locked in.

It had been almost a decade since I'd seen Jed and his twin brother, Jay. When we all graduated from high school, Jed and Jay got on a bus heading straight for New York City. I can't even imagine what it was like for them when they moved there at eighteen years old, by themselves, with no jobs and no one to pave the way for them. For me, that says a lot about the power of dreaming big and shooting for the moon. Jed had gotten a job delivering telegrams for Western Union. After bringing one to Andy Warhol at his famous art studio, he wound up getting a job with him. He worked his way up the ranks, and eventually he and Andy developed a relationship, and Jed moved in with him.

Now I was contemplating moving to New York City, and Jed was excited to show me what life could be like there. When he arrived at the hotel to pick me up, Andy was with him. Wait—was this really happening? Andy Warhol was going out to dinner with us? They took me to an elegant French restaurant, and as we made our way toward our table, I noticed heads turning as people realized that Andy Warhol was entering the room. Jed had always been extremely soft-spoken, an introvert, and I was now seeing that Andy was also very soft-spoken and had a similar personality. They were like two peas in a pod; it was easy to see how they ended up together. They also seemed excited about the prospect of my moving to New York and said they'd love to help me get settled in the city, which was comforting, though admittedly a bit mind-blowing. Little did I know what an amazing life and career would be ahead for me, but I've always been thankful for Jed's unwavering friendship and encouragement to follow my dream.

The next morning, I flew back to Sacramento with a variety of fantastical thoughts dancing in my head. The exposure to the exhilarating sights and sounds of New York City, the WABC-TV studio, and the fancy-shmancy night out with Jed and Andy had started me thinking that this was the right job for me.

Maybe New York City was exactly the place I needed to be.

Maybe the people at KCRA didn't fully understand my "talent." (Remember, this was a brand-new word for me.) Soon I might be shaking the California dust off my shoes and moving into the exciting world of Manhattan, where a job at a major television station awaited.

Back home, as I analyzed the situation, I reminded myself that my experience couldn't possibly match up with that of other job applicants. I felt I'd done well in the interview and the taped audition, but realistically my chances of getting the job were slim at best. With that bit of rationalization in place, I could go back to work the following morning and face the inevitable questions, which I knew would boil down to two: My friends would ask "How did it go?" and my colleagues at the station would likely just say "Didn't get the job, eh?"

I was to be spared the second set of comments, since that same night the phone rang. The secretary on the other end of the line said, "Please hold for Mr. Nye." My heart was in my throat. I hadn't expected to hear anything this quickly, so I wasn't prepared.

"Hello, Joan, it's Phil Nye calling," he said.

"Hello," I answered, searching for some special inflection in his voice, but I couldn't read anything.

"I wanted to let you know that you've got the job if you want it," he said. "I just got off the phone with your agent, and we've made a great offer, which he'll go over with you. We'd like you to come to New York as soon as possible."

Oh my God . . . the job was mine, and they wanted me there ASAP!

I thanked him and said I'd love to take the job and that I'd call Richard right away. It was the most exciting thing that had ever happened to me. A few minutes later, Richard called me with the details.

"You begin in two weeks, and they're going to pay you thirty-six thousand a year plus extra money for each time you're on. That extra money is called on-air fees," he said. "And that means you can easily make sixty thousand a year. That's not bad for a start."

"Are you kidding, Richard?" I said. "That's great."

"That's what a good agent is for," he said. This is a line I've heard many times since.

"What's the next step?" I asked.

"I'll have the contracts in a few days. When you get here you can sign them," he said.

"That's amazing," I replied. "In the meantime, I have a friend in New York who has volunteered to help me find an apartment."

He said, "Good luck on that one. You'll need it."

I could hardly wait to hang up the phone so I could call my mom and friends and tell them the good news. As I dialed my mother's number, I worried about how she would react. While she would be happy for me, I wouldn't live close to her anymore, and she wouldn't be able to see me each day on the local news.

And then there was my boss, Paul Thompson, who'd be losing his female anchor—his new, successful anchor who had been bringing the broadcast good ratings.

As soon as I got to the station the next morning, I told Harry first, who was of course thrilled for me, and then I went into Paul's office. As I took a seat across from him, I couldn't help but think about the first time I sat in his office and asked him what a woman could do in the news business. So much had happened in less than two years, and Paul's belief in me and his unwavering support were at the heart of it all. It was almost hard to get the words out of my mouth—to tell him I was going to be walking out on him.

I took a big breath and remembered *L-O-W and S-L-O-W*. "Paul, the news director at WABC called me last night and offered me the job. I hope you can understand that I just had to accept it. It's the number one station in the country. I still can't believe it myself, but I had to say yes."

For an instant, I could see the disappointment on his face, but then he bolted from his chair and came around the desk to envelop me in a congratulatory hug. He was a huge mentor and cheerleader of mine, and he clearly recognized what a tremendous opportunity this was. "I'm so proud of you. I'm also sick over losing you, but of course you had to say yes."

I gave him a kiss on the cheek and told him they wanted me to start right away, so I was giving my two weeks' notice. I ended with, "I hope that someday I can return some of what you've given me."

I told the rest of the people at KCRA that I was going to be a field reporter (something they all knew I'd never done before) and a weekend anchor. While my friends were excited for me, my detractors nearly choked. Here they were trying to get jobs in San Francisco, LA, or Denver, and I was going to New York to work for ABC's flagship station.

Their reaction was predictable. One said, "Are you nuts? You've never been a reporter. How are you going to know what to do?"

I said, "I've been producing the noon news, anchoring, and doing consumer reporting—and I'm a quick study. That's how I'm going to do it."

Another male reporter said, "But you've never covered a fire, a murder, a demonstration, or even worked with the camera crews."

He was right, of course. He knew my credentials, but he didn't know my determination. I was learning that when opportunity knocks, you might as well answer the door and have at it.

Next came my mother.

When she and I spoke, it wasn't nearly as hard as I had thought it would be. She said, "Of course you're taking the job. It's an

IF I CAN MAKE IT THERE, I CAN MAKE IT ANYWHERE

incredible opportunity, and you'll be wonderful. And I'll come to New York to visit as often as I can." She was proud of me, but I could tell that she wasn't delighted at the prospect of my moving so far away—nor was she thrilled with losing the celebrity status that my being on local television gave her in Sacramento. She really got a kick out of seeing me on TV each day. With me working in New York, she would lose that. Still, I could always count on Mom to say the right thing.

Two weeks isn't much time to change from one life to another. I began packing what I thought I would need in New York; held a huge garage sale where I even sold my little red 1975 AMC Gremlin to Harry Martin, one of the KCRA anchors; and, of course, I had the traditional farewell lunches. The exhilaration of the move kept me from worrying too much about what was in store for me, and before I knew it, I was headed for the airport and another flight to New York.

Once again, I kissed my mother goodbye at the gate and boarded my plane.

Joan's Special Report, "Women in Business"

Chapter 11

SMALL-TOWN GIRL ON THE MEAN STREETS OF NYC

Nothing is impossible. The word itself says "I'm possible!"
—Audrey Hepburn

I was a little more subdued on this flight to New York than I was on my last, and though I had plenty of time to read the magazines I'd brought along, I spent most of the flight just staring out the window, trying to block out any thoughts that I might have made a huge mistake. I'd been so wrapped up in getting things in order before leaving Sacramento that I'd given almost no thought to the task of getting settled when I got to New York or to the realities of the job I would be starting the next day.

In just two weeks, I'd accepted the offer from WABC to work as a street reporter for *Eyewitness News* and moved all the way across the country. My career had been fast-tracked in Sacramento, and my short tenure there had never taken me outside the studio to cover stories. Now I was going to cover the mean streets of Gotham! Had it been a mistake to accept the offer so quickly? Once they figured out that I had no prior street-reporting experience, would they send me back home with my tail between my legs? Between the recirculated air in the plane and my downward spiral into self-sabotaging thoughts, I needed a soothing cup of hot tea, so I rang for the flight attendant.

Why was I letting negative self-talk take hold? I'd never let doubts stand in the way of my saying yes to an opportunity before, and now that I had this terrific job, I wasn't going to start. I pictured Mom juggling daunting lawsuits, foreclosures, and Dad's complicated estate while raising two teenagers. I could rise to this challenge too. When the attendant brought the tea, I drank it like liquid courage.

After all the horror stories I'd heard about looking for an apartment in Manhattan, I was happy it was no longer on my to-do list. As it turned out, my childhood friend Jed had done the impossible. I was surprised and grateful when he immediately stepped up and offered to find a place for me, even though we hadn't been in contact for years. I think it speaks volumes about close friendships—the kind where you can just pick back up wherever you left off as if no time had passed at all. I also assumed Jed had fond memories of how my mom had been such a steady, supportive force during his somewhat turbulent childhood years, and this was an opportunity for him to support me in what was now his hometown.

Jed lived with Andy Warhol on East Sixty-Sixth Street in the prestigious Upper East Side of Manhattan, and he had heard about a small furnished apartment for rent in the Beekman on Park Avenue at Sixty-Third Street, just a few blocks from their place. I was really surprised when he told me that Andy had gone along to check it out.

SMALL-TOWN GIRL ON THE MEAN STREETS OF NYC

I flinched when I heard that it was going to cost $750 a month, as that seemed high to me, but everyone told me New York was going to be expensive. Believe it or not, Jed said that an apartment on Park Avenue at that price was considered a bargain. In retrospect, I probably should have known that Jed and Andy likely had a different perspective than I did on what constituted a "good deal." Once Jed mentioned that Dan Rather also lived in the building, I felt like it was meant to be, and I agreed to sign the lease sight unseen.

Unlike my first trip to New York for the audition, this flight landed in a downpour, obscuring my view of the city. Not an omen, I told myself.

My taxi pulled up to the Beekman, a striking mix of red brick and limestone with an ornate canopied entrance. Before the car had fully stopped, the doorman rushed out, loaded my bags onto a trolley, and ushered me inside.

Opening the door to my new home, I finally understood what people meant by small New York apartments. My living room window overlooked the traffic jam on Park Avenue, while my bedroom window looked directly into another apartment—Halston's bedroom, I would later learn. The kitchen was little more than a countertop with a mini-fridge, sink, and microwave. But when the bellman informed me that the phone in the living room connected not only to the front desk but also to the French restaurant downstairs, I figured my tiny kitchen problem was officially solved.

The next day, I would walk into *Eyewitness News* for the first time, completely unaware of the storm I was stepping into. Rumors were already swirling that I had been hired because I was young and blonde—not because I deserved to be there. My immediate outsider status wasn't just about being a "newbie" (or a blonde, for that matter); it was because this wasn't just any newsroom.

I didn't know it yet, but *Eyewitness News* represented a revolution in television journalism. For decades, television news had been the domain of white, Anglo-Saxon men—Walter Cronkite, Chet Huntley, David Brinkley. Local news was no different. That changed in 1968, when WABC hired a visionary named Al Primo to be its news director.

Primo, inspired by his walks through the city, saw New York for what it was—a melting pot. He wanted the news team to resemble the people watching at home. WABC transformed local news by assembling a team of reporters that reflected the diversity of New York itself—across race, ethnicity, and religion. Rather than relying on the traditional model of anonymous, interchangeable reporters, Primo built a cast of distinctive, relatable personalities viewers could connect with on a daily basis.

Audiences began tuning in not just for the headlines but to see familiar faces—reporters who brought warmth and presence to the news. He hired Melba Tolliver, one of the first Black female reporters in the country. Then he tried to hire a Puerto Rican reporter named Gloria Rojas away from the CBS affiliate in town, but she wasn't willing to join the new team yet. She suggested Primo check out a Jewish Puerto Rican lawyer who was "fighting for the little guy" with bombastic flair. His name was Gerry Rivers. Primo tracked him down and hired him, on one condition: that he use his birth name, Geraldo Rivera, on air. The rest is history.

While critics dubbed the format "happy-talk news" and dismissed the casual banter between newscasters as unprofessional, viewers embraced the more human approach. The ratings soared, and soon the model was being replicated in cities across the country.

This newsroom was a family. Tight knit. Fiercely protective of one another. And into that mix, the station dropped me—a young, blonde, California-bred reporter with zero street experience.

When I arrived at WABC in 1975, Phil Nye, the news director who had plucked me out of obscurity, never told me that I would be filling a gap in the *Eyewitness News* team as the blonde WASP. Apparently, he wanted to raise the ratings in the bedroom communities, which were weaker than the urban numbers. But the tight-knit *Eyewitness News* team embraced their ethnic identities and those of their colleagues.

On my first morning, I walked into the bullpen wearing a peach pantsuit (so California, and so wrong for New York City). The newsroom was a sea of men and women wearing navy, gray, and black. Without introductions, I was met with active disinterest at best, icy coldness at worst. It wasn't at all like the movies, in which the curmudgeonly news editor with the soft spot for beginners puts his arm around the young reporter and introduces her to the staff, who, realizing the new recruit is a little insecure, show her the ropes. Nope, not at all.

To compound the situation, Peter Bannon, a reporter from Atlanta, was also hired that week, and he also happened to be blond. He had more news experience than I did, but that didn't seem to matter with this group of reporters. It wasn't long before we began hearing whispers: "Why the heck did they hire Ken and Barbie?" (Cute, maybe, if it isn't you they're talking about.)

Had the news execs listened when I said I had no experience in street reporting? What would the other reporters do with that bit of information?

Five minutes later, I was sent out with a veteran reporter, Doug Johnson, to cover an event honoring a retired boxer. In the car, Doug studied the wire copy in silence. I was too intimidated to ask questions. When we arrived, the three-man camera crew sprang into action, setting up lights and sound equipment in a well-rehearsed ballet. Doug fired off a few questions, shook the boxer's hand, and we were done. I filed everything away in my mental notebook.

The next morning, before I even reached my desk, the assignment editor called me over. "You're going with Bob Lape today; he's covering a prison story. They're leaving now."

Wait—wasn't Bob the food critic? Were we covering prison food?

I didn't have time to ask. Thirty minutes later, I was inside a high-security prison, surrounded by steel bars, clanging doors, and gray-painted walls. I'd never seen the inside of a jail before, let alone a high-security prison.

When Bob and I returned, Phil Nye waved me into his office. "We'll have a story for you tomorrow," he said, then hesitated. "But first, we need to talk about your name."

I swallowed hard. My name?

Phil said, "When 'Blunden' is written quickly, the *n* at the end of *Blunden* can look like an *r*, and we wouldn't want a reporter to be a '*Blunder*.' The critics would have a field day." As it turned out, they had one anyway, but I didn't have to give them a written invitation.

When Phil said "Blunder," it did stir up some old memories.

When I was a little girl, our family used to go out to dinner from time to time, and when the restaurant was crowded, my dad would leave his name with the hostess while we sat down to wait. Occasionally we'd hear, "Dr. Blunder, table for Dr. Blunder." Dad used to get very upset—a doctor couldn't be a blunder! Well, if "Blunder" wasn't a good name for a surgeon, it was also not a good name for a reporter.

That night I called my mother to tell her what I'd done so far and to break the news about the name change. "Mom, remember how Dad used to get so upset when someone said his name wrong and called him 'Dr. Blunder'? Well, my news director seems to have the same concern, and he wants me to pick a new name."

I was met with a telling silence.

The next morning, word had already spread that I was changing my name. Reporter Gloria Rojas suggested "Joan Cartwright," using the surname of the family on *Bonanza*, a Western TV show at the time. Puzzled, I asked her why. "You're from California, so everyone will think of the hit show, and it was the Cartwright family who presided over the Ponderosa Ranch, right?"

Right. Did she think that all of California looked like the Ponderosa Ranch?

I have a feeling some other names were suggested that I didn't hear.

Doug Johnson, the veteran I'd shadowed on my first assignment, had a simpler idea. "Drop the B. Call yourself 'Lunden.'"

It stuck.

A few minutes later Joan Lunden was on her way to her first assignment in New York City, a trial that was taking place in the New York State Supreme Court in lower Manhattan. I was in a car with a three-man crew. We introduced ourselves and were off. I was a little giddy, with a tinge of panic and exhilaration, so I focused on the wire copy about the bombing and conspiracy trial. There had been many protests over the Vietnam War during the past few years, and some more radical protesters had bombed Army recruiting centers. This was a trial for one of them.

We stopped in front of an impressive Greek Revival building with huge columns and a long, wide staircase leading up to its doors. Herb Todd, the cameraman on this assignment, asked, "Joan, how many mags will you want?"

Mags? Did he mean magazines? "I don't think I'll have time to read any magazines while I'm in the courtroom."

All three men looked at me in disbelief and smiled, trying their best not to break into laughter. The sound man couldn't help himself; he laughed so hard he may have peed his pants.

Herb took it in bemused stride. "I'm talking about film. Do you think you'll want six hundred feet, or more?"

I still didn't have the slightest idea what a mag was, so I said, "Oh, I don't know. What do you think, Herb?"

What Herb thought was that I didn't have the slightest idea what a mag was, and I most likely didn't have any idea what I was doing in general. Herb was a kind-looking man, fatherly, and he gave me a quick look, then a little smile. "We may need a four hundred and a six hundred," he said, then he grabbed his entire bag and we headed toward the steps of the court building.

As we walked, I got close to him and whispered, "Herb, what's a mag?" I was fessing up to being a real greenhorn. Instead of screaming with laughter, he explained that *mag* was short for *magazine*, the name for the big round canister on top of the camera that contained the film. The canisters all looked the same, but they contained various lengths of film.

"Most stories take at least one four-hundred-foot mag," he said, "which gives us enough film for you to edit it down to anywhere from one to three minutes for air." Lesson one for Lunden.

Lesson two came right on its heels. Herb said, "They don't allow cameras in the courtroom. We can go into the building with you. You go into the courtroom and take notes, and when you come out, we'll find you somewhere near the door."

"Where will you be, exactly?" I asked. We had walked up two flights of stairs and turned three corners by then; I was anxious not to lose them.

"Don't worry—we'll find you."

I didn't know how that would work, but I didn't have time to think about it because I was too busy listening to the rest of his instructions. "When it's all over, if the woman is found not guilty, you stick with her like glue, since she'll be able to exit the courthouse. Stay right next to her and don't move away from her for any reason. If she's found guilty, she won't be able to come out of the courtroom. In that case, you stick like glue to her attorney. Make sure you know where he is in the courtroom and *stick* with him," he emphasized again. "Remember, we'll find you."

I checked my watch. It was 10:30 a.m.

I steeled myself for what lay ahead, walked toward the courtroom door, and then looked back to see which direction Herb and the crew had gone. They had vanished in the crowd. I opened the door and found the place packed. I had never been to a formal court proceeding so I didn't know where to go, but when I saw a row of people taking notes, I figured they were press too. I awkwardly made my way through a crowded aisle and sat next to a man who turned out to be from the local CBS affiliate.

He leaned over and said, "Here's what's happened so far." I quickly learned that many of the reporters from competing stations and newspapers were helpful and quite nice, and I became friendlier with my so-called competition than with my own colleagues. After all, I spent more time with them at story locations. At any rate, whether he was simply being nice or flirtatious, he brought me up to speed, and I made notes on the rest of the trial.

In the five hours I sat on that hard bench, I had plenty of time to identify the defendant. When the gavel struck and the defendant was found guilty, I did just as Herb had told me. I got right next to the woman's attorney and walked out of the building. Despite the throng of other TV crews and journalists, Herb's crew had indeed found me. The sound man handed me a microphone as I edged my way close to the attorney and stuck it in front of his face. It only took the lawyer thirty seconds to say what he wanted to say. I'd spent the whole day there for a two-minute story.

That's when I did my first New York sign-off. I should say "sign-offs"; the first time I said, "Joan Blunden, KCRA-TV." The second time I said, "Joan Blunden, *Eyewitness News.*" The third time I got it right: "This is Joan Lunden, *Eyewitness News.*" My baptism by fire was over; I had met my first big challenge and survived.

I'd come to New York at the height of the worldwide oil crisis, and the following evening I was sent to cover a meeting between Secretary of State Henry Kissinger and the leaders of the OPEC[1] member nations at the United States Mission to the United Nations, which is not far from the United Nations Headquarters. The mission is essentially the US embassy for the UN. Before I left the office, Joe Coscia, the assignment editor, warned me, "You're not going to be allowed inside the mission. You don't have credentials. You're going to be out in front with the demonstrators. And you won't be allowed to talk to Kissinger."

We'll see about that.

When our car pulled up in front of the US mission, there were several hundred people being held behind police barricades. They were carrying placards protesting OPEC oil policy while yelling and chanting protest slogans. We got shots of the demonstration and then walked closer to the barricades to talk to the protesters. I barely needed to ask a question—one after another, they started shouting into my microphone.

"We're paying a fortune for gas. Kissinger needs to do

---

1 The Organization of the Petroleum Exporting Countries.

something to fix it."

"I waited in line for more than an hour, and by the time I got to the pump, the station had raised the price three times."

One especially loud and angry protestor turned out to be a truck driver who was understandably distraught over how the crisis was crippling his industry. "How's a guy supposed to make a living when our gas prices are going up and the speed limits are coming down?"

As the decibel level from behind the police barriers rose, my crew and I moved away pronto. We crossed the street, where network crews were moving through the Secret Service security check at the door. I watched as the agents opened cameras and lighting equipment and rifled through personal bags.

At one point I was the only reporter still out in front, and as one limousine after another pulled up, I began to get nervous. "How will I know when Kissinger arrives?" I asked.

"Don't worry; you'll know," my cameraman Ronnie said.

About five minutes later, four unmarked cars with flashing red lights and a half dozen motorcycle cops pulled up at the same time.

The sound man handed me the mic and said, "Guess who?"

From my vantage point on the steps of the mission I could see a man get out of the limo, but he was immediately surrounded by a cordon of Secret Service agents. "How do I get to him?" I asked Ronnie in a panic. It didn't look to me as if there was any way to break through that wall of bodies.

But Ronnie said, "Don't worry—when the lights go on, you'll see why they call it the magic of TV."

The crowd of protestors jeered. Then the camera lights turned on, and like Moses parting the Red Sea, the light opened a path. I had gotten much closer than I'd imagined I could, and somehow through the mayhem our eyes connected—and yes, I mean my eyes connected with those of Henry Kissinger.

The first thing that came to my mind was that he looked just as he did on the evening news. I shouted (politely), "Excuse me, Mr. Secretary." Secret Service agents moved in to shield him. As one pushed me back, he barked, "You can't talk to the secretary out here." But Kissinger saw me too, and he paused; in fact, he gave me a real once-over. Then he came toward me and said with a boyish grin, "It's perfectly all right. I'll talk to the young lady."

Oh my God . . . Henry Kissinger seems to be flirting with me. (This was the beginning of an ongoing flirtation Kissinger would maintain for the next two decades. Always harmless, I might add, since he was happily married.)

My heart nearly stopped, because now that I had him, I had to think of what to ask him. I was like the dog that chased the car and finally caught it. With my adrenaline pumping, I pulled myself together and said, "Mr. Secretary, the Syrian foreign minister has charged that negotiations are dividing the Arab nations. Could you respond to that?"

He replied, "Well, I'm seeing the Syrian minister tomorrow morning, and I'll have to have a talk with him. That's not our intention."

It was all over in a few seconds. It was short, but I had done it: *I got Henry Kissinger on tape.*

That night, my interview aired on the network news. I sat in the newsroom, waiting for someone to acknowledge my *major* scoop.

Nothing.

But I knew. Four days on the job, and I had covered a New York Supreme Court trial and Henry Kissinger all by myself. Maybe I *was* cut out for this after all.

For the next several weeks, I saw a lot of exciting stories on the evening news, but none of them were mine. If you look up New York City in the 1970s, you'll see that the city was mired in a major financial crisis and was nearly bankrupt. Deteriorating and abandoned apartment buildings, due to what was termed "white flight" and economic stagnation, were everywhere. As the city's crime rate soared, a vigilante group called the Guardian Angels took to the streets, making citizens' arrests for violent crimes. I wasn't looking at the big picture, though; I was taking it story by story, honing my street-reporting skills. I was also getting to know the inside of most of the police precincts and fire stations in New York, and the smoky aroma of my clothes attested to that.

In fact, it seemed as though every time there was a fire, they sent me, the rookie. I'll never forget the very first fire I was ever sent to cover. I hadn't been in New York long, and as we pulled up to a massive blaze in an apartment building on the Lower East Side of the city, flames were shooting out the windows and smoke was everywhere. As the film crew pulled their equipment from the car's trunk, I tried stopping a fireman who was moving from one position to another at that moment. He glanced at me very briefly, like I was an annoying kid sister, and then refocused on aiming his fire hose at the blaze. I would soon discover that you were allowed to get reports only from the man in the white helmet—the fire chief—*not* from the guys who were busy fighting the fire.

Okay, so that was lesson three.

Joan snags an interview with Secretary of State Kissinger.

Chapter 12

ACCIDENTAL ANCHOR

Confidence grows out of challenging yourself in new ways and from saying "yes" to unexpected opportunities—even if it scares you.

—Tory Burch

One day, I got a surprising and random opportunity to anchor the six o'clock news. It came about because of a dispute over a device called a Klieg light, also known as an eye light. Bill Beutel, one of the anchors on our 6:00 p.m. broadcast, had heard that Barbara Walters had a tiny light placed in her anchor desk that magically erased any dark circles beneath her eyes and smoothed out lines. Beutel, a strikingly handsome man who really didn't need a lot of help but was incredibly vain, became obsessed with getting Klieg lights added to the *Eyewitness News* set.

However, he anchored the show with Roger Grimsby, who was older than Beutel and personified the image of a grizzled veteran reporter. Grimsby was adamant that looks shouldn't matter more than your experience and your credibility. He couldn't care less what people thought about his on-camera appearance, and he forbade anyone to install an eye light on his side of the set.

The expense of the eye light for Beutel was ultimately authorized, and everyone thought that would be the end of it. However, the day the new lighting was installed, it was Roger's turn to do the news tease. (That's when, ten minutes before the newscast, one anchor is on set to promote the stories in the upcoming show.) When Roger arrived in the studio, he discovered to his great horror that the electricians had installed the eye light on the wrong side of the news desk—his. In a fit of anger, Roger marched back into the news director's office, threw his script into the air, and screamed, "You don't like the way I look? Then get someone else to do the damn show!" and stormed out of the building. (And that's the PG version of what Roger really said.)

Everyone went into a panic. The producers in the studio control room were calling the newsroom, saying, "Roger stormed out! We need someone to fill in; we go on the air in less than ten minutes!"

Don Dunphy Jr., the assistant news director, jumped into action. He ran through the halls of the newsroom, looking into offices, and that's when he spotted me—the newbie who was the most recent hire at the station. But at that moment, it didn't matter.

Dunphy literally grabbed me by the back of my suit collar and lifted me up from my chair, telling me, "You're anchoring tonight. Let's run!" We ran out of the newsroom and down Sixty-Sixth Street to the studio as fast as we could. A makeup artist was standing by to quickly do what she could as I jumped into the anchor chair next to Beutel. I was handed the script for the hourlong show, but because of Grimsby's tirade, the pages that had been thrown in the air were now all out of order. Page twenty followed page one, which followed page five. And worse, some pages were missing. "Stand by; in five, four, three, two, one." I took a breath and read what was before my eyes on the teleprompter and then reorganized the script during the commercial. Ironically, the new eye light did strange things to my face that night.

By the next afternoon the lights had been switched and Roger returned to work. But I'd gotten an early taste of my future anchor career, all because someone installed a light in the wrong place.

* * * * *

I became an accidental anchor on yet another occasion during that first year in New York. It happened on a Saturday night when the anchor for the abbreviated fifteen-minute evening newscast at 11:00 p.m. failed to show up. A young writer named Alan Weiss was getting his first shot as a producer that night, but he began to worry when he still had no anchor thirty minutes before airtime. The regular anchor, Gil Noble, had always arrived late, so no one worried too much when they didn't see him in the newsroom.

As eleven o'clock drew nearer, the rookie producer started to get so nervous that he checked the vacation schedule, and sure enough, Gil was off. No one had caught that detail and replaced him.

In a panic, Alan borrowed someone's jacket and tie and was about to do the broadcast himself when he remembered I lived across the street. It was almost eleven o'clock when my phone rang. "Joan, I'm desperate," Alan said. "I need you to anchor tonight, in eleven minutes. Can you get here in time?"

I'd been bicycling in Central Park that warm evening and had showered and washed my hair earlier; it wasn't even completely dry yet. I'd just set a bowl of hot popcorn on the coffee table to eat while watching a movie. But I heard the anxiety in his voice and said I'd be there as fast as I could. I threw on a blouse, snatched up my purse, jumped into the elevator (I lived on the twenty-eighth floor), and ran down the block to the studio. I had jeans and sneakers on, but anchors were never seen below the desk anyway.

The atmosphere in the studio that night was like something out of a movie. The rookie producer was sitting at the anchor desk, white as a ghost at the thought of having to do the live show himself, when I breathlessly bounded through the door. He looked up and said, "Thank God you're here. One minute to air."

I slid into the anchor chair and turned my purse upside down on the desk. As items came rolling out, I grabbed a lipstick, pulled my freshly washed hair into a ponytail, and shoved everything else onto the floor. Then, with less than a beat to catch my breath, I was on. "Good evening; the top story tonight is . . ."

The late news program on Saturday nights was a short broadcast, only fifteen minutes long. I hadn't had time to see a script, so I read whatever appeared on the teleprompter. During the first commercial break, I quickly read the upcoming copy and put on some blush and a little mascara. In the next commercial break, I put on some eye shadow. By the end of the program, the people watching at home, if they were paying attention, must have wondered what in the world was going on—I was transforming myself in front of their eyes. I was also saving the newscast; we whipped through the news, weather, and sports without a hitch, and at 11:20 p.m. I was on my way back to my apartment, where the popcorn was almost still warm.

The station's confidence in me seemed to be rising. I was assigned to cover one of the candidates in the mayoral campaign, a relatively unknown politician named Ed Koch. I followed the Koch campaign through the primaries and was at his headquarters on election night when he won the nomination of the Democratic party. It was exciting to be in on an upset victory like that, and I fully expected to continue to follow his campaign until the election in November. I was wrong in that assumption. I later realized that no one had expected Koch to win, and that's why they had assigned the new kid to his campaign. As soon as he became a viable candidate, a male reporter took over the assignment.

During this maturation period, I remember being sent to cover the early-morning story of an apparent murder. The police had found the body of a woman lying in a dirt-filled vacant lot on Manhattan's Lower East Side, an area of tenements and burned-out buildings. We were the first news crew on the scene. We were barely noticed as the police searched the area, so we inched our way toward the tarpaulin that was covering the body. When one of the officers spotted us, he walked over and told us he was the officer in charge. I asked, "Have you determined the cause of death?"

The officer nonchalantly pulled back the tarp to reveal the lifeless bluish-purple body of a young woman and said, "She had her throat cut, so she either choked on her own blood or she bled out."

I was shaken as I stood looking at her, but before I allowed any bile to creep up in the back of my throat, I tried to cover up my shock by saying, "Do you have any identification yet?"

At that, the officer pulled the woman's sweater up toward her face. "No; she's not wearing a bra," he said. "She was likely a prostitute."

She didn't look more than eighteen or nineteen years old. She was someone's daughter. The insensitivity of the officer's actions and that remark really floored me. I couldn't understand how not wearing a bra equaled being a prostitute, but it certainly did in the mind of that policeman. I realize that people who work in certain fields—doctors, nurses, police officers, fire fighters—can become somewhat desensitized to death, but there must be a level of insensitivity beyond which, as human beings, we do not go.

I know that as reporters we're supposed to be objective, but who isn't moved by the plight of an old woman who has just been kicked out of the house she's lived in for fifty years, or by the anguish of a young mother whose child has just been killed by a car? I was learning how to be a street reporter, but no one was training me how to knock on the door of a mother whose son had just died by suicide and ask for his photo without it tearing me up. I found it difficult to separate my work from my feelings, and I never seemed to get hardened to the human tragedies I was covering.

It became obvious after a while that there was a fine line between covering a story to get the information out to the public and invading someone's privacy. In 1976, New Yorkers were on edge during the "Son of Sam" murder spree. The people of the city were terrorized for more than a year. Because the serial killer targeted attractive young women with long brown hair, hundreds of women cut their hair short and dyed it blond. Twenty-four-year-old David Berkowitz was eventually charged with killing six people and wounding eleven others. We would be sent to the homes of victims to get interviews only a few hours after the bodies had been identified. The families of these young victims were totally devastated, and often unable to respond at all. Yet the news demands that we cover these types of stories. Whether there is a moral question about a person's right to privacy is still an issue that needs more investigation.

Somehow, though, things started to fall into place for me. I was covering important press conferences, interviewing public figures, and covering city and federal government actions. I was moving around from story to story in a "let's get down to business" fashion.

In time, I finally got the assignment I'd been promised, anchoring the Sunday-evening broadcast. There was even some whispering that I was possibly in line to get a permanent anchoring spot on the Monday-through-Friday weeknight news at some point.

But that future could have been greatly jeopardized if it weren't for my coanchor Doug Johnson. Doug was an experienced and legendary reporter at *Eyewitness News* and one of the few who befriended me. It was December and I was still new to anchoring the Sunday program—and, more important, I was still new to the various traditions of New York City.

New York is a melting pot of many different ethnic groups, and words that originated with some of those groups eventually worked their way into general speech. For example, many non-Jewish New Yorkers spiced their everyday speech with Yiddish expressions. That December evening with Doug, I was slated to tell the story of Chanukah, the Festival of Lights, which often correlates with the Christian holiday of Christmas. Being from Sacramento, I looked at the word *Chanukah* as it was written in the script, and in my head, I pronounced it to myself as "Cha-*new*-kah." Doug noticed what page I was reading and leaned over, saying, "You're doing the *Ha*-na-kkah story, right?"

Wait—he'd just pronounced it "*Ha*-na-kkah."

"Right, I've got that one," I said.

"Don't forget to say *Ha*-na-kkah," he repeated slowly and distinctly. It was a subtle and thoughtful way of telling me how to say the word—a word he realized I may never have heard before. And he was absolutely right on that one. "Oh God, you just saved my life," I said.

He smiled as he replied, "Or at least your career. You're welcome."

From that night on, I've always asked about any word I was unsure of before going on the air with it. When I walked back into the newsroom after the show, I saw the writers snickering and looking my way. One of them, seemingly a nice Jewish boy from Brooklyn, said with a smile (or was it a smirk?), "Hey, you did okay on that Cha-*new*-kah story, Joan."

Was it a setup? It sure felt that way.

As the giggles continued, I knew that it had been a setup for sure.

Joan on WABC Eyewitness News, *1976*

Chapter 13

STEPPING OUT IN THE BIG APPLE

*In New York, you're always just
one cab ride away from a new adventure.*

—Attributed to the character Carrie Bradshaw
(played by Sarah Jessica Parker) in *Sex and the City*

Moving to a new city for a job is daunting. I was lucky to know Jed upon arriving in New York, and he and Andy graciously invited me out. But my erratic schedule, which involved early mornings sometimes and late nights at other times, made socializing difficult. While I was gaining confidence at work, my social life was nonexistent.

I was also discovering an unexpected reality women in the news and entertainment industry faced: The more well-known we became, the less likely it was that men would approach us. The result? I had so few dates I that can remember every single one.

The first was at a party I covered at an embassy, where a suave young Italian diplomat asked me to dinner. I said yes. He picked me up in his Ferrari, took me to an elegant restaurant, and, over dinner, we had a pleasant conversation. Then, out of nowhere, he said, "Let's go back to my place, and tomorrow morning we'll fly down to Bermuda on my plane. I have a house there."

I replayed our conversation, wondering what I had said to give him the impression I would be amenable to that. I was flustered but also insulted, and I ended the date right then and there and left the restaurant. As I shut my apartment door behind me, I thought, *Did that really just happen?*

My second date was, thankfully, less distressing and far more interesting. I had been assigned a story about an extraordinary penthouse built in the airspace above the Atrium, a high-rise on Fifty-Seventh Street. In New York, people can buy the rights to build atop existing buildings—a concept that fascinated me. The penthouse belonged to Stewart Mott, an eccentric General Motors heir and self-described "avant-garde philanthropist" who used his fortune to fund progressive causes.

As I toured the space, Stewart explained that the workmen outside were moving in plants for his rooftop *farm*. His philanthropy was often upstaged by his unconventionality; his garden would eventually boast 460 different plant species, a chicken coop, and a compost pile, all perched above Manhattan.

Stewart was charming. As he showed me around, he asked how long I'd been in New York. I told him I had recently moved from California. "How do you like it here?" he asked.

"It's been an adjustment—so much concrete, not enough trees. And I miss my cat."

"Want a great shot of the penthouse and garden from above? My office is on the top floor of the General Motors Building. Meet me there, and you'll get an exclusive view."

STEPPING OUT IN THE BIG APPLE

That final shot from his office concluded both the workday and our flirtation. But when I returned home after the eleven o'clock news, I opened my apartment door to find a dozen green plants and, inside a pet carrier, a beautiful white Persian kitten. Seriously! There was a live cat in my apartment!

There was also a card: "Welcome to New York. Best, Stewart."

A few days later, he called and asked me to dinner. He was kind and unpretentious—certainly a step up from the overconfident Italian diplomat.

Later that week, my mother visited for Christmas. When Stewart learned she was in town, he invited us both to dinner. Mom, ever practical, saw the potential upside of my marrying a billionaire.

Stewart was a staunch Democrat; my mother a lifelong Republican. I worried about the conversation turning into a debate. But before I could warn her, she promised, "I'll be a good sport."

The evening began at a Park Avenue gathering for Senator Frank Church, a Democratic presidential candidate up until Jimmy Carter became the party hopeful. As I nervously watched my mother, I heard voices rising—hers among them. I whisked her into the bathroom for a quick mother-daughter chat.

Next, we attended a fundraiser for Morris (Mo) Udall, an influential representative from Arizona also vying to be president. The event was held in a sprawling Central Park West duplex. I glanced over and saw Mom seated between Mo and Gloria Steinem. She caught my eye and gave me a reassuring smile. Later, I found her deep in conversation with Congresswoman Bella Abzug, an outspoken feminist. Somehow, she was keeping her opinions to herself—an incredible feat.

A few weeks later I told my mother I wasn't continuing to date the heir to billions; we came from totally different worlds. I wasn't sophisticated in his political arena, and, more important, the chemistry just wasn't there. And besides, finding Mr. Right wasn't even on my radar at that point; I was far too busy proving myself in my career.

I'd been at my new job for only a short time, and I was working twelve to fourteen hours a day, which didn't bother me. However, I was getting no help or encouragement of any kind, except of course from the camera crews. Equally troubling was the fact that I hadn't been able to make any personal friends at work. This was a first for me—I'd never had problems finding friends before. I'd tried striking up conversations, but I just couldn't seem to crack the code with this tightly knit group of reporters.

My social life remained centered around my friend Jed and his partner, Andy, since they were the only people I really knew outside the newsroom—and because they let me tag along with them. Like the night we went to Studio 54.

We stepped out of a cab onto West Fifty-Fourth Street, where a crowd of socialites, aspiring rock stars, and stylish nobodies was gathered outside the black doors of the infamous club, all hoping to get in. The bouncers knew Andy and Jed by sight and waved the three of us inside as a woman in a silk halter jumpsuit with a plunging neckline complained that she'd been waiting for an hour now. Her glittering eyeshadow caught the neon glow of the club's marquee, and I felt conspicuous in my simple black cocktail dress and subtle makeup compared to the women wearing barely there disco dresses, feather boas, body paint, and sequins.

I was relieved to have Andy in front of me and Jed right behind as we found our way to the stairs. The scent of Charlie cologne fought with thick cigarette smoke and a hint of something illicit from the corners, making me cough a little on the way to the VIP balcony. All the while, the bass line of Donna Summer's "Love to Love You Baby" thrummed against my sternum.

Everyone on the balcony hailed Andy and Jed and offered to share their tables, but Andy had arranged for a relatively quiet space just outside the spotlight for the three of us. Andy said he would hold down the table while Jed took me over to the rail to look down at the dance floor. It was, of course, filled with scantily clad people grinding against each other to loud disco music and pulsating lights. I could tell Jed was embarrassed by the level of uninhibited human sexual behavior on display, so I suggested going back to the table. As people stopped by to say hi to Jed and Andy, they both seemed to enjoy introducing me to their friends, who stood a bit more at attention when they heard I was a TV reporter. "Oh my, we didn't know we had a big-time news lady here; we better behave ourselves or we might end up on your show."

I actually felt conspicuously naive amid the glitz and glamour and the gaudiness and tawdriness. Even so, I had to chuckle a little when I thought about the fact that while I may have faded into the background in a place like this, I was, outside these walls, an intrepid woman trying to break a thick glass ceiling in a man's industry.

It was a fascinating night, in a sometimes-freakish way. I was certain that when rumors got around to the newsroom that I was clubbing on the VIP balcony at Studio 54, my colleagues likely wouldn't believe that Jed and Andy were acting as my protectors all night. While you could be sure there were drugs at the club, you could also be sure they weren't anywhere around us, since Jed and Andy would never have wanted to get me in trouble. But I resolved to not even bother trying to set the record straight.

I was still feeling insecure and unaccepted at work. I'm not sure whether it was the fact that I was considered an intruder by my colleagues or the lack of direction from anyone, the long hours, or the loneliness, but I was questioning my decision to pull up stakes and leave my anchor position and all my friends in Sacramento behind.

It had been a pretty cushy job anchoring the noon news back in California. My job here in New York City often required me to be in the newsroom by 6:00 a.m. (the plight of a newbie), and I was often out on the street working until midnight in all kinds of weather, surrounded by police, dead bodies, devastation, fire and smoke, prostitutes, and demonstrators. Not to mention I was still learning how to be a street reporter. It was daunting, but I couldn't just throw in the towel.

No way. I had to persevere.

Chapter 14

THE FIRE ISLAND FIASCO

Harassment is about power—the undue exercise of power by a superior over a subordinate.
—Michael Crichton, *Disclosure* (1994)

Phil Nye, the man who had hired me and was my mentor at *Eyewitness News*, was replaced by Ron Tindiglia, who also seemed to be quite supportive of me. He brought in several colleagues he'd previously worked with, one of whom turned out to be the first person to ever offer me advice. Let's call him Ted for the sake of this story.

Ted spent a fair amount of time working with me in the editing room, showing me different ways to construct a story. He explained how to mix up the video and the sound bites (statements made by people on the scene) and how to change the opening and closing shots to avoid repetition.

When the work schedule got crazy, we'd occasionally dash out to get a quick lunch together. But as time went on, things started to feel uncomfortable. It felt like he was trying to turn our work relationship into something more personal. It may have been naive of me to think that you could work with a man and have a few lunches with him without his beginning to have other thoughts on his mind.

Then there was the Fire Island incident. My new trusted mentor told me that there was an *Eyewitness News* get-together planned for the weekend. "You should come along, Joan," said Ted. "It will be a good opportunity for you to socialize with the rest of the team."

Not having any close friendships in the newsroom, I was concerned that I would feel awkward and uncomfortable, like a tagalong. With some encouragement, I agreed to go. I'd never been to the famed Fire Island before. I'd heard that no cars were allowed on the island, so you had to take a ferry to get there. "I'll be going, and I have a car so you can go with me," Ted said.

When we arrived at the ferry, he parked the car, and we made the short trip to the island, then walked to the house where the gathering was to take place. When the door opened, I recognized the host as a local WCBS reporter whom I'd met on stories and who was clearly friends with Ted. He welcomed us in and introduced us to his girlfriend, but they were the only ones there. His house was like most of the other shingled cottages on Fire Island, often referred to as bungalows. I took in the "casual island ambience" with a lot of blue-and-white textiles and graphics of anchors, starfish, and shells. The dinner cooking on the stove smelled delicious. As time began to pass and no one else showed up, I asked where the rest of the reporters were or if we'd come early.

"Well, as it turns out," said Ted, "everyone had something else going on, so it's just the four of us!"

What? I looked at the others, and they seemed to be doing

their best to avoid me. Oh my God, was this really happening? How had I fallen for this?

I was embarrassed that I'd been so naive as to let this situation unfold, and I was offended as a woman that a guy—my superior at work—thought he could get away with this! He assumed that I would just go along with it. I was also scared because it felt like there was no way out. It was evening and the sky was getting darker by the minute. You can't just walk outside a home on Fire Island and hail a cab to take you back to your apartment. Remember? No cars.

"Ted, you know this is not what I signed up for," I said, trying to be strong but not too offensive, since he was my boss. I was praying he would say "Oops, my bad, I'm sorry, let me take you back home."

Instead, he tried to be charming and make light of it. "Look, maybe the original plan fell through, but we're all here, so let's just enjoy ourselves." Did he think I was buying this? But I had no choice other than to sit and have dinner with this small group—this overnight double date. I tried to be pleasant, to *go along to get along*, as they say. Ted was my superior, so I tried not to appear too bitchy (though I'm not sure if I succeeded at that). After dinner, the hours seemed to drag on forever, and all I could think of was how I hadn't seen this coming. Had it just been a matter of time before this happened?

Eventually, the hour came to turn in. The other couple peeled off to a bedroom, and I sat down on the couch and folded my arms. Growing angrier by the minute, I said, "This is not going to happen, Ted. You can go on into that bedroom, but I'm staying right here on this sofa." Now he had the audacity to act angry. I guess he felt it was going to make him look bad in front of his buddy. I'd never seen this guy angry before—his face was turning red, and he wasn't giving up. "Okay, I get it, but at least just sleep in the bedroom."

Really? Was this guy serious? I was flabbergasted. At this point, he was still trying to wrangle me into an uncomfortable—and unethical—situation just to help him save face with his friend. No way.

It was a long, stressful, uncomfortable night on that sofa with no blanket or pillow. As the sun was coming up, I snuck out of the house before the others awoke and made my way to the ferry. Thankfully I was able to jump into one of the taxis waiting at the other end.

I was nervous walking into work on Monday morning. I still couldn't believe Ted had thought I would go along with his plan. But I would have to work with him; he was my immediate superior. And I was about to find out that hell hath no fury like a man scorned. Ted started killing my stories—meaning he kept my stories from making the show lineup for one reason or another. I knew that they were all good stories and all of them were on deadline, but he had the power to keep them off the news.

I felt vulnerable and helpless. Not only that, but my reputation also took a hit because a) it had become known that I went to Fire Island with my immediate superior, and b) it was obvious to everyone that my stories weren't making air. This fact also meant I wasn't making on-air fees, so Ted was now affecting my income. Remember, a television reporter at that time was paid a base salary and an additional fee for each story that appeared on the air. If your stories didn't get aired, you earned less money.

But even more disturbing than the loss of pay was having to put up with his attitude and what it said to me and other women who only wanted to work as equals. His behavior clearly sent the message that women were not equal to men, and that when I'd refused his overtures he was free to seek revenge. This was clearly sexual harassment and sexual discrimination, but it was also 1976 and women weren't well-versed in how to handle these situations. And, sadly, these situations felt almost acceptable back then. If Ted had asked a male reporter to join him for lunch and the guy didn't accept, it wouldn't have been taken as a sexual rebuff. But that wasn't true for a woman.

He pursued his grudge for a couple of months, and while I'm a very nonconfrontational person, even I reached the breaking point. When I heard him yucking it up in the hall one day, I shouted from my desk for him to come into my office. He swept in with a smug look on his face. "What do you want?"

"First, shut the door." I took a deep breath. "This has to stop. Now. I'm not putting up with it another day."

His expression barely changed, but he could play dumb all he wanted—he knew exactly what I was talking about.

"We both know you're keeping my stories off the air for no valid reason," I said. "I know it and you know it, and everyone else in the newsroom knows it. It's pure revenge on your part, and it happens to be discriminatory, not to mention you're affecting my income. I've spoken with my agent and my lawyer, and they've both advised me to file suit against you and WABC-TV for sexual harassment and sexual discrimination, and they say I'm going to win."

That got his attention. He understood that this could spell real trouble. I could see by the look on his face that my punch had landed. I had him.

Before he even had a chance to respond, I closed with, "Against my lawyer's advice, I'm going to give you one chance, today, to rectify this situation. It's not because you deserve it; it's only to avoid the legal process. But hear me: If I detect even a whiff that this is still happening, I promise you I will tell the lawyers to go ahead and file the suit they have prepared."

He just stood there for a minute, his face becoming more and more flushed. Then, to his credit, he said, "You're right. I'm sorry. It's unprofessional of me, and it won't happen again."

He walked out, and we both went back to work. Sometimes you just have to put on your big-girl pants and stand up for yourself, even if it feels incredibly uncomfortable and scary.

It all stopped, but from then on he spoke to me only in the line of duty—and if looks could kill, he fired enough shots for me to die many times over. But since he didn't ambush any more of my stories, I felt vindicated.

I hope he's reading this.

I'd like to be writing only about how this wonderful mentor had helped me be a better reporter, and how he helped hone my creative skills, because he did do that. I'm immensely appreciative. It's such a shame that he couldn't take that win—that he had to ruin what had been a wonderful friendship and working relationship up to that point.

Chapter 15

THE GLASS CEILING WON'T BREAK ITSELF

Teach your daughters to worry less about fitting into glass slippers and more about shattering glass ceilings.

—Melissa Hurrington

In late September 1976, I was finally settling into my new life in the city. After a brutally hot summer, this fall day was shaping up to be quite pleasant, sunny but with slightly brisk temperatures. Not a bad morning to be hitting the streets of New York as a reporter.

As I walked through the newsroom, our news director, Ron Tindiglia, waved at me through the glass wall of his office to come in. When I entered, he literally jumped out from behind his desk, obviously excited to tell me something. He wanted me to fill in the next week for the station's popular anchorman, Bill Beutel, on the 6:00 p.m. news while Bill was on vacation.

As I stood there in frank disbelief, I hadn't noticed that Bill's partner, anchorman Roger Grimsby, was also in the room. Roger was a gruff old guy who had anchored for decades with the younger Bill. In retrospect, they were a bit like *The Odd Couple*, but the two of them were an incredibly popular duo who had a stranglehold on the local news ratings.

When Grimsby heard—clearly for the first time—that Tindiglia was offering me the chance to sit in the seat next to him on the 6:00 p.m. news during Bill's absence, he exploded, leaping off the sofa and across the room until he was nose-to-nose with me. He began to sputter, hardly able to put a sentence together, he was so furious.

Inches from my face, he began to yell at me. "You don't deserve to sit next to me and to anchor the goddamn New York *Eyewitness News*! You haven't been to the school of hard knocks, for Christ's sake. You're still wet behind the ears. You haven't paid your dues—the price to sit at that anchor desk. You haven't worked your way up to this coveted broadcast the way all of us have!" Then he angrily threw the show script that had been in his hands onto the floor and stomped out of the office, leaving me standing there, totally shell-shocked.

I looked down at the newspaper on the sofa Roger had just vacated, the same one I'd just read with my morning coffee. All the papers were filled with articles about Barbara Walters' move from the *Today* show to ABC news, an unprecedented shift that would make her the first woman to anchor a network evening newscast and the first news anchor ever to receive a million-dollar-a-year contract. She was set to debut the following week.

A huge glass ceiling was breaking.

And, apparently, it was breaking for me too!

But as I collected myself, remembering that I'd be sitting next to Roger at the news desk, I turned back to Ron. "Wow, I didn't see

THE GLASS CEILING WON'T BREAK ITSELF

that one coming. Does his outburst change your mind at all, or does your offer still stand?"

"It absolutely still stands, Joan," he said. "And don't worry about Roger. He's always a grump; he'll get over it."

But will he? I thought.

I walked down the corridor toward my office, thinking that maybe I *was* too inexperienced to anchor. Maybe Roger did have a point. He had come up through the ranks as a newspaper writer, then worked in radio and finally TV. He was a media veteran; he'd kept *Eyewitness News* number one for years. He was truly a legend in New York City. I had come to this number one newscast from a small local station where I'd gone from cleaning weather maps and getting coffee for people to anchoring in two short years. It had been quite a meteoric leap.

Gulp.

No. Stop those thoughts! I told myself. *You don't have to believe everything you think.*

New thought: *I got this.*

Media and cultural forces were with me. Despite the pushback and anxiety, there were a few intrepid female broadcasters in addition to Barbara Walters leading the way, including Lesley Stahl, Connie Chung, Judy Woodruff, and Jessica Savitch. It was a groundbreaking time to be a woman in television broadcasting.

The women's movement had been careening ahead at full speed ever since it exploded onto the scene in the mid-sixties. On college campuses, young women were marching and protesting for equality. The newly formed National Organization for Women (NOW) was lobbying Congress and bringing lawsuits against several large media companies to give women more opportunities in the workforce. Changes were beginning to happen for us, including legislation that outlawed gender discrimination in education, college sports, and finance and employment discrimination against pregnant women. There was also the legalization of abortion and birth control. As the feminist movement took aim at the media world, demand for more female presence in magazines, in newspapers, and on television had grown louder.

However, there was still a considerable amount of resistance from news executives. The president of NBC News at that time, Reuven Frank, had been quoted as saying, "I have the strong feeling that audiences are less prepared to accept news from a woman's voice than from a man's."

And it wasn't just the execs who were rankled by this latest development—so were the male newscasters. ABC network news anchor Harry Reasoner had made no secret of his displeasure with the plan to team him with Walters.

In a press interview with *Newsweek*, he said, "I was with her [Barbara Walters] on Nixon's China trip, but I never actually saw her work. All I know about her from that trip is that she rides a bus well."

There were rumblings going on all throughout the ABC-TV building, and a well-known male ABC News correspondent was said to have been seen running through the network newsroom yelling, "The women are coming, the women are coming!"

Roger clearly wasn't alone in his ire with co-anchoring alongside a female.

As Barbara Walters stepped onto the elevator in the ABC newsroom the following week, Harry Reasoner happened to step in right behind her. According to others who were on that elevator ride, there was a palpable chill in the air. Harry wouldn't even look at Barbara, let alone speak to her. It was not a good omen for how that pair was about to present on air.

THE GLASS CEILING WON'T BREAK ITSELF

If this is how the great Barbara Walters is being received and treated, where does that leave me? I wondered. What should I be expecting as I took my place next to grumpy Grimsby?

Realistically, I guess I should have expected that Roger wouldn't go easy on me either. But in my wildest dreams, I never could have imagined what ensued.

There was an eerie and unusual silence on set. Everyone felt the tension in the air. There was none of the usual joking around as we got closer to airtime.

Then the stage manager started the countdown. "Ten . . . nine . . . eight . . . seven . . . six . . . five . . . four . . . three . . . two . . . one . . ."

After opening the broadcast with his usual "Good evening. I'm Roger Grimsby; here now the news . . ." he teased the lineup of stories, then turned to me and, with steely, menacing eyes, bluntly said . . . "Barbara."

Wait, did he just call me Barbara?

Yep, he really did.

For a moment, I wondered if he was even older than I'd thought. Had he forgotten my name?

No, it couldn't be that. But I didn't dare correct him live on the air. I just had to ignore the slip of the tongue and go on. I looked into the camera and began talking.

And then it happened again. "Barbara."

And again, and again, and again, each time he ended a story.

Roger just couldn't help himself. I suppose he thought that behavior was warranted, given the outrageous onslaught of females daring to trespass into the male-dominated world of news on that evening. What surprised me even more was that he was able to persuade the other male reporters on the show that night to join in with him, each ending their stories and throwing back to me with "Barbara." Not once during that broadcast did the show producer or the news director walk into the studio and tell them to knock it off.

In retrospect, it was clear that a monumental change was afoot in television news at both the local and national level, and I was at the cusp of that change. As I relay my workplace encounters here, it's with an acute awareness that there are women all over this country today who are dealing with unfair, messy, discriminatory situations that are far worse than mine ever was. We still have a long way to go, but, thankfully, there's a lot more awareness in the workplace today, as well as protective laws that didn't exist in 1976 when I felt like I was left to handle threatening situations by myself.

While that night was an uncomfortable and embarrassing experience, I also think it was an opportunity to grow. It showed me that my path would be full of unexpected challenges. It also strengthened my belief that I was capable of doing anything I set my mind to. It reminded me of something I'd once heard: "If you weren't going anywhere, they wouldn't be trying to stop you."

In fact, now that I think about it . . . thanks, Roger.

Chapter 16

TWO-TIMING

*Every next level of your life will demand
a different version of you.*

—Leonardo Di Caprio

One of the advantages of working in local television news in New York City is that producers of network TV shows live in your town and can see you every night on the air. One day I got a call from one of those producers, Woody Fraser, the executive producer of *Good Morning America*. "I'd like to talk to you about doing some spots on *GMA*," he said. "Could you come over and meet with me?"

"Absolutely," I answered. "When do you want me there?"

We made an appointment for the next morning, and after I hung up, I remembered that just before I came to New York for my interview with WABC-TV I had turned on the ABC station in Sacramento just to see what their programming was like. One of the shows I watched was *AM America*, their early-morning news program with Bill Beutel and Stephanie Edwards. As I sat watching it, I imagined what it might be like to work on a show like that.

It was the first time I'd allowed myself to dream about the potential of a career in television at a higher level than anchoring the news in Sacramento.

AM America hadn't taken off in the ratings. ABC had replaced it with a new early-morning news program, *Good Morning America*, whose executive producer was Woody Fraser, a pioneering veteran of the talk show industry. Fraser is credited with inventing the daytime talk show format in the late 1960s. He realized more than most that "it's when people get bored that they change the channel," and his life's work had been about making sure that never happened.

Now I was sitting in the office of this "producing genius" (as everyone called him). Unlike other execs who sat at expansive wooden desks, he preferred a circular table large enough for a full staff meeting. He couldn't have been any more enthusiastic about his new show.

Woody was a fast talker who made big hand gestures and called everyone "Babe"—even the men. He began telling me about the vision for *GMA*. "We've purposely designed our studio to look like a home, one that any of our viewers might live in, rather than a traditional news desk in front of a blue background. In fact, you'll notice that the furniture on the set is all in warm golds and oranges, like a home."

I had occasionally snuck a look at the set, since *Eyewitness News* shared the same studio. It was covered in plastic sheeting while we broadcast our show in the evening.

"We're also taking a new approach with our hosts. We've brought in David Hartman, who's had a very successful acting career in prime-time television."

I knew David from his leading roles on *The Bold Ones* and *Lucas Tanner*.

"We also got Nancy Dussault; you may know her from Broadway!"

I hadn't heard of her, but I learned she'd been an actress and singer.

Woody continued: "We're putting together a family of contributors. So far, we've got Rona Barrett on Hollywood gossip, Jack Anderson on Washington politics, Howard Cosell on sports, and Erma Bombeck, who's just plain funny. I got two field reporters, former New York mayor John Lindsay, and Geraldo Rivera, whom you already know from local news."

So, wait—was he thinking of me for that family?

"My idea is for you to report on new products and new ideas."

He leaned in and flashed his signature smile. "I think you could be perfect spotlighting new products and trends in the American lifestyle."

He wasn't any more specific, because, frankly, he didn't know exactly what these spots would look like. Woody was creating this new format for early-morning television. Nobody had ever done anything like this on the *Today* show or *CBS Morning News*. He had unprecedented creative freedom, since the show was part of ABC's entertainment division. The news division was a partner in the program, but the entertainment division was calling the shots, and there was great anticipation around changing the face of early-morning TV.

"So, whaddya think? Wanna come on board? It'll be fun!"

"Absolutely!" I said. "I'd love to be a part of the program. Out of curiosity, how did you happen to choose me?"

His eyebrows inched up. "C'mon—you're on the news every night!"

I cautiously leaned forward. "I'm actually more qualified for reporting on new products than you may even have realized."

Again, his eyebrows shot up.

"I was a consumer reporter at KCRA in Sacramento before I came to work for *Eyewitness News*."

He stood and walked me to the door. "Great! You'll be terrific. I'll call your agent and set everything up."

It was one of the easiest career negotiations ever.

Woody would have to call my *Eyewitness News* boss and reassure him that all the stories would be done live, so I'd be finished by 9:00 a.m., and therefore the *GMA* assignments wouldn't interfere with my news work at the station.

This may appear to be a simple act of corporate communication, but there was long-standing animosity between the local station and the network. WABC resented it when the network poached their talent. This was especially galling because *GMA* had also poached Geraldo Rivera, who had been a huge star at *Eyewitness News*. What had supposedly been a part-time job for Geraldo quickly morphed into a complete defection.

With that in mind, I knew my semi-regular appearances on *GMA* covering "new products and new ideas" could possibly land me a full-time job there, and might even put me in a position to fill in for the female host when she was out on the road. Come on—a girl can dream, can't she?

WABC was equally aware of that possibility. So, part of my new job became keeping both parties happy. This meant always being available for *GMA* and never missing my regular assignments on *Eyewitness News*. As a result, my days often began at 5:00 a.m. in the *GMA* studio and ended after the eleven o'clock news signed off.

In fact, on my *GMA* mornings, it seemed to me that my *Eyewitness News* stories would often be arbitrarily scheduled to run on both the 6:00 and the 11:00 p.m. news. That sure felt like retaliation for starting my day at the network instead of the local station. But I did both jobs for more than three years, and it was worth it.

This additional network exposure opened up some other new possibilities. First there was a call from Dustin Hoffman—yep, *the* Dustin Hoffman. He wanted to discuss a possible role for me in his upcoming movie. My agent, Richard Leibner, quickly reminded me that I wasn't an actress. But when I told him I'd agreed to meet Hoffman for breakfast the following morning, he said, "I'm going along." It was fun hearing him describe the movie, which was about a divorcing couple (played by Hoffman and Meryl Streep) fighting over custody of their child, and the role he saw for me as the attorney who'd be representing him. Then, Hoffman told us the part in which his character and the attorney become involved, and that the scene would require nudity. Okay, that was a pass. It wasn't so much fun when the movie hit the theaters and it turned out to be the Oscar-winning *Kramer vs. Kramer*, though!

I'm ambitious, but, admittedly, I'm not an actress.

The next call resulting from my newfound exposure was from Norman Lear's office. He was preparing a new prime-time situation comedy for NBC to be called *Coast to Coast*, patterned after *The Love Boat* but taking place on an airplane.

I was again flattered, and I called my agent, who didn't know whether to laugh or be aghast. "Joan, you're *still* not an actress," he said.

I knew he was right. Acting had never intrigued me; however, this time the role and the offer were too big to not at least pursue it just a bit. Richard reluctantly said he would speak with them about the fee for doing a pilot and the logistics of doing a show for another network. He ended with "You know I have to tell them we're not interested, but I don't want to hear from you six months from now if this thing turns out to be a big hit. Promise you won't give me any of that 'I told you so' stuff."

I promised I wouldn't.

But a few months later I opened a copy of *People* magazine and saw an article that predicted the major female star of the next television season would come from a new show called *Coast to Coast*.

I couldn't resist. I clipped the article and sent it to Richard anonymously.

The very next week, *Us Weekly* carried an article about Fred Silverman, president of ABC's entertainment division, moving to NBC, and it went on to say where the ax was going to fall when he arrived at his new job. The first show that *Us* predicted would be eliminated was the new prime-time sitcom *Coast to Coast*. I kept expecting Richard to send me that article, but he never did.

Chapter 17

READY IN THE WINGS

Be so good they can't ignore you.
—Steve Martin,
Interview on Charlie Rose (2007)

The opportunity to do the new-product and new-lifestyle stories at *Good Morning America* had opened the door there a crack, but it would now be up to me to put my shoulder against that door and force it open all the way. I had to make the most of my short and sporadic appearances. They needed to be so interesting and appealing that the program's executives would take notice.

I wanted to be seen by the producers as a person who was ready and waiting in the wings if one of the cohosts was ill or perhaps even quit or was fired. This may sound brash and aggressive, but I've learned that a certain amount of brashness is necessary if one is to get ahead in television, and though I wasn't willing to step on people on the way up, I was aware that I had to make my presence known and press any advantage that might come along.

I can't help but think of the legendary story of how Shirley MacLaine became an Academy Award–winning actress. It happened only because she was an understudy in the Broadway show *The Pajama Game* for the star, Carol Haney. Shirley practiced and perfected the role on her own, just in case she was ever needed to fill in. Then, after Haney suffered an onstage ankle injury, MacLaine stepped into the role and gave an impressive performance, which was noticed by Hollywood film producer Hal B. Wallis, who happened to be in the audience that night. That's when Shirley's acclaimed film career began.

My initial assignment at *GMA* was to figure out what would make a memorable new-product story—in other words, it was up to me to uncover products before they were offered to the public. As usual, there was no precedent—no model to follow—so I had to blaze my own trail. I met with Woody Fraser to talk over ideas, and he told me that one of their producers had found a brand-new kind of spare tire that was about to hit the market.

Before you laugh, this was in 1976, and because there was a national rubber shortage, auto companies were selling cars without spare tires. The tire companies had now come up with a new small-size spare meant to last long enough to get you to the nearest gas station, where the normal-size flat tire could be fixed or a new tire could be purchased. My job was to create a live segment that would introduce the new spares and demonstrate how to use them.

I did this by picking one up, rolling it around, and bouncing it on the floor. This would prove that they were manageable—*even for a woman*—and durable enough to make it those few miles to the next garage. It turned out to be a rather lively segment that was useful, relatable, and timely, given the much-publicized rubber shortage, so everyone seemed to like it.

After that initial appearance, I was on my own to come up

with the next idea. Going forward, I presented my ideas to the producers, and once they decided which ones to pursue, it was up to me to research the products and determine whether they were fit for a national broadcast. The hard part was building a network of contacts who would inform me of new products before they were introduced to the news media.

This was a challenging task while still working my shifts as a reporter and weekend anchor. Fortunately, I was contacted by a young high school student, Michael Horowitz, who was looking for an internship opportunity for school credit. Bringing him into the fold was the perfect answer, so while I was out covering fires, my young intern was doing the legwork for the new product spots.

I hit the jackpot when Michael began working for me. Even though he was still in high school, he was bright and tenacious and not at all reluctant to approach big companies, which was the only way to find out what products were on the horizon. He helped me tremendously, but his presence at my desk at the local station became another source of irritation for the *Eyewitness News* staff. They simply couldn't figure out why the newbie reporter now had an intern. Little did they know that I'd simply had the good sense to not ask anyone if it was alright to hire an intern. When Michael approached me about an internship, I just said yes.

Michael and I were able to establish a network of contacts by obtaining directories of American trade associations and writing personal letters to hundreds of product development departments. We contacted the public relations departments of major manufacturers of consumer goods and asked to be added to their lists of people who would receive news about products being introduced in the coming months. The response was tremendous. I was appearing on *GMA* several times a month while still working full-time at WABC. I was getting great feedback from the *GMA* producers, and before long they asked me to start shooting the new product stories in the field. The only issue with this exciting development was the need to get time off from my day job at *Eyewitness News* so I could shoot the stories.

Uh-oh. That wasn't part of the deal we'd made with WABC, and it meant that other reporters would have to fill in for me, which didn't make me too popular in the newsroom. But hey, I wasn't so popular there to begin with.

When my field pieces began to air, *GMA* started receiving positive mail about me (only snail mail existed back then; no email and no social media platforms on which to comment or criticize). If it's possible to pinpoint a time when your career started to blossom, this might have been that moment for me.

In the next few months, I became a full-fledged part-time member of the *GMA* family. Now, if the female host was sick, on vacation, or on location, the show producers would often ask me to sit in for a segment called "People in the News." This segment was just a few minutes long and entailed delivering short quips about celebs who were in the news that day, but it gave me a taste of the hosting role without the full responsibility. It was essentially a fabulous training period for me, and it also allowed the producers to watch me become more comfortable and confident in the role. I could also now be tapped to do the live commercials that were always done by the female host on the show.

The live commercials were for the cotton industry and for Alpo dog food. Back then, commercials for Alpo were done both in our studio and on the *Today* show set. At around 6:00 a.m., the star dog of the day would arrive with its handler. You dared not offer that pup a morsel, because they wanted the dog to be hungry when the bowl of Alpo was put before him.

READY IN THE WINGS

Many years earlier, when Barbara Walters was hosting the *Today* show with Dave Garroway, it had been her job to do the live commercials on the show. I heard a story about what happened one morning before the live Alpo commercial.

The *Today* show stagehands had rolled a demo table out onto the set, and the stage manager was standing by with the bowl of Alpo. At the same time, a beautiful golden retriever named Lucky was obediently waiting for his cue, the placing of the bowl of food. Barbara got into position behind the demo table, and with fifteen seconds remaining, the dog handler put Lucky up on top of the table. The stage manager began the countdown—ten seconds, nine, eight . . .

. . . At which point Lucky pooped right there on the demo table.

Seven, six . . . The crew and staff looked on, horrified, staring at the fresh pile of doggie-doo.

"Five seconds," said the nervous stage manager.

When no one moved, the show's executive producer, Stuart Schulberg, who happened to be standing nearby, quickly stepped up.

"Four seconds." Without hesitation, Schulberg stretched out his arms and scooped the poop into his hands. "Three seconds." He stepped away. "Two; one." The bowl of Alpo was placed on the table, and Lucky rushed to gobble it up.

Cue Barbara: "My, what a hungry dog Lucky is this morning," she said.

Thirty seconds later, the commercial was over.

Schulberg then walked over to the staff and young interns, held out his poop-filled hands, and said, "This is the difference between what you do and what I do. I get the show on the air, no matter what."

Okay, back to me and my Alpo commercial: I was happy to get the chance to costar with the *GMA* Alpo dogs because doing so might put me one paw closer to possibly cohosting with David Hartman. (Sorry, I couldn't resist.)

This was happening at a time when David's sidekick, Nancy Dussault, was on her way out at *GMA*. Coming from Broadway, Nancy had spent her nights on stage, and she just wasn't a morning person. She would come in with puffy bags under her eyes and lament how miserable the early start time was. It was becoming apparent that a change was imminent, and it seemed as though Nancy couldn't wait to be relieved of the early-morning gig. Would fate take me by the hand and give me a shot?

When it came time to finally name a female anchor for the 6:00 p.m. *Eyewitness News* broadcast, I was in a position to possibly get the role, but I was passed over for Rose Ann Scamardella. (By the way, those execs made the right choice. I mean, come on—who better to sit at the helm of the eclectic team than the nice, folksy Italian girl from Brooklyn? She was absolutely perfect. Rose Ann grew into the anchor role very quickly, and New Yorkers loved her. She also became the inspiration for Gilda Radner's Roseanne Roseannadanna character on *Saturday Night Live*.)

However, the decision to pass me over had likely sealed my fate in local news.

Rose Ann Scamardella gets the anchor job.

Rose Ann inspires Gilda Radner's Roseanne Rosannadanna.

Chapter 18

I'LL HAVE MY PEOPLE CALL YOUR PEOPLE

*If the plan doesn't work, change the plan
—but never the goal.*

—Daniel Hurst

I was putting the finishing touches on one of those "three-handkerchief" stories for *Eyewitness News*, this one about a Columbia University honor student who was beaten to death with a baseball bat by a gang of teenagers who wanted his portable radio.

I had just written, "His friends described him as a well-rounded young man who was not only a brilliant mathematician but also a fine athlete, a young man who . . ." but before I could complete the sentence, my desk phone rang.

"Miss Lunden, please hold for Mr. Shanks," said the very businesslike voice of an efficient secretary. It took me a second to connect the name with ABC corporate headquarters. A moment later, Bob Shanks, the ABC network vice president in charge of *Good Morning*

America, was on the line. Over the last year, while reporting for *GMA*, I may have said hello to him once or twice on the set. Still, he opened the conversation as if we knew each other well. "Hi, Joni," he said. "How's everything in the news business?"

"Fine," I answered, and I felt a little ridiculous as I said, "And how are you doing?" I was on deadline and tense and had the urge to say *Hurry up and tell me what this call is all about,* but I managed to restrain myself.

In a very matter-of-fact tone, he said, "We're thinking about making a change in the host of the show, and we're considering you. Would you be interested?"

"Absolutely," I said, trying to put a national-television timbre into my voice.

"Good," he said. "I'll get back to you to set up lunch." It was short, sweet, and absolutely thrilling, though far from what could be considered a job offer. I tried to temper my excitement so I could finish my news story, but I wanted to shout to everyone in the newsroom that little Joni Blunden from Sacramento, California, might be the new face on *GMA*.

I quickly returned my attention to the sad story I'd been working on about the young Columbia University honor student. I finished it by writing that he was a Rhodes Scholar and had planned to work in international finance after graduation next June. Were it not for that call from Bob Shanks, I'd normally have been near tears by this time, but I was excited by my new job prospect and felt I had done Harvey's memory some justice in this piece as well.

It's hard to keep a secret in the television business; most people connected with the industry in New York had heard the rumor that *Good Morning America* was looking for a woman to replace Nancy Dussault. We all wondered whether Nancy had also heard the rumor.

I'LL HAVE MY PEOPLE CALL YOUR PEOPLE

A week later, Shanks called again to set a date for lunch. As I walked into the Warwick Hotel, I saw him waiting across the lobby. He looked exactly how I pictured a network executive would—impeccably dressed in a dapper three-piece suit and wire-rimmed glasses, with thinning hair. Our lunch was a bit unnerving in that we seemed to be talking about everything *except* my possibly working at *GMA*; for example, "What do you think of the new set and format we're using to counter the traditional shows like *Today* and *CBS Morning News*?" Then, finally, between bites of his raspberry sorbet dessert, Shanks said, "Joan, we'd like to consider you for Nancy's job."

Okay—there it was. I tried to sound calm and collected as I said, "Well, I love working on the show, and with David, so I'd love to be considered." That was essentially all there was to it. The conversation had been cordial and as light as the raspberry sorbet. I left the lunch full of hope but with no idea of what to expect next.

So now what? I tried to picture myself in the role, but one of the things I noted was how poorly the producers seemed to treat Nancy. She didn't get much time on the air, and the time she did get was mostly devoted to interviewing minor celebrities or doing homemaking segments and any other soft stories David wouldn't necessarily want. Did I think things would be different for me? But c'mon—the job was so enormous. Should I even let that bother me? I needed to get my foot in the door before I worried about anything like that.

A few days later I was handed a phone message that simply said, "Call David Hartman," with his office phone number written on it. When I called, his secretary asked, "Would you be available to meet David for breakfast at Wolf's Delicatessen at ten a.m.?"

Wolf's was mostly a tourist spot, but it was a dead giveaway that David was a regular when the waitress took our order and he said, "I'll have the usual."

I didn't have a usual, so I ordered French toast with well-done bacon, orange juice, and coffee. We made small talk until his usual—a toasted English muffin with butter, a glass of juice, and a cup of coffee—arrived along with my large platter of French toast. Yes, a little embarrassing.

I thought it was going pretty well, because he was friendly and full of curiosity. Then again, I'd seen him respond with a genuine sense of wonder to some of the least interesting people in the world. The conversation then turned serious. "I'm sure Bob told you we're looking to make a change on the show. I wanted a chance for the two of us to chat. You've really stepped up when we've needed you, so it seems like you might be ready. What do you think?"

I'd thought about it a thousand times since the call from Shanks. I felt ready, but I'd also heard that he was a taskmaster and expected perfection. Would I be able to measure up, to be whatever it was that made a perfect cohost?

"It's been a great opportunity to sit in for Nancy. It gave me a chance to dip a toe into the water and see what it's like. And I consider myself a quick study. I'd be watching you carefully, so I'm pretty confident I'd be able to handle it."

As he looked at the check and laid down an ABC-TV credit card on the table next to it, he said, "We'll be making a decision very soon. I'm glad we got a chance to talk." That's how he left it. David wasn't a network executive or a producer of the show, but he'd come from Hollywood, where he'd had success in prime time. He was buddies with all of the network honchos and wielded a tremendous amount of power over the program.

ABC then went radio silent for three weeks, until one day Edwin Vane, a senior vice president at ABC, called to ask if I could meet with David's agent, Felix Shagin, to talk more about the job.

Ed Vane was Bob Shanks's boss—did that mean that I was one step closer?

I quickly called my own agent, Richard Leibner, who was dumbfounded by the request that I be interviewed by David's agent in order to secure the job. "You've gotta be f***ing kidding me. Nobody does that! Meeting with producers is one thing, but meeting with the host's agent? No way. You're not doing that. No way!"

"But, Richard, come on—this is for the *GMA* cohost job! Work with me here!"

"I'm telling you, prospective hosts are never, *ever* asked to audition with the other host's agent. Ain't gonna happen. It's absurd. I'll call Shagin and set him straight."

When he paused for breath, I said, "Richard, calm down. That's not what you're going to do. I want this job. Do *not* make that call. I need to take this interview."

"Well, if you're going to his office, I'm going with you. No way you're going into another agent's office without me."

I've since learned that sometimes agents are far too willing to advise clients to turn down jobs the clients really want on principle—but they never forget the 10 percent commission they get from the jobs the clients take against those agents' recommendations.

The big day arrived. We shared a cab, and Richard talked nonstop. "Don't give this putz too much. Try to just answer his questions. Be a little like your idea of a bad interview. Go ahead and try to look interested, but at the same time be a little noncommittal. Be your bright self but just be careful. Oh, and also, be pretty but not too gorgeous."

As our cab crept down Broadway, my palms started to sweat; I hate being late for anything. The driver stopped in front of one of those big old nondescript office buildings that line Broadway in the theater district. Richard opened the heavy brass door and repeated himself: "You got this, doll. But if he asks something really outrageous, just look at me and I'll take it from there." (For all of you clutching your pearls that he called me *doll*, are you telling me you've never watched an episode of *Mad Men*? In 1976, this was just how men talked to women.)

As we rode up in the elevator, I couldn't help but think that my whole future in television was possibly going to be decided in the next few minutes. Shagin's hallway was dingy, not at all the kind of place one would expect to find an agent who handled the likes of David Hartman. As in many of those vintage New York buildings, the floor was made of small black-and-white tiles that were the standard for bathrooms in the 1920s, and my high-heeled steps sounded like tiny gunshots. The doors on either side of the hallway were mostly unmarked and made of that opaque glass that shows only shadows and rattles when the door slams shut. I thought I recognized the profiles of both Philip Marlowe and Sam Spade as we walked toward my future. The door to Shagin's office was like all the rest, except that his opaque glass said FELIX SHAGIN in gold letters outlined in black.

I opened the door and there was Felix. No secretary, no staff, only a small, unassuming office with a desk, side chairs, and a lot of memorabilia. Shagin was very cordial, though he was obviously surprised by Richard's being there. I introduced them, and Shagin offered us chairs.

Shagin sat down behind his desk and started twirling a pencil in his fingers. He was looking at the pencil as he said, "I wanted to talk to you because when we choose someone to work with David, we want to make sure that it's someone who can work well with him and who will look right next to him. So I'd like to ask you a few questions, if you don't mind."

His first question was, "Would you be willing to change your hair color?"

Really? That was his opener? You can't make this stuff up.

I hadn't known what to expect, but man, it sure wasn't that. That's like starting a television interview with "I notice you wear false teeth" or "Don't you think you should go on a diet?" It came out of left field.

Was he testing my attitude? My flexibility? Would I do whatever was asked of me? Or did they really think a brunette would look better alongside David?

I looked at Richard. He was shell-shocked. His mouth was wide open, but words failed him. I was glad he didn't say "What the f*ck!"

I replied in my best quizzical tone, "I'm not quite sure I understand why you're asking, but if blond hair doesn't show well on TV, or if the producers felt my hairstyle wasn't appealing to a mass audience and I thought what they were saying was valid, I would be willing to make changes. I'd just need to better understand the reason for the request."

I kept trying to catch a glimpse of Richard's face to see if he approved or disapproved of my answer.

I added, "But, frankly, I'm a little surprised by the question. Why do you ask?"

"One potential problem we see is that you may look too young, which could make David look old."

How does one respond to that?

He moved on. He wanted to know about my aspirations and what I thought my role on the show might be. "Do you understand that you'll be the second banana? You'll be like Ed McMahon to David's Johnny Carson. Any problem with that?"

"I realize David has been with the show since its inception, and this job doesn't get equal billing." I smiled and added sincerely, "But it is a very good position for a woman, so I'll be happy with it the way it is." After a slight pause, I had the guts to add, "And of course, depending on how women's roles grow in the industry and in society as a whole, I would imagine the role would grow proportionately."

Richard had to be impressed with me on that final note; however, he might have also been concerned about Shagin's reaction. He had sat on his hands long enough. "What Joan is saying is that we realize this is a wonderful opportunity for her, and she is willing to make necessary changes. But I want you to know that she is also a good student and learns quickly, she likes David and the way he works, and they already get along very well together. I think it would be a good relationship and good for the ratings to team them up."

Richard and I hit our stride with the rest of the questions, saying the right things to close this deal. The whole thing took less than thirty minutes. When we got up to leave, everyone shook hands, but I didn't know what to make of the meeting. As we walked toward Eighth Avenue to catch a cab back uptown, Richard said, "Hey, doll, you aced that one. There is no way that Shagin was put off."

Although I had no concrete reason to think that I would get the job, I was feeling somewhat confident about the prospects. Did that mean my chances were fifty-fifty? Later, in my apartment, I reflected on what had happened that day. There weren't many jobs like this available in the world. Then, almost immediately, I felt nauseated at the thought of doing it. Taking the job would require me to awaken at 3:30 every morning, five days a week, and do multiple live interviews for two hours every day. I knew how nervous I got when I did my live two-minute product pieces, and then I pictured myself sitting on the set calmly chatting with heads of state, movie stars, musicians, artists, doctors, and leaders from all walks of life. It was responsibility on a grand scale.

At that point I told myself, *Oh God, I hope I don't get it, because if I do, I don't know that I can pull it off.* The ego side of me wanted to hear them say "It's yours," and the other half of me was hoping and praying that I wouldn't get the job. I also knew that there had to be other people under consideration—likely people with more experience than I had. Still, how could I not start thinking about how I was going to spend my big raise in salary?

Less than a week later, just before leaving the newsroom after the evening broadcast, I stopped in the ladies' room. The men's and women's bathrooms happened to share a wall, and as I was washing my hands, I couldn't help but overhear a loud conversation in the men's room. That conversation went like this:

Man's exuberant voice: "Hey, have you seen the new girl they hired to do *GMA*? Wait till you see the legs on that broad." There was some mumbling in the background, and then the man's voice resumed: "I heard she might be doing some stuff for *Eyewitness News* too. She's an anchor from the West Coast. Her name is Sandy Hill." More mumbling.

In one stroke, this gorgeous girl with long legs had gotten "my" job on *GMA*—not to mention the fact that she could be cutting me out on *Eyewitness News* as well.

Time stood still.

I wasn't supposed to hear what I heard, and I didn't want to have heard it, but nevertheless there it was, and there was no taking it back. I knew it had to be true, even though I didn't want to believe it.

Sandy Hill gets the GMA *anchor job.*

Chapter 19

IF OPPORTUNITY DOESN'T KNOCK, BUILD A DOOR

Life is all about how you handle Plan B.
—Suzy Toronto, Author

In April of 1977, Sandy Hill was introduced as the new cohost of *GMA*. She'd done a few interviews about taking over the *GMA* role and was said to have told several reporters that being a news anchor, she intended to bring news credibility to the show. Everyone knew that wouldn't sit well with David. While he'd come from Hollywood as a successful actor, he'd worked hard to become a credible anchorman too.

Okay, so let's see how this pairing works out.

In addition to that, there was the constant rub from the press and the news industry about how *GMA* fell under ABC's entertainment division, while the other morning shows were run by their networks' news divisions. Sandy could have used more diplomacy when announcing her move to *GMA*.

Meanwhile, no one from ABC or *GMA* ever called me back to say, "Thank you for taking all the meetings, and maybe something will come from them sometime in the future, but at the moment we're going in a different direction." Nothing; not a word, ever. In time I came to learn that this was standard industry practice.

Again, I was left straddling both sides of the fence, reporting for and anchoring the weekend broadcast of *Eyewitness News* and working some mornings for *Good Morning America*. While I hadn't gotten the cohost role this time around, my star did still seem to be rising at *GMA*. The waters, however, did not remain calm for long. For the previous year and a half, I'd been dating a coworker at *GMA*, and we'd decided to get married. He'd been a producer on the show for years, but he had just jumped networks to NBC, where he was now the producer of the *Today* show, *GMA*'s prime competition.

It seems that the ABC execs felt this "mixed marriage" was cause for concern—so much so that I got a call from an ABC executive asking me to come see him at corporate headquarters. It was like getting called to the principal's office.

When I went to see him, I spotted a copy of the *Daily News* on his enormous desk, opened to the entertainment page, where I knew there was an article about the *GMA* producer who'd just jumped networks to be the new producer at *Today* and how he was planning to "whip the pants off *GMA*."

"We can't ask you this officially," the executive said, "but now that your fiancé is going to be producing the *Today* show, can we be certain that you won't reveal *GMA* secrets when the lights are out? When two people are under the covers, they say things they might not say otherwise."

IF OPPORTUNITY DOESN'T KNOCK, BUILD A DOOR

Did he just ask me that?

I was totally taken aback that he would say something like that to me, but at the same time I thought it was funny, and I started to laugh.

He added, "Hey, if you don't want to answer that, you can tell me to go to hell."

I said, "If all my husband and I have to talk about under the covers is morning shows, then we're going to be in serious trouble." That broke the tension in the room, so I went on. After all, I was only a fill-in cohost, I explained. I never went to *GMA* production meetings, and I didn't even have an office at *GMA*.

They let the matter drop, but that kind of scenario gives you an idea of the extent of paranoia that exists in the television business, not to mention the poor treatment of women. My fiancé over at the *Today* show wasn't called in by the NBC execs, nor did anyone ever ask him a question like that.

Believe it or not, there was never even a hint of a conflict of interest. A few years later he left the *Today* show. In retrospect, I'm not sure I would ever have been offered the job at *GMA* as the permanent cohost if he'd still been the *Today* producer.

Meanwhile, I felt like I was edging closer and closer to getting a full-time role at *GMA* as a correspondent.

One morning I was in makeup before the show, and one of *GMA*'s guests came in for makeup. He was part of a new segment on *GMA* called "Face Off," in which two people would sit opposite each other and debate a topic in the news. He was a skilled debater who could take either side of an issue, something of an intellectual chameleon. For example, if we were going to talk about abortion, he'd say, "Which side do you want me to be on?"

While we sat next to each other in the salon chairs, he struck up a conversation, casually mentioning that he was writing an article on women who were making it on TV. He said, "I think you're a good example. Can we talk about it?"

I was flattered and said, "Of course. I'll be glad to."

Since I was inexperienced and naive at the time, I answered all his seemingly straightforward questions. I thought they were perfectly legitimate. For instance, he asked about my growing up in Sacramento: "What kind of hobbies did you have growing up? Were you already thinking about being a reporter?"

I answered, with all the pride in the world, that I was like any young girl; I took dancing lessons after school, performed in dance and musical recitals, and marched in parades. All perfectly acceptable activities in a young girl's life.

He assured me that it would be a very positive article, and I couldn't wait to read it.

About two weeks later I heard that his article about me had appeared in the *Los Angeles Times*. It was anything but positive. I instantly learned how innocent (and, let's face it, naive) quotes could be taken out of context, how words could be twisted, and how a perfectly normal remark could be used to make a person sound silly. Here are some examples:

Interview question: "Did you read newspapers much as a young child?"

My answer: "Not too much, because newspapers weren't a big part of my life as a young girl."

Article: "I was not an avid newspaper reader, and I was bad at keeping up with current events."

Interview question: "Did they give you any kind of training at KCRA when you started?"

My answer: "Not much, actually. I had to learn on the job."

IF OPPORTUNITY DOESN'T KNOCK, BUILD A DOOR

Article: "Joan Lunden didn't exist. She was invented by the people who run the local television news business to serve their needs."

Interview question: "Did you know much about television news when you were hired?"

My answer: "Frankly, I'd never thought about being on television, let alone the news, until a friend at our local NBC affiliate suggested I talk to the news director about the expanding role of women."

Article: "The real person behind the pretty blond[e] reading off the teleprompter for New York's *Eyewitness News* . . . couldn't have cared less about news."

He had questioned me about my habits as a *child*, and then he made my answers seem as if they were about my *adult* life. The reporter labeled me a baton-twirling beauty queen who ended up, apparently by mere chance, on a news program.

That was my first taste of an interview with a professional critic whom some might say was a hatchet man. Take your pick.

I soon found out, however, that I was in good company. This is the same writer who did the interview with former president Jimmy Carter for *Playboy* magazine in which he got Carter to say he "had lust in his heart"—something that would haunt Carter throughout his political life. Even when he passed away, that line would be included in his final TV profile.

The next morning I got a call from Bill Fyffe, then head of news for the ABC-owned stations, telling me to come to his office. As soon as I walked in the door he started raking me over the coals. "How can you be so naive, Lunden?" he yelled. "If you can't give a decent interview, then the next time we'll have to send someone from PR to go with you."

I opened my mouth to explain that the article came out of a casual conversation in the makeup room, nothing official. But he wasn't having it.

"And with this guy, of all people! You gave him all the ammunition he needed to shoot you down, and he used it." Finally, in frustration, he said, "You should have at least known better than to say you had been a beauty queen in high school, for God's sake."

It was a sucker punch. I couldn't even answer Fyffe, because he spoke the truth. Beauty contests and baton twirling are always held against women who later seek professional careers. I left his office with my tail between my legs.

Fortunately, Woody Fraser, the executive producer, knew how to handle the situation. He called me into his office not to dress me down but to lay out a constructive plan to combat the smear. "Joan, we're going to fight this by putting you on the air to substitute for Sandy while she's out next week."

My blood pressure normalized.

He smiled and continued, "Don't worry—that newspaper will get yellow and blow away, and you'll still be on television. Oh, and by the way, that jerk's never gonna be on our show again."

Woody's support was the boost of confidence I needed. Sitting in for Sandy the following week helped me overcome the rookie mistake of tangling with a snake and get my mojo back.

* * * * *

I continued doing *GMA* consumer reports and working my full-time job at *Eyewitness News*. Woody, ever my mentor, left the show and was replaced by George Merlis, who also became one of my strongest supporters.

IF OPPORTUNITY DOESN'T KNOCK, BUILD A DOOR

Then, early one morning, I was sound asleep when the phone rang. I reached over, picked up the receiver, and said "Hello" as I stared bleary-eyed at my clock radio to see if I'd accidentally overslept.

Nope—it was 5:15 a.m., and I wasn't due in for my shift as a reporter until 9:00 a.m. On the other end of the line was the frantic voice of George Merlis, a *GMA* producer. "Sorry to wake you up, Joan. Can you do the show today?"

"Sure, George. What part?"

"All of it."

I threw off the covers. "I'll be right in."

I flew out of bed, reached into my closet, chose the first suit and blouse my hand hit, ran a comb through my hair, and dashed out the door. By 5:45 I was in hair and makeup and a producer was running through the morning's two-hour script. As it turned out, David Hartman had called in sick that morning, and while George assumed that cohost Sandy Hill could handle the show alone, she had arrived that morning with laryngitis.

As I rolled into the second hour of the show, I was feeling more comfortable handling everything by myself. As I prepared for an interview that David was supposed to lead, a producer came on set to give me a heads up about the next guest. "You'll be interviewing that woman sitting over there with all the kids. She just opened a new show on Broadway called *Runaways*. The kids are in the show. She seems a little quiet, so you may have to pump her. Here are the questions; take a look. We're back out of commercial in three minutes."

I sat down opposite the guest, got the cue from the floor director, and said to camera, "Broadway producer Elizabeth Swados is here with us this morning to talk about her new show, *Runaways*. Good morning, Elizabeth."

She had a WTF look on her face, clearly having expected to see David instead of me. After all, David was a former Broadway actor, and I was just a substitute who had been brought in at the last minute.

When I turned to her and said, "Tell me about *Runaways* and what it's like having to direct a large group of young kids," she knew it was the perfect question, but she seemed so rattled by the chaos that had put me in the seat across from her that she was having a tough time leaning in to the interview—not to mention being cordial. But I get it.

I made it through the show with no major problems, and everyone in the studio applauded after the sign-off at 9:00 a.m.

It was truly one of those occasions when the understudy had come out of the wings and given a great performance. When I acted on that opportunity and went into the studio that morning and took over the entire broadcast, those network producers saw me, for the first time, as a real potential host.

I'm sure it was on George's recommendation that I soon received a call from Squire Rushnell, the ABC vice president in charge of *GMA*.

"Joan, we're considering bringing you on full-time, so we need to know you would appeal to our advertisers," he said. As mentioned earlier, some of the commercials on the show, such as those for Alpo and Cotton Incorporated, were done live in the studio. Apparently, this could be part of the new role I was being considered for.

He booked a private production studio to tape some sample commercials. The taping session went well, and it sounded like the advertisers were on board, giving Squire the green light to make me an offer to join *GMA* full time.

But when the official offer was made, I had to say no. *What?*

IF OPPORTUNITY DOESN'T KNOCK, BUILD A DOOR

you might ask. How could I say no to that kind of opportunity? How could I say no to a job I'd wanted for so long? What could possibly be the problem? The offer seemed to be primarily for commercials more than field reporting. My agent was a news agent and questioned whether that was a smart move. What would happen if *GMA* decided after six months or a year to make a change? Where would that leave me? Would any news division take me seriously as an anchor after months of seeing me sell dog food?

On top of that, it was not a good financial deal for me. I was making twice what they were offering working for both *Eyewitness News* full-time and *GMA* part-time. How could I justify losing 50 percent of my current salary even if the job was what I wanted?

After I weighed the pros and cons with Richard, he responded like any good agent would. "I know you want this job, but these commercials could spell trouble. Networks can be fickle. You could find yourself in a tight spot if *GMA* decided not to keep you and you had to go looking for another news job."

I knew Squire Rushnell wouldn't be too happy about having to go back to his advertisers with the news that I was turning down the offer. I was petrified to tell him.

We met in one of the executive dining rooms on the fortieth floor of the ABC headquarters. I tried to be as ingratiating as I could as we took our seats at the table and unfolded our linen napkins. "Squire, thank you for the opportunity to talk this through together."

It was difficult to even think about how to start this conversation, since I knew Squire's job offer was implicitly a mentorship offer as well. I could tell by the warmth of his expression that he wasn't prepared for where I would be taking this conversation. I gathered myself as the waiter filled our water glasses and left menus on the table. "I love *GMA*, I enjoy everyone on the show, and I really want to work on *Good Morning America* full-time."

Squire's face fell a bit. He saw the "but" coming.

"But I just can't take the chance of primarily doing commercials at this point in my career." I studied his changing expression, making it even harder to continue. I rushed it out. "If I took the job, I'd also be cutting my pay in half."

I hated saying it, but it had to be said.

"Well, I must say, this is not the answer I expected. I thought we were on the same page, which is why I pitched you to our advertisers."

I couldn't really blame him for his disappointment, but he'd also put me in a no-win situation. I felt nauseated. Had I drifted away from being the golden girl of *GMA*'s future? In fact, turning down the offer could shut me out of any future consideration. The program still needed to hire someone to do the job I'd just been offered and turned down. And God knows there were plenty of women lining up for the position. In no time, they found a young woman named Jeanne Wolf for the job. With that move, my appearances on the show were significantly reduced.

However, I also saw that my fears had been well placed when we all heard that, after a very short stint, Jeanne was being replaced by a woman named Candace Hasey. Even more disconcerting was hearing through the grapevine that not only was Candace joining *GMA* but she was also being represented by Richard Leibner—my agent!

Later that day I got a call from Richard. "There's a woman from Texas who wants me to represent her for the job you turned down at *GMA*. Would you mind?"

"Would I mind? Are you kidding? That's a direct conflict," I said. "You know that by turning down that job—*on your advice*—I've lost all my leverage at the show, and I want to regain it. Richard, are you seriously asking me if I mind your representing the woman looking to take my place?"

Richard pressed his case. "If you really look at this objectively, Joan, I don't think your chances of gaining ground are very good right now. It was Squire Rushnell who recommended that Candace call me for representation. Squire is angry at you for not taking the offer when he made it."

"I know he's mad," I said, "but that's what agents are for, isn't it? To smooth things over and, in the end, get what their clients want?"

Employing the convoluted logic that agents often use, Leibner said, "I think if I'm able to get Candace in there, I'll have my foot in the door, and then I'll eventually be able to get more for you at *GMA*."

"Great concept, Richard—one that only an agent would come up with," I said. "If you decide to represent her, there won't be any conflict, because you will no longer represent me."

As it turned out, by trying to play both ends against the middle, Leibner ended up with neither client. Candace Hasey went with someone else, and I hired Jim Griffin at the William Morris Agency to represent my interests. Sadly, Richard's bad judgment brought our wonderful collaboration and close friendship to a screeching halt. I've always regretted that it went down that way.

The morning after that traumatizing call with Leibner, I ran into Sandy Hill in the hallway at *GMA*. She took one look at me and said, "All right, you look upset. What's up?"

I was on my way to my *Eyewitness News* assignment desk at the other end of the block, so I cut to the chase. "Well, I won't be doing very much on the show anymore because, as you must know, they're going to hire Candace Hasey for the sub job."

"Candace Hasey? Who's that?" Sandy asked incredulously, and then added vehemently, "Nobody said a word to me about a change."

I recounted the story as I knew it. She thanked me and then went straight to Squire's office, where she exploded like a bomb because no one in management had told her. On further reflection, she must have feared that Candace could become a prospective replacement for her at some point.

Squire then called Richard Leibner and exploded as well. In turn, Richard called me, and yes, another bomb went off. He said, "Sandy went to Squire and told him everything you told her and that she's mad as hell at everyone because they didn't consult with her."

What surprised me was that Richard wasn't upset about what was happening to me, but rather he was mad at me for telling Sandy.

"Richard," I said, "how was I supposed to know that Sandy hadn't been told? You people move us around like pawns in a chess game, and now we're at a stalemate."

I knew I had to do something to advance my position. I decided that I really wanted the *GMA* job, at whatever financial sacrifice, and I just needed to figure out how to go back after it now.

Chapter 20

AN EXERCISE IN DIPLOMACY

*And the trouble is,
if you don't risk anything,
you risk more.*

— ERICA JONG, *FEAR OF FLYING* (1973)

I was being driven by two forces. First, my contract with *Eyewitness News* was coming up for renewal, and they'd passed me over for the evening anchor role. I could see that a squeeze play was coming. The local management thought I was more loyal to *GMA* than to them (and, let's face it, that was honestly the case). Meanwhile, *GMA* wasn't happy with me because I'd turned down their offer.

While all this was going on, another news director had been hired at *Eyewitness News*, and he'd barely said five words to me in the five weeks he'd been there. Seemingly, he'd been told that my loyalty was to the *GMA* job. I was no longer getting the best assignments, and I could feel that my time at the station was coming to an end.

I didn't want to alienate anyone at *Eyewitness News* in case *GMA* fell through and I needed to stay there, so I made sure I was available whenever the local assignment editor needed me. At *GMA*, I faced a bigger problem in that I had to win back Squire's support.

I tossed and turned all night weighing my options. I could decide to be happy as a street reporter and weekend anchor at ABC's flagship station. But the more I thought about it, the more I had to admit that I wasn't a street reporter at heart. At *GMA*, my star had faded a bit by my own hand. Should I call Jim Griffin and ask him to put out feelers at other networks? Suddenly I knew the answer: I couldn't rely on someone else to make it happen for me. I needed to go straight to the top myself.

Before reporting for my afternoon shift at *Eyewitness News*, I summoned up all my nerve and called the president of ABC, Elton Rule, and asked for an appointment to speak with him. We weren't total strangers—we had met a couple of times at ABC functions—and I knew he was from Sacramento; I felt that sharing the same hometown might be a good icebreaker.

When Rule's assistant answered the phone and heard that it was me, she said, "Well, Ms. Lunden, Mr. Rule is in the office today. Let me see if he's available to speak." In less than a minute, Elton Rule was on the line. "Hi, Joan, how can I help you?" Slightly surprised that he'd picked up so quickly, I composed myself and said, "Mr. Rule, I'd like the opportunity to discuss the situation that I'm in here at ABC with you. I feel as if I'm about to be eased out of two jobs, and I think it would be a shame for me—and, frankly, for ABC—if that required me to start negotiations with a competing network."

He listened, and then he said extremely graciously, "I always enjoy you on the air, and I wouldn't want that to happen. I'll be glad to talk with you about it, so if you'll just make an appointment with my secretary for three o'clock tomorrow afternoon, we can have a talk."

The next afternoon at 2:55 I walked up the front steps of the midtown headquarters of ABC with my heart in my mouth. I pressed the elevator button for the thirty-ninth floor. I had been to the ABC executive dining rooms on the fortieth floor once before when I told Squire I wasn't taking his offer, but I had never been to the executive suite. As the elevator rose, I kept telling myself that I hadn't come this far to only come this far.

I stepped off the elevator onto a carpet that seemed about four inches thick and approached the secretary, who was sitting behind a mammoth desk. I told her I was there to see Mr. Rule and, instead of asking me to take a seat, she announced my arrival and pointed to his office. The door, which extended from the floor to the ceiling, opened with a slight *whoosh* as if breaking a vacuum seal, and I was inside.

I've seen some nice offices, but this one was spectacular. It was bigger than some entire apartments, with windows that offered a breathtaking view of Manhattan. The walls were done in rich wood, and Rule's marble desk sat well away from the wall. One of the signs of corporate power is the distance between a person's desk and the wall—and Elton Rule's desk was a *long* way from the wall. He had a commanding presence; he was tanned and athletic and oozed confidence. As well he should—he had taken ABC from a distant third place to number one.

We greeted each other and I sat in a plush leather chair in front of his desk. I planned to play it cool. I wanted to be strong, but I also wanted to evoke some sympathy for my position without breaking into tears.

After the briefest of chats about the weather, I began what I had rehearsed the night before and again on the elevator ride up. "I feel caught in the middle of a situation," I said. I hesitated for a moment to try to get a read on his face, and he seemed to be attentive and caring, so I went on. "After five years as a reporter at *Eyewitness News* I'd been led to believe that I was in line to be the first woman anchor, but Rose Ann Scamardella got the job, and she's great at it. I'm still working my shifts as a reporter and weekend anchor, but it's probably fair to say *Eyewitness News* doesn't have any future plans for me."

He had been nodding along at points, and now he sat forward in his chair, seeming to have a concerned and supportive look on his face. Or was that just my hopefulness? I steeled myself for the next part of my plea.

"*GMA* did offer me a position, but it came with a huge pay cut, and it was primarily doing commercials, which concerned me since I've been working hard for years now at being a journalist and a news anchor. I felt like I had to turn the offer down. I didn't want to turn it down; it just felt too risky. But I'm sure it left the *GMA* executives with a bad taste in their mouths."

I wanted him to say, *God, Joan, we need you; let's figure out a way to keep you.*

Instead, he said, "I think I'm beginning to get the picture."

That would do. I continued. "Mr. Rule, I'm now being advised by my agent that I should start talks with the other networks, which I don't want to do." At this point, he could easily have said, *If that's the way you feel, go right ahead.*

Instead, he said, "I'm going to look into the situation, because it would be a shame for us to lose you. You're a delightful young woman who has worked hard. As soon as I know something, I'll call you."

AN EXERCISE IN DIPLOMACY

Elton Rule had given me half an hour of his time to plead my case, and I didn't know if I'd pulled it off or not, but I'd done it, and I kept it together in the process. I'm not the type who cries easily, but I was filled with a tremendous amount of emotion because so much was riding on this conversation. I'm not sure, but I think he may have caught a glimpse of the tears welling up in my eyes, and perhaps that spurred him to take a mentor position for me. As I got up from my chair, he rose too, came around his desk, and walked me to the door. While I was swallowing hard and trying to keep my emotions in check, I was also feeling like I'd found a friend on the plush thirty-ninth floor.

Late the next afternoon, back in the newsroom, while working on my story for the six o'clock news, I trembled slightly each time I heard a phone ring in the office. Then, with minutes to spare before going to the set, my phone rang. It was Elton Rule.

Mr. Rule cut right to the good part. "It was nice talking with you yesterday. I've made a couple of calls, and I suggest that you pursue *GMA*. I've spoken with them."

I thanked him and hung up, not sure exactly what that meant. I could interpret his advice in several ways. Was I supposed to just forget about WABC because I was finished there anyway, and this was his sensitive way of telling me? Or did he mean that he had smoothed things over with Squire Rushnell and set things up for me at *GMA*?

It didn't matter. Whatever Elton Rule said to the execs at *GMA*, it worked.

Chapter 21

TWO PHONE CALLS

*There is no force equal to
a woman determined to rise.*

—Adapted from W.E.B. Du Bois (1910)

A few weeks later, I was putting the finishing touches on a story for the 6:00 p.m. news when the phone rang in my office. Jim Griffin, my William Morris agent, excitedly said, "Joan, ABC just called. They've made you an offer to join *Good Morning America*. And Joan, implicit in the offer is that you'll take the cohost role when Sandy Hill leaves in a few months."

"It's really happening? Oh my God, I want all the details, Jim, but I've got only twenty minutes to finish my story for the six o'clock show. I'll have to call you back."

My heart began racing. There were so many people I wanted to call with this news, but I had to try to concentrate on what I was writing or I would never have it done in time for the upcoming show. Just as I was finishing the last line and absorbing the weight of Jim's call, the phone rang again.

It was my gynecologist. "Miss Lunden, congratulations! The test came back positive. You're pregnant."

I sat there in a stunned, happy daze while the newsroom clattered on around me, unaware that my world had just tilted on its axis. A wave of joy was quickly followed by a stab of uncertainty. Would ABC still want me on air, visibly pregnant? I immediately picked the phone back up and called my entertainment attorney, Marc Chamlin. "*GMA* offered me the cohost job, but then my gynecologist called, and I'm pregnant. Will the *GMA* offer still stand when they find out?"

Marc said, "Calm down—and congratulations on both fronts!" Then he explained the legal landscape. "Lucky for you it's 1979, because just last year a federal law was passed that prohibits companies from discriminating based on pregnancy or childbirth.[1] So, legally, ABC can't rescind the offer."

My heart rate returned to normal shortly after hearing this, but the question remained: Would I be able to do both at the same time? Of course I couldn't say no to this job offer. So I would say yes and figure out how to do it. Like I always did.

In January 1980, I packed up my office at *Eyewitness News* and moved a few blocks over to my new office at *GMA*. I started as a reporter and substitute cohost while Sandy Hill's contract wound down. In February she left to cover the Winter Olympics in Lake Placid but never returned to the studio, staying on the road through the rest of her contract. It seemed the animosity between her and David was so toxic that she had no desire to come back.

In the meantime, I shared hosting duties with our entertainment reporter, Pat Collins, who, coincidentally, was also pregnant. We were able to cover each other's maternity leaves, which allowed me to ease into the role without the immediate pressure of being the official cohost.

---

1 The law was an amendment to the Civil Rights Act of 1964.

TWO PHONE CALLS

As I settled into my new position, I quickly learned that morning television wasn't just about delivering the news—it was about setting the tone for the day. And that meant leaving my personal struggles at the door. I recognized the importance of putting on a happy face, no matter how I felt or how little sleep I'd gotten. (Pregnant women would understand why there were saltine crumbs in the pockets of all my clothes!) I had to walk into that studio, sit behind the coffee table, and bring warmth and energy to millions of viewers who were just waking up, still groggy, maybe hitting the snooze button one last time. I had to be their gentle nudge into the day.

Beyond adjusting to early mornings on the job, I was also preparing for my new role as a mother—one decision at a time.

After interviewing so many pediatricians and La Leche League representatives over the years, I was convinced that breastfeeding was the best choice for me and my baby.

"We've learned so much about the long-term benefits," one La Leche League expert had told me. "Breast milk really is the perfect food for babies; it has the ideal balance of fat, protein, sugar, and water, and it even adapts to suit each baby's needs."

Back in the 1950s, when my mother had me, formula was the norm. Heavy marketing had convinced new mothers—and even doctors—that it was the more modern, scientific choice. Without groups like La Leche League advocating for breastfeeding, many women would have been unaware of its benefits. So, I wasn't entirely surprised by my mother's reaction when I told her my plan to breastfeed and to bring the baby to work with me.

"Seriously, sweetheart?" she said. "There are formulas that are just as healthy—not to mention that using one would make it a whole lot easier for you in this big new job."

"Mom," I said, keeping my voice patient, "breast milk has

antibodies that protect against childhood illnesses. It even helps prevent ear infections and stomach bugs. Formula just can't do that."

She hesitated, then sighed. "Well, when you were born, that's not what we were told."

"I know," I said gently. "But there's been so much research since then. And it's not just about nutrition—I don't want to miss out on the bonding, which they also say is important."

She seemed to accept that, but I still heard sincere concern in her voice. "And you really think you can bring a newborn to work while hosting a live national show?"

I didn't have a great answer for that one. "The network seems open to it," I said, though even I wasn't sure it would work.

"Well, I'm sure you know what you're doing, sweetie. It just seems . . . ambitious."

She wasn't wrong. And deep down, I was wondering the same thing. Could I really juggle both?

Jim Griffin had been the one negotiating the details of my contract. When I had called him to discuss my plan, he'd been quiet on the other end of the line. "Jim, I just don't see how I'll be able to breastfeed my new baby if I don't have her with me. I know it's a big ask, but I need you to support me on this."

Jim not only went to bat for me but he also got ABC to agree to provide my baby, Jamie, with a nursery at the studio and to let me bring her on the road with me during her first year. I tried to imagine what those discussions must have been like for the male executives at the network, talking about my breastfeeding, since at that time you couldn't even say the word "breastfeeding" on television.

But the network had agreed, so now I had to devise a plan for getting a baby to the studio with me . . . by five o'clock in the morning.

TWO PHONE CALLS

Balancing work and motherhood would never be easy, but I realized early on that I wasn't the only one facing that challenge. Every woman, no matter her job, has to learn how to separate personal responsibilities from professional ones. Of course, it's much easier to do that when everything in life is perfect—and we all know that's not always the case. You may have a headache, a sick baby, a sore throat, yet you still have to pretend everything is fine in front of your colleagues. I empathize; I really do. In my case, I had to keep those things to myself in front of millions of viewers.

I don't consider myself an actress, but when the red light went on, I guess I became something of one. I had to set aside exhaustion, morning sickness, stress—whatever was happening in my personal life—and deliver the news in a way that gently ushered in the day for the people at home and let them know what was happening in the world.

Through it all, I reminded myself *I can do this. I can do this.*

It wouldn't occur to me until years later that viewers who watched me stay on the air throughout my pregnancies and then balance my career with family responsibilities might have been thinking *If she can do it, maybe I can too.*

And maybe, just maybe, that was the most significant role I would ever play.

GMA *promo:*
America's talking about
Joan's pregnancy.

Chapter 22

LEARNING THE ROPES

I never dreamed about success.
I worked for it.
—Estee Lauder

When I worked as a street reporter doing interviews on location for *Eyewitness News*, I had the luxury of time. I could afford to let people ramble because I would return to the studio and work with an editor to choose the best parts for the broadcast. *GMA* was a completely different format—we did live interviews, bloopers and all. Interviews ranged from three to five minutes, so I had to learn how to get the guest through their story and finish in time for the commercial break. The show's writers spoke to the guests beforehand and briefed us the night before on what to expect. There was a real learning curve! There's no way you can develop the skills to stay calm and appear confident and competent on live television without actually doing live television.

Fortunately, I had a five-month initiation before taking over the role full-time in August.

Perhaps the most important skill I had to master on a live program was to always stay focused and totally engaged in every interview, whatever the subject. One morning, my first executive producer, Woody Fraser, made my learning curve abundantly clear. "I guess you've never been to or watched an ice hockey game," he said.

"You're right," I replied.

"I could tell by the interview you did with the hockey player this morning."

Uh-oh.

He continued, "If you don't care about the guest—or, in this case, ice hockey—then the viewer will pick up on that, and they won't care either. Maybe they'll even turn to another channel. Your job is to be *fascinated* with ice hockey and hockey players for four minutes—two hundred forty seconds, that's all—but you need to be all in."

In that moment he made me a much better interviewer, and I've never forgotten that advice—even in my personal life. Have you ever been talking with someone, standing there nodding like one of those ducks that dip their beaks in the water but not hearing a word the other person is saying? You recognize the feeling, don't you? Well, you can't let that happen on live television or you're a dead duck, because you won't know what to say next.

I'm sure that when this sort of lapse happens to you, your body immediately fires a full burst of adrenaline into your veins and you become instantly alert. You have total recall of everything that's happened for the last twenty years, but unfortunately you can't remember a thing that happened in the last sixty seconds.

LEARNING THE ROPES

Well, that's the way it is on live TV all the time; you cannot let your concentration falter in front of millions of people. If you do, even for a few seconds, you get a hyper-overdose of adrenaline. There may be a dozen people on the set and another dozen in the control room, but they're powerless to help you. While I wore an earpiece on live TV, in all my years on *GMA*, I never had a producer come to my aid and suggest a question.

Mastering the ability to focus was no insurance against fading out and losing my place in a conversation, however. Sometimes when an interview was flowing beautifully, the realization would hit me that I was so "in the moment" with this fabulous conversation that I wasn't thinking about the list of questions and had lost track of where the interview was headed. What was the next question supposed to be? It can be hard to get back to the scripted interview in those moments.

I did develop some tricks that helped me avoid those semiconscious states, though. Rather than simply reading the questions from the script, I would handwrite the questions for each interview on five-by-seven cards. Somehow, as the words passed from the written page, through my brain, and onto the card by my own hand, the process made them truly my questions. Then I read them aloud to myself at least twice. I didn't memorize them, but I knew them. I would place those cards under my leg in case I needed them. The cameramen always joked that I had a funny way of reading the cards.

Next, let's talk about eye contact. Not everyone is used to looking another person in the eye. I remember one interview that illustrates this point. While speaking with a financial expert who had been on the show several times before, I could see that he was blanking, and I feared maybe he was even going to pass out. After about thirty seconds, his eyes were completely vacant. I didn't know whether he was hearing a single word I said. As I continued, I essentially gave him his answers within the structure of my questions. He was sweating profusely and began to breathe rapidly, and I knew his mouth was as dry as sandpaper. The only way I got him through the interview was by telegraphing support with my body language and eye contact. He was embarrassed afterward, but—seriously—it can happen to anyone.

In fact, it happened to a woman that David was interviewing one morning. She was an attorney, someone who was very bright and had seemed fine when she said "Good morning" before the segment. But when the cameras went on, you could tell that she was having trouble, and at one point the camera cut to a close-up and caught her just as her eyes rolled back and her head slumped against her chair. She had fainted dead away. We went to a commercial immediately. This kind of thing was rare; I can't think of another time when it happened. In this case, the woman knew her material and was well prepared, but the early-morning hour, several cups of coffee on an empty stomach, the bright lights, and the excitement combined to get the best of her.

That story leads me to another aspect of live television: dealing with unpredictable moments. Cooking demos, by their nature, were full of those. We loved having Julia Child live in the studio. Besides being one of the world's greatest chefs, Julia was wildly funny; anything could happen. One morning she was making crepes and she suddenly realized they might be burning. She slipped her spatula under one of them and said, "Oh, too hot," then flung it over her shoulder. The hot crepe plopped against the wall behind her and slid to the floor. All. On. Camera.

Well, when something is funny, it's funny. Yes, it was slapstick humor, but everyone in the studio was in hysterics. We got a ton of

LEARNING THE ROPES

mail after that show, mainly because viewers could see we were all having fun—and besides, what Julia did is something that all cooks secretly want to do from time to time.

It was also a lot of fun when Julia was cooking up yummy recipes that called for alcohol. The entire crew would crack up behind their cameras as Julia added alcohol to the dish and just kept pouring . . . and pouring . . . all while she continued talking. Julia knew exactly what she was doing—going for the laugh.

Speaking of funny, handling interviews with people who are paid to be funny—comedians—could sometimes be tricky. I had assumed they would naturally be funny during their interviews, but that wasn't necessarily the case. For instance, Steve Martin—whom I always envision wearing that headpiece that made it look like he had an arrow through his brain—surprised me one morning by being serious and deadpan. Maybe he was just sleepy because of the early-morning hour, but I had to immediately adjust my expectations—and my interview—the minute I realized that he may have been there to promote a film, but that didn't mean he was going to make an effort to make me or our audience laugh. Converserly, a comedian like Billy Crystal or Robin Williams was so spontaneous and outrageous that you could prepare all you want, but you never knew what to expect live. Robin's ability to jet off into a funny and sometimes bizarre stream-of-consciousness rant was uncanny.

Another thing that would throw the studio crew into hysterics was something we called a "verbal typo"—those mistakes that occur randomly somewhere between the brain and the mouth. You'd like to think they would just end up on the cutting room floor, but that's not the case with live television. I'll never forget the time at KCRA when one of the younger weathermen said "There's a cold mare's ass coming down from Canada" when he meant to say "There's a cold air mass coming down from Canada."

An interesting side note: In live television, there are no do-overs—well, except sometimes. While *GMA* aired live in the east, it was on a tape delay out west in order to begin at 7:00 a.m. PST. If we made a mistake on East Coast time, we'd occasionally stick around after the show and wait for the exact moment that mistake was about to air out west so we could cut in live and fix it. We used to joke that people on the West Coast thought we were perfect, while everyone back east knew better.

That's what live TV is all about—flexibility, adaptability, being fast on your feet, and remaining calm through it all.

Joan's interviews Robin Williams on **GMA**.

Chapter 23

GOOD MORNING, I'M JOAN LUNDEN

Stay afraid, but do it anyway. What's important is the action. You don't have to wait to be confident. Just do it and eventually the confidence will follow.

—Carrie Fisher

On August 27, 1980, I awoke a few minutes early at 3:15 a.m. and showered and dressed quickly so I would be ready to lift seven-week-old Jamie from her crib, change her diaper, and bundle her up in the bunting I'd laid out the night before. With my office bag over one shoulder and a diaper bag on the other, we headed out into the night, where an ABC limo sat ready to take us to the Manhattan studio. After I exchanged good-morning greetings with the driver (even though it wasn't really the morning yet), he gestured to the eighty-page script on the back seat and then closed the limo's darkened privacy glass so that I could nurse Jamie on the drive to the studio.

The ride from my quiet suburb, where I'd moved when I was pregnant, into New York City could take an hour or more in morning commuter traffic, but at that hour it would usually take just forty minutes, which was enough time to read my script, make notes, and fill the baby's tummy. However, that day, of all days, the limo broke down halfway to the city. I'm always jittery about being on time, so this misfortune kicked my nerves into overdrive. I didn't want anyone to think I couldn't be on time for my job as a new mother.

Thankfully, a nice driver stopped to help. He drove us to a nearby taxi stand and we went the rest of the way into the city by cab. Once we arrived at the studio, there were "Good morning"s all around, and everyone wanted a peek at baby Jamie. As graciously as possible, I asked them to wait until after the show so she wouldn't wake up, and then took the stairs to my second-floor dressing room, which was a humongous walk-in closet. There were shelves filled with shoes, more shelves filled with sweaters, hanging racks for dresses and skirts, and drawers for underthings and jewelry. Beside my dressing room was Jamie's little nursery, where I gently placed her in her crib, careful not to wake her before the baby nurse came on duty.

I headed straight to the makeup room, where the hairdresser and makeup artist waited in what was a small beauty salon. It was outfitted with four swivel chairs, so the guests could also be groomed and styled there. It included an inventory of makeup, nail polish, and everything else you could find at one of the cosmetic counters at Bloomingdale's.

Throughout the morning, producers came into the makeup room with script changes or last-minute additions, and at around 6:00 a.m. I was handed a newly revised version of the day's script. The guest list and the interview schedule didn't typically change after this unless something as serious as an international incident or a national crisis occurred, or a guest was arriving late. Fortunately, my first day back from maternity leave didn't involve any of these exigencies.

6:50 a.m.: Once I was dressed, I took one last glance in the mirror and then made my way into the studio. We'd picked out a wine-colored wool jacket, a pale pink blouse with a bow, and a coordinating plaid skirt—so 1980s, and in retrospect, so dorky! As I settled into my chair, the cameramen and stage managers all gave me a welcoming cheer, and a stagehand handed me coffee in a *Good Morning America* cup. (I would find that the very efficient stagehands continually filled my cup all throughout the morning. By the end of a show I might have had three cups or more, so after a week of that I switched to hot tea.)

6:59:50 a.m.: David rushed into the studio with flair and settled into his chair next to me. A few feet away, Vice President Walter Mondale sipped coffee as he waited for his interview, and outside, limousines were arriving with the morning's other guests.

The stage manager motioned to the camera in front of us and, since stage managers never want their directives to be heard live on air, he stage whispered, "Quiet on the set, please." The ten-second countdown began. "In ten . . . five, four, three . . ."

At home the audience saw the *Good Morning America* opening montage with its symbolic rising sun and heard our melodic theme music, which was written by Marvin Hamlisch, the legendary composer of Broadway and film scores. Next on screen was what we called the "*GMA* face," a person or group that would give a friendly greeting from somewhere in America: "Hello, I'm Stephen Adams in Kansas City, Missouri. *Good morning, America.*"

7:02 a.m.: Another stage manager pointed her finger at us, the red light on camera two lit up, and we were on the air. I made sure to sit up straight but still look relaxed. Remembering the advice I'd gotten when I first started anchoring in Sacramento, I took a cleansing breath and said to myself, *L-O-W and S-L-O-W.*

"Good morning, I'm David Hartman. It's Monday, the twenty-seventh of August, and I'm delighted to welcome Joan Lunden to this broadcast."

"I'm excited to be here with you, David, and with all of you at home who are joining us this morning." Whew. The introduction was over, and I felt my muscles relax. I had prepared well, and the show went off without a hitch. Now that I'm reflecting on it, the producers didn't really give me much to do that first day, and I'm thankful for that. As the clock edged toward 9:00 a.m., I could finally exhale. When it was all over, David signed off with his signature closing remark: "Go out and make it a good day."

A press conference was scheduled right after the show to officially announce that I would be joining David on the program. The *GMA* stagehands were setting up for it. Rows and rows of folding chairs were placed in front of the set where David and I opened the show each day. As the press arrived, they were offered breakfast along with champagne and orange juice. Meanwhile, the PR director for *Good Morning America*, John Goodman, pulled me aside before things got started. He warned me to downplay the fact that I was a new mom and told me to definitely not say that I had my baby with me at the studio. "Stay away from that. If they think you have your baby here with you, they'll question your ability to focus and do the job," he said.

"No problem. I won't say a thing about baby Jamie."

David and I made our entrance, he welcomed the press and said a few words about the program, and then he introduced me. I talked about how thrilled I was to be able to work with David on such an important broadcast, and then I opened it up for questions.

The first question came from *Time* magazine. "We hear ABC is letting you bring your new baby to work with you. Can you tell us about that?"

Uh-oh. Now what?

My eyes shot to the back of the studio, where the ABC and *GMA* execs were standing, along with the PR director who'd just told me not to talk about baby Jamie. But I had no choice; I had to answer the reporter from *Time*.

I told him that ABC had graciously allowed me to bring my new daughter, Jamie, to work with me, since I was a new mom and I was breastfeeding. (Oops, I said *breastfeeding*; what will they do with that sound bite?)

The second question was from *Newsweek*.

"*Good Morning America* travels the world; how will you handle that with a baby in tow?"

Again I had to answer the question, and the answer was that ABC had contractually agreed to let me take Jamie with me anywhere we went in the world. (And a year later, just before her first birthday, she went with me to London to cover the wedding of Prince Charles to Lady Diana.)

As the questions kept coming about how I was going to blend early-morning television with being a new mom, it became clear that the breaking story that day was that a giant media company was allowing a woman to bring her baby to work with her.

As the press conference was starting to wind down, out of the corner of my eye I saw John Goodman coming into the studio with my little Jamie in his arms. He made his way up the center aisle through the sea of reporters and gently handed Jamie to me as the cameras began flashing.

That was the picture on the front page of newspapers and magazines across the country. It was also the beginning of an onslaught of women's magazines asking for interviews and photo shoots.

It was an exciting time, although it was also a bit overwhelming. I think it was also something of a surprise to the ABC executives and the *Good Morning America* producers that the press was so interested in the story. I don't think they truly understood what they were saying yes to. And I also don't think they realized what impact it would have—that it would resonate the way it did with the audience and especially with women everywhere, and even throughout the corporate world.

Joan's first day as official **GMA** *cohost.*

Chapter 24

BEHIND THE SCENES AT *GMA*

*Make the most of yourself by fanning
the tiny, inner sparks of possibility
into flames of achievement.*

—Golda Meir, first female prime minister of Israel

The most common question I get about my years at *GMA* is: "What time did you wake up?" Most people can't imagine a 3:30 a.m. alarm. Even I sometimes hit snooze, clinging to the last moments of a dream. During those extra minutes, I would wonder why anyone would be willing to do this five days a week.

I would sometimes mentally weigh the options of a normal life—a nine-to-five job, grocery shopping, cooking, entertaining in the evening, watching the late movie—versus a schedule that had me finishing half my workday as most people were just settling in for the morning. Still, even on the worst mornings, the scales would always come out tipped in favor of what I was doing.

The job really started on the car ride into the city as I read through the script the driver had brought me and browsed through the daily newspapers—*The New York Daily News* and *The New York Times*—scanning the headlines and reading the stories I might be covering that morning as well. Then there were the packets of research for each scheduled guest—remember, we didn't have laptops or iPads or even cell phones back then, so everything came to us in paper form . . . lots and lots of paper.

At the studio, we'd head straight to hair and makeup. We were a tight-knit team, but the room was usually quiet as we focused on scripts and interview notes. That same team traveled with us wherever we went, whether it was to Yugoslavia for the Olympics or to Normandy for the fortieth anniversary of D-Day. No matter where we were, the routine stayed the same: early mornings, makeup brushes, and a flurry of last-minute prep.

I was always surprised by the amount of mail that came in every day asking about my hair, makeup, and clothes. Who makes that dress? What about the shoes you were wearing on Tuesday?

It didn't take me long to understand the public's fascination with every aspect of my personal life, including what I wore each day on the program. I also got requests for pictures of my hairstyle—front, side, and back views—so people could take those photos to their hairdresser to replicate.

On *GMA*, an extensive wardrobe was essential—at least for the female host. David's dressing room was more of an office, with just a small closet for a couple of suits and shirts. His biggest decision? Navy or gray. Add a white shirt and tie, and he was done. Meanwhile, my wardrobe took up entire walls, complete with a tracking system to avoid outfit repeats.

We also kept track of outfits I wore for interviews taped after the show. I would change into a new outfit for each interview, and once it was scheduled into an upcoming show, I'd make sure that whatever I'd worn during that pretaped segment was what I was wearing on the day the interview aired. This was intended to provide visual continuity for the viewers at home. It would otherwise be confusing to watch the show and see me in one outfit at 7:15, another at 7:40, and then back in the one I'd worn first at 8:10.

I was always surprised when someone wrote in to point out that I had worn the same dress not that long ago. Really? Most often, though, women wanted to know where they could shop for the clothes I wore. ABC had cut a deal with the Lillie Rubin chain of women's stores, which provided my clothing and a stylist to oversee it all. Ellie Dell was petite, always smartly dressed, and a sophisticated buyer who knew the fashion district well and was quite a taskmaster.

A few times a year, my personal assistant, Elise Silvestri, and I joined Ellie for a grueling three-day marathon through various designer showrooms. It might sound glamorous, but trust me—it was exhausting. The designers hung dozens of sample pieces on the walls, pointing out color options. Since everything was in model sizes, I had to figure out my fit ahead of time by trying on similar pieces in department stores.

As we made our way through the fashion district on those days, Ellie kept a master list of what we'd ordered and what we still needed so I would have a diverse wardrobe for the following season. (Yes, it meant we were buying wool in the middle of hot weather; it's weird, but it worked.) When these selections arrived at the studio, a sweet, gentle man named Ducky was there to press each item and take care of any necessary hemming. Ellie would stop by and lend her expertise on putting outfits together. From then on, it was up to me to decide what should be worn that day.

This is where all my assistants became indispensable, beginning with Elise Silvestri. She had started with me as a college intern and graduated just as I got the *GMA* job—so we were both brand-new to how things worked at the network. I was fortunate to have her support for four years, and even after she left *GMA* to become a talk-show producer, we remained the best of friends. In fact, her daughters and mine have also remained close and are now mothers raising children of the same age.

We would meet at the studio each day, and she would make the changes to the wardrobe board so that my mornings could go smoothly. I didn't want to be making clothing decisions as last-minute script changes and makeup and hair touch-ups were happening.

And there were those unforeseen problems that could cause anxiety (mostly in the control room), like the live interview from London with legendary actor Charlton Heston. He was stuck in traffic and couldn't get to the ABC London studio on time, so the interview kept getting delayed until he finally arrived, a bit breathless, during the last half hour of the show. These kinds of circumstances cause all sorts of last-minute reshuffling in the show lineup. It's live TV, so we would often be told only seconds before whether an interview at a remote location was a go or a no-go at the moment. Our job was to keep the chaos behind the scenes and never let the viewers catch on.

One morning, that challenge hit its peak when the Beach Boys were scheduled for a live interview from Los Angeles. I had been a fan of their music when I was younger. In fact, one of their albums had been recorded live at a Sacramento concert I attended at age fifteen. Although I hadn't seen them in years, I'd heard stories about how they had acted rather oddly on other shows (and I'm being kind with that description).

BEHIND THE SCENES AT *GMA*

Moments before the interview, I sensed something was off with the remote feed. It was usually some minor sound issue or a satellite that wasn't in the right place, but not this time. What I couldn't see on our studio monitor was the Beach Boys knocking over chairs in mid-brawl with their manager and hurling more four-letter words than the FCC would allow. The New York control room watched in stunned silence, wondering if they would settle down in time for the interview.

They finally did, but they all sat back down in different chairs, and some of them were no longer wearing their microphones. Meanwhile, out in the studio, I didn't know that any of this had happened.

The *GMA* writer who briefed me had only been able to pre-interview the Beach Boys' manager, so she couldn't construct a meaningful series of questions directed to anyone in particular. She gave me some general questions suitable for any member of the group. On the surface that might have seemed safe enough. It was not.

When the stage manager cued me, I said, "Now joining us live from Los Angeles are the Beach Boys." I still had no idea anything was amiss, so I proceeded to introduce each of them. Of course, they were all in the wrong seats, so the close-up shots didn't match the names I was saying. But that was just the beginning of this train wreck.

When I introduced the manager, the camera panned to an empty chair, because he hadn't rejoined the group. One of the Beach Boys yelled, "Hey, Jack, get in here." Jack, the manager, sat back down in his chair. Okay, so not exactly off to a roaring start. But I was still unaware that they'd all changed places, which meant the seating chart under my leg was totally off.

When I asked my first question, I could see that the person I thought I'd asked wasn't saying anything. Another member of the group was talking, but there was no sound because his mic was off. When I threw out the next question, someone else answered. *What the heck was going on?* Thinking I could rectify the situation, I said, "So, Brian, what do you think about that?" Unfortunately, it was Brian who'd just answered, so he looked at me blankly and said, "I am Brian." Crap. Oh my God, this ship was sinking. At this point, I could hear uproarious laughter coming through the headsets of the stage managers. It was the producers and technicians in the control room who were almost peeing in their pants as they watched this disaster live on the air.

As it turned out, the one guy I'd been told wouldn't talk much was the only one who seemed to have the mental capacity to hold a conversation. There was simply no way to fix this interview, so I ended it by saying, "Goodbye, fellas; it's been . . . uh, fun."

Seconds later, the control room staff poured out onto the set in hysterics. Half of them were in tears from laughing so hard. Then they told me about the fight and the mix-up in seats, to which I said, "Thanks a lot for letting me in on your amusing morning."

And yes, I heard from friends after the show who called, still laughing. "We just couldn't believe anyone in the entertainment biz would act like that on live television. They were outrageous."

Despite unnerving interviews like the one with the Beach Boys, I began to get comfortable in my seat at *GMA*, so I wasn't that nervous before each show. However, as 7:00 a.m. neared, I could always feel the adrenaline starting to flow. About five minutes before airtime, just as we settled into our chairs, the audio technicians would set up our mics. They'd clip a tiny microphone to my lapel or collar, or sometimes to the back of the waistband of whatever I was wearing. As you may have sensed by now, audio technicians basically have their hands all over you.

I remember one day when Dolly Parton was booked on the show, and as she came into the studio during a commercial break, she said in her Dolly voice, "Which one of you lucky fellas gets to put the mic on me?" She was a hoot, and so incredibly down to earth and friendly.

During the last couple of minutes before the show went live, the crew was always busy putting flowers on the set's coffee table, moving cameras, adjusting the lighting, and shifting furniture from place to place. David often came in with a flourish about one minute before airtime. A little behind-the-scenes secret: the audio technician always played "I Feel Good" by James Brown in our earpieces; he knew it was a surefire way to get us pumped up.

Then it was time to sit up, perk up, be alert, and put a smile on our faces.

"Quiet on the set, please, everybody. Now, in ten . . . five, four, three . . ."

"Good morning, I'm Joan Lunden."

Well, actually, let me clear that up right now: In the early years I wasn't allowed to say the words "Good morning, I'm Joan Lunden" because David's contract not only prohibited me from calling myself a cohost, it also explicitly stated that only he could open and close the show. So, while you at home may not have noticed, only David would say "Good morning, everyone, I'm David Hartman *with* Joan Lunden." *The Washington Post*'s television critic, Tom Shales, did notice. "Hartman is definitely the star, all right," he wrote. "There is officially no cohost on the program, unlike other networks. Hartman, the host, is, according to ABC publicity, 'joined in the studio each morning by Joan Lunden.' Hartman's female companion on the show has always been so expendable, so anonymous, that *Today* show wags refer to her as the lamp."

JOAN: LIFE BEYOND THE SCRIPT

Shales wasn't the only one to notice the disparity. The writers at *Saturday Night Live* caught on to it right away. One Saturday night, when I could actually stay up late, I was watching the show. A few segments in, comedian Joe Piscopo appeared on a set that looked exactly like ours. It seems that David's opening sequence each morning, along with his obvious control over the program, had inspired an *SNL* skit that was spoofing our show.

In the skit, Piscopo played the part of David, impersonating his signature low speaking voice: "AWWWWWW good morning, good morning, everyone, AWWWWW I'm David Hartman here with Joan Lunden." In Piscopo's comedic style, he made David sound like the cartoon character Bullwinkle.

With that brief introduction of me, Piscopo nodded in the direction of the seat next to him. The camera widened out to show, in my seat . . . wait for it . . . a large plastic blow-up doll, who, of course, could say nothing—it just sat there motionless. I don't know where they got that blow-up doll with blond hair, but it was uncanny how much it looked like me.

At the time, *SNL* was a must-watch for me. Seeing myself parodied? Equal parts mortifying and thrilling. Looking back, I realize that satire is a powerful tool; it wasn't just about making fun of me, it was about calling out the deeper gender dynamics at play in the media.

I would get a more personal lesson in gender politics one morning from a woman who'd been in the ring fighting gender battles for years—Barbara Walters. I was getting coiffed when I saw in the mirror that she had just arrived in the studio. Even though she had worked the early schedule for years on the *Today* show, I thought I noticed her having a hard time wiping the sleep out of her eyes as she stopped by the makeup room to say good morning. As she turned to make her way down the hall toward the coffee room, what really opened her eyes was the sight of baby Jamie nestled in her crib in a room adjacent to my dressing room. There was Barbara standing over my little girl in total disbelief. She looked at me and said, "I can't even imagine what my bosses back at the *Today* show would have said if I had tried to bring my daughter to work with me. Boy, times have changed!"

I was excited that I was interviewing her that morning about one of her specials. I don't remember the exact special we discussed, but what I'll never forget is the advice she gave me. She pulled me aside after the segment and quietly said, "Don't try to demand equality—that time is just not here yet. There will be many big interviews that your bosses will not be ready to give you. But you see where fighting City Hall got your predecessor—out the door. Just take each story that they're willing to give you, as small as it might be, and make it a gem. Make it shine. That is how you will grow your role here."

That advice has served me well in my career and in every aspect of my life. Over the years, Barbara and I cohosted *GMA* many times—and we shared stories about being moms and trailblazers in this business.

Chapter 25

PERFECTING THE BALANCING ACT

You go through big chunks of time where you're just thinking, "This is impossible"…and then you just keep going and sort of do the impossible.

—Tina Fey, *Bossypants* (2011)

When I look back on those early days of *Good Morning America*, finally taking my seat next to David and at the same time being a brand-new mom, I actually marvel at myself a little. I imagine there were people holding their breath as they waited to see if I would pull it off. For me, I just put one foot in front of the other and learned how to do it all in real time.

For the first seven weeks after Jamie was born, I was fortunate to have a baby nurse who taught me the ropes. Once I started at the new job, though, we agreed that she would just meet me at the studio each morning and stay through the show and for a few hours after in my office so I could finish my work. Most mornings went off without a hitch, but when the baby nurse was late—and she was certainly not as on time as I was—I would find myself rocking Jamie in my arms as the producer briefed me on a late-added guest and the makeup artist applied my mascara and lipstick.

When the show would end each day, Elise and I went to my *GMA* office, where Jamie had a swing, another changing table, and another crib. I used to joke that Jamie had more beds than Conrad Hilton. Elise helped me execute my Herculean plan to balance my new role at *GMA* with the demands of motherhood. For example, when I needed to breastfeed Jamie, she would hang a sign on my closed office door that said "Breastfeeding Mom." Whenever I was being briefed by writers or interviwed by the press and Jamie needed to be entertained, Elise would take her around the office. Jamie was like a little mascot, often delighting staffers who were stressed from the grind of booking interviews and writing scripts.

The *GMA* staff used to joke that I would start *Good Morning America* each day as Joan Lunden, but I'd always end the show as Dolly Parton. I'll give you a minute to let that visual settle in your brain. I'll never forget one morning when I was interviewing a US senator about then-president Ronald Reagan's "trickle-down economics." You may remember that theory, but what I remember about that interview is that suddenly I was experiencing inflation and "trickle down" firsthand. It was time for baby Jamie to feed, and my boobs knew it. I was wearing a silk printed blouse, so the camera didn't really see it, thank God, but I did need to have my hairdresser run into the studio during the commercial with his hair dryer to dry me off. As they say, the show must go on.

It was one of the first times when I had to make some quick decisions about how to handle the juggling act. In the end, the producers, who cared only that we were in the middle of a live national broadcast, had a good laugh with me about it and were completely supportive—and I think that's because I weathered it

PERFECTING THE BALANCING ACT

with a sense of humor. I dried off, kept smiling, and kept going. Jamie was given a bottle despite my discomfort, and I didn't bail on the job. It was a good lesson for me on how to find a balance with my employer through a sense of fairness, sanity, and responsibility. Oh, and did I forget humility?

Honestly, I think I connected with the American public so quickly because they saw me balancing motherhood and work in real time—navigating the chaos and figuring it out as I went, complete with dirty diapers, spit-up, and all.

I was surprised by the amount of mail that came in every day asking questions about Jamie and how I was dealing with the balancing act. I soon needed a larger staff solely to answer all that mail.

The year 1981 was big for the news: the Iran hostage crisis, a space shuttle launch, and an assassination attempt on President Reagan sixty-nine days into his presidency. The biggest event of the year, however, turned out to be the royal wedding of Prince Charles to Lady Diana Spencer on July 29. For me, still learning to navigate motherhood and my new *GMA* role, I was about to go on the most exciting assignment of my career—the royal wedding—with baby Jamie in tow.

Admittedly, I'm a bit of a royal watcher, so I loved this assignment—and it was my one-year-old daughter's first trip abroad. Through my hotel, I arranged for a British nanny so Jamie would be well cared for as I was out and about with camera crews shooting stories.

On the day of the wedding, David and I were in two different locations so we could give Americans a look at the pageantry from the time the carriages left Buckingham Palace to when they arrived at St. Paul's Cathedral. The show producers had booked British royal watchers from London newspapers to sit with each of us and provide details only they would know—color commentary, if you will.

At one point in the broadcast, when we were in a commercial break, the royal watcher assigned to me, Nigel Dempster, drew our attention to a carriage that was approaching the cathedral. He said, "Oh, look—this next carriage has the most interesting guest of all, Camilla."

Camilla? Who was that?

"Camilla, oh my; she's the real love interest of Prince Charles . . . and, incidentally, that's who he's still seeing, despite this marriage."

Wait—*WHAT?*

Wasn't this a real-life royal fairy tale, with young Lady Diana marrying the prince of her dreams? As the commercial break was ending, we were all still in shock over this jaw-dropping remark, but we couldn't say anything about it during our live coverage of the wedding without facts to back it up. Of course, over the ensuing years, Nigel's words would ring true as Charles and Camilla's story unfolded.

* * * * *

In 1983, my second daughter, Lindsay, was born. The morning after I delivered her, I woke before dawn in my hospital room to get myself ready to present my new little girl to the world. As the sun began to come up there was a knock at the door, and a *Good Morning America* video crew came in to set up cameras and pull video cable in through the hospital window from the satellite truck on the street below so I could say "Good morning, America" from my hospital bed with my newborn daughter.

That was what my life was like—the line between my public

and personal life was completely blurred. It was an unusual existence, but a wonderful one. Just stop and think about the amazing moments you've shared with the people in your life—weddings, births, etc. Now multiply that by twenty-six million; that's how many viewers the show had each week. Hundreds and hundreds of congratulatory cards and gifts poured into my office with the birth of each of my daughters. Yes, I do mean actual baby gifts: children's books; hand-crocheted sweaters, bonnets, and booties; handmade leather baby shoes; and on and on.

It felt as though I'd formed an almost familial bond with the American public. The notes and letters from well-wishers were written almost as though I were a cousin or maybe a neighbor that they knew well. And I must tell you that with so many viewers sending well wishes, each of the wonderful events in my life was amplified.

Now, of course, I had to adjust to life with a toddler *and* a newborn. One day I was sitting in my glider with Lindsay on my shoulder (Would you please burp already?) and trying to conceptualize an acceptable timetable for returning to the early-morning grind. I'd been on maternity leave for more than a month when persistent thoughts about the May sweeps began nagging me. The ratings during sweeps are crucial to a network's advertising revenue, which is why all the morning shows were under a lot of pressure to take their shows on the road. With Lindsay's March birthday and my five weeks of maternity leave, my return would now be right up against the May sweeps. It wasn't reasonable to think that I could go back to work and take Lindsay with me with all the travel I was facing.

But there was no way I would miss sweeps; it would be absolutely unthinkable. While I felt guilty that Lindsay wouldn't get the extended bonding and breastfeeding time that Jamie had, I knew what I had to do. I thought to myself, *Come on, Joan—there are women who have to go back to work a week or even days after delivering, so buck up and tell them you'll be back in your anchor seat next week.*

In today's world, new parents are protected by the Family and Medical Leave Act, which guarantees parental leave not only for birth parents (including dads) but also for adoptive parents. Before its passage in 1993, not only was there no such legal protection but workplace expectations were also entirely different. If you wanted both a career and a family, the job had to come first. We've come a long way since then, but we still have more to go.

Lindsay finally let out a big belch, and I put her down in her crib. As I leaned over her, that's when it struck me: *OMG, I still have my mommy belly.* Of course I hadn't dropped all the weight from giving birth just weeks before. When I went back to work the following week and finished the first show, the ABC vice president in charge caught up with me on the way to my dressing room. Lowering his voice to almost a whisper, he asked, "Can I assume you're back in those workouts of yours, getting yourself back in shape?"

Wait, what? Buddy, I just had a baby forty-one days ago.

I felt like saying *Fine—I'll just go back home and return after all the weight is gone. See you in a couple of months.* I didn't do that, though, since I'm not a confrontational person. I simply said, "Don't worry, I'm working on it."

By the way, let me be honest: I never really lost all the baby weight until years later. I just got better at camouflage dressing. Thank God we all had big hair and shoulder pads in the eighties!

When my third daughter, Sarah, was born in 1987—by cesarean section—I needed to remain on maternity leave for longer, since my recovery was slower. I've heard women talk about how they found a cesarean birth easier—"Zip me open and zip me closed." Really? Well, I can't relate to that *at all*; they cut my stomach open, and it hurts every time I sit up in bed.

Even though Sarah had been born in late summer, which gave me a bit of a reprieve, the show's fall lineup and my upcoming travel plans were looming, and clearly they were going to be challenging. I remember having many conversations with my then-assistant Debbie Bierman weighing the pros and cons of succumbing to my own internal pressure to get back in the anchor chair. Debbie had been with me long enough to be more than an assistant. She was, and still is, one of my closest confidantes.

"You had a cesarean, Joan. Give yourself some slack. And I really don't think the producers expect you to bounce right back."

I knew Debbie was giving me good advice, but I felt such pressure to return to the show. In retrospect, I think I was bullying myself into going back sooner than I should have, and as Debbie said, even sooner than anyone was expecting. I felt like I had dueling angels on each of my shoulders. One was telling me to be a good employee while the other was telling me to be a good mom, and only now can I see how being good to *myself* had no room on either shoulder.

It was an emotional roller coaster; I felt joy and elation with each new baby, but there was also a physical struggle to make it all work together logistically. In the end, I caved, weaning Sarah much earlier than I had my other two daughters, and much earlier than I knew I should. As an adult, Sarah has struggled with some autoimmune issues, and I can't help but wonder if they're attributable to the early weaning. I do kick myself today for having given in to the pressure *I put on myself*, compromising my life—and my daughter's—in order to meet the show's shooting schedule.

My stories of juggling work and motherhood are really no different than those of millions of other women across this country and around the world: telling your boss about your pregnancy, negotiating maternity leave, finding good childcare, and dealing with mother guilt. My life as a working mom just played out each day on TV and in the press.

Meanwhile, at home in the morning, my girls would dress for school and then, at the breakfast table, they'd say good morning to me on the kitchen television. This morning ritual was created by our wonderful nanny, Bonnie Coddington, who began working for me when the girls were very young and stayed until their preteen years. "I always have the show on when the girls come down for breakfast, and they always check out what you're wearing and then kiss you good morning—literally on the TV screen," Bonnie told me.

Isn't that sweet? But here's the rest of the story: once they kissed me, they usually asked to change the channel to their favorite cartoon.

As my daughters got to be a bit older, it became easier to take them (and Bonnie, of course) along with me as *Good Morning America* traveled to far-off locations. We would pack bags of toys and coloring books to keep them occupied on flights. Amazingly—and thankfully—they always seemed to go with the flow. In fact, when we'd land in a new city or country, the *GMA* staff traveling with us would often applaud because the girls hadn't fussed.

Bonnie would take them sightseeing while I prepared for the show and went live on air. Then we would all meet up in time to hop on a train or a plane to the next destination. I always felt that this was an amazing perk—not just to be able to have them with me but for them to see the world . . . and me at work.

GMA travel also frequently meant leaving the girls at home, which killed me. But at least I didn't have to worry, knowing they were in good hands with Bonnie. Admittedly, though, I worried about the effect my job might have on them. Was I away too much?

And my biggest worry was, *Did my job ever put them in danger?*

Magazine writers were always looking for details about my personal life, and while it can be intrusive, you could say that I signed up for it. But my kids didn't. And so that left me feeling like a mama bear, always wanting to protect them and always worrying about whether something I said to a writer would have a negative impact on them.

As the girls got older, I knew they would be more aware of what was being written about me—and about them. While I sometimes allowed the girls to participate in a photo shoot for a magazine, I wouldn't allow them to be in a cover shot. My thinking was that if some pervert was walking down a New York street, he would never stop to buy a *Ladies' Home Journal* and look at the photos inside, but if the girls' faces were on a cover, it could be seen by anyone, and that could possibly put them in danger.

There were also times when the producers asked the girls to participate in our show, especially during our *GMA* travels. For instance, when we broadcast the show live from Amsterdam in May 1989, I was sent to shoot a story at Anne Frank's home, where she had hidden from the Nazis. The producers decided it would be an interesting angle to include Jamie and Lindsay since they were young, just as Anne Frank had been when she had to hide in that attic. They thought the girls could ask questions from a child's point of view.

In one scene, they had nine-year-old Jamie sit in the room where Anne Frank had lived in silence so as not to be detected. Jamie read passages aloud from the diary that Anne Frank kept during that period. At one point during the shoot, six-year-old Lindsay asked, "Why did the Germans hate the Jewish people?"

Couldn't she have asked an easier question? I answered, "They were led astray by the lies of one hateful man who was determined to kill all those who weren't exactly like him." It was an incredibly powerful moment.

In 1990, I took all three of my daughters on a two-week road trip to Scotland, England, and Ireland. I imagine ABC execs and my producers wondered whether traveling with them would be a distraction, but thanks to careful planning—largely with the help of my *GMA* colleague Sonya Selby-Wright, who was from England—it wasn't. Their itinerary was packed: watching the changing of the guard at Buckingham Palace, seeing Prince Charles compete in a polo match, riding horses at Jane Seymour's estate while I interviewed her, and even exploring a Blunden family castle in Kilkenny, Ireland, and meeting relatives I hadn't known I had. (It was actually very educational for them—or at least that's what I told their school when I pulled them out of class for two weeks.)

Meeting distant relatives was surreal, but the experience gave me a deeper understanding of my dad's family's journey from England to Ireland and Australia. If not for this *GMA* trip, I never would have learned this rich history.

My girls also loved coming with me in the early morning on the days when we had a guest on the show they found interesting. While I brought them to work with me daily only when they were babies, they did continue to come for a visit every now and then. In fact, they grew up with quite an understanding of the workings of our show and the *GMA* studio. The cameramen taught them to focus the cameras—not live on air, of course—and superstars picked them up as babies and cuddled them. Whether it was Jim Henson or Sammy Davis Jr., it was only years later that Jamie came to understand, through pictures and video, what that time was like.

One morning, when Barbara Walters was cohosting with me, Kermit the Frog was a guest—along with Jim Henson, naturally.

PERFECTING THE BALANCING ACT

Jamie, who was then five years old, was a huge fan of Kermit and Miss Piggy, so she had come in with me that morning clutching her beloved Miss Piggy doll.

As we counted down out of commercial, Jamie peeked over the counter at which we were seated—and locked eyes with Jim Henson as he crouched below Kermit. Barbara shot me a panicked look. Would Jamie expose Kermit's secret on live TV? My mind raced. I leaned in.

"Jamie, you know how you have an imaginary friend? Well, that's Kermit's imaginary friend."

Incredibly, she bought it. She beamed at Kermit and never looked down again. Kermit chatted with her, and Jamie was over the moon. Barbara and I finally exhaled when we cut to commercial. Thankfully, my child hadn't forever destroyed the magic of Jim Henson and the Muppets. Whew!

Moments like these reminded me how intertwined my professional and personal lives had become. My daughters had front-row seats to history and television magic—sometimes as participants, sometimes as wide-eyed observers. It wasn't always easy, but looking back, I wouldn't have had it any other way.

Joan and daughter at Anne Frank house in Amsterdam

Chapter 26

EARLY MOMFLUENCER

In a gentle way, you can shake the world.
—Mahatma Gandhi, central figure
in India's nonviolent struggle for independence

When I think back on bringing Jamie to work with me as an infant, I'm amazed by how it all played out. There had been no model to follow. And then later, when all my little girls were able to travel domestically and abroad with me, it became clear what an unprecedented request I'd made of a television network. Early on, I started to wonder whether my producers and colleagues would truly support this unconventional work plan, or if it would become an Achilles' heel.

Truth be told, I did feel tremendous support from my colleagues and even from my producers. Of course, the juggling act still wasn't easy to pull off. But, certainly, none of us could ever have anticipated the enormous amount of press that my pregnancy and my "baby deal" with the network generated.

While the media attention was positive for *GMA*, me, and women in the workplace, it heaped additional responsibilities onto my already demanding schedule. Week in and week out, I found myself on the phone with women's magazines talking about balancing motherhood with working in live television—something that continued for years.

Photo shoots became routine, and let me just say that they're more challenging when you're doing them with a young child in tow. I came prepared with a well-stocked baby bag and a separate toy bag, and we always had duplicate outfits in case of spit-up mishaps.

As I was being shaped into "America's Mom," an expectation of perfection took hold—both from the outside world and within myself. I didn't want to let people down, but behind the scenes, I was sleep-deprived, sometimes impatient, and unsure how to handle toddler meltdowns. Unlike *GMA*, motherhood didn't come with a script.

The press attention also brought an unexpected opportunity: an offer to do a commercial. In 1982, when Jamie was a toddler, my agent, Jim, called me to say he'd been contacted by the toy company Hasbro. "They want you to do toy commercials for them," he said.

This was the first time I'd ever been asked to do a commercial aside from those I did on the set of the show. "Can I do that when I'm working on *GMA*?"

"Well, at first I assumed you wouldn't be able to, since you're working on a news program. Broadcast journalists have always had strict clauses in their contracts prohibiting product endorsements in order to maintain credibility and avoid any conflicts of interest."

I could tell there was a "but" coming in the next sentence, so I waited.

EARLY MOMFLUENCER

His voice carried a smile. "But then it occurred to me that your contract is with the entertainment division, not the news division, so I actually think you can do it."

That detail about my ABC contract—that there would be no conflict if I did a commercial—would open a door that would lead to many new opportunities and a new aspect of my career, not to mention meaningful additional income. I shot dozens of commercials for Hasbro, Revlon Care for Kids, and Beech-Nut Baby Food.

While no one at the network raised objections, I worried initially that my commercial work would raise a few eyebrows. However, our viewers seemed to appreciate the authenticity of seeing someone they knew as a real working mother in commercials for toys and baby food. The commercials seemed to reinforce the connection I was building with my audience.

It wasn't just about selling products, however; I was also sharing valuable parenting information. This combination of blending consumer endorsements with valuable advice—which, of course, I'd garnered from expert guests on *GMA*—would years later become known as "momfluencing."

What began as a surprising opportunity to appear in commercials quickly evolved into something deeper. I wasn't just lending my face to brands—I was beginning to use that platform to connect with parents on a more meaningful level. The line between endorsement and education started to blur, and I realized that the trust viewers placed in me could be used not only to recommend products I believed in but also to share knowledge that could genuinely help families.

One of the most powerful examples of that shift came in 1983, just before Lindsay was born. I opened a segment with a representative from the American Lung Association by asking viewers, "Did you know that a pregnant woman who smokes two packs a day is cutting off a good twenty-five percent of oxygen and nutrients to her baby?" It was a startling statistic—one I hadn't known myself until I was preparing for the segment. Like many of our viewers, I was learning in real time how smoking in early pregnancy could lead to asphyxiation or cause birth defects during the critical first trimester, when many women didn't even realize they were expecting.

The camera pulled out from a single shot of me to include not only the doctor but a pregnant woman in a medical gown lying flat on an examination table. I introduced her: "We are also joined today by a woman who wants to simply go by Susan. She is pregnant and is a smoker, and she has agreed to take part in a demonstration so we can see the actual effect of smoking on the fetus."

An ultrasound technician sat beside Susan's exposed belly and narrated what we were seeing. "Take a look at the ultrasound screen; this image is the developing baby inside Susan's uterus."

By 1983, ultrasound technology was advanced, but the images were nothing like the digital ones of today. The image had a grainy quality, so it took viewers a moment to locate the curved fetal spine glowing faintly against the dark backdrop of the uterus and the limbs that moved in jerky, slow-motion waves.

Susan took a moment to catch a glimpse of the screen and smiled. That was my cue. "Okay, if you're ready, Susan, go ahead and inhale from your cigarette."

We all watched as the grainy image of the fetus suddenly writhed and constricted. Everyone on the set gasped. It was as though the baby was fighting for breath—and, in fact, that's exactly what was happening.

Susan had yet to see the image. "Susan, do you want to take a look at the screen so you can see what we're all looking at?"

The segment producer knew Susan personally and had asked her if she would be interested in learning about the effects of smoking during pregnancy. Susan had been eager to do so; this was a new frontier in medical science, after all. But now she was on national television, where this graphic illustration couldn't be unseen. I worried that she might have felt embarrassed or even shamed. I asked gently, "Did you ever imagine that's what was happening every time you inhaled?"

"Oh my God, I had no idea. I've got to figure out how to stop," she replied.

The response from our viewers was unlike anything I'd seen before; letters poured in for weeks, showing just how much the topic resonated with our audience. To build on the public awareness we raised, the American Lung Association approached me and suggested that I, "America's Mom," become the national spokesperson for their campaign against smoking during pregnancy. It didn't take much convincing!

When I started digging into the research, I was shocked to learn just how dangerous smoking is during pregnancy. It raises the risk of miscarriage, stillbirth, and low birth weight—and kids exposed in utero can even show lower math and reading scores later on. The science had been clear since the 1950s, but the message just wasn't reaching women. In the 1980s, the Roper Center for Public Opinion Research found that nearly half of all women didn't know smoking during pregnancy could lead to serious problems like premature birth, SIDS, and long-term developmental issues. The risks were real—but the awareness just wasn't there.

My campaigns with the American Lung Association helped bridge that knowledge gap on billboards and through flyers that were distributed in schools, restaurants, and bars. In an effort to reach women in rural areas, we also created public service announcements to run on local stations.

Statistics show that our campaigns made a difference. In 1987, when I was pregnant with my daughter Sarah, I wore a pastel-pink two-piece maternity outfit with a bit of Chanel flair to create a poster for the campaign. That year, approximately 19.5 percent of pregnant women reported smoking. By 2000, that figure had dropped to 12.2 percent. With the success of campaigns like these, I learned a valuable lesson about using my platform to deliver messages and make a meaningful impact on the health and well-being of Americans.

Through these experiences, I came to appreciate the privilege of having a platform that could be used for more than entertainment—it was an opportunity to inform, inspire, and make a difference. I don't know why I hadn't thought about this, but as I was writing this book, my now-grown daughter Jamie said, "You were a momfluencer before the word was even coined." I hadn't set out to be an influencer—there wasn't even a word for it then—but in hindsight, that's exactly what I was. Unlike today's influencers, who build their platforms from scratch, mine was created by my daily presence on national television. Offers for endorsements came to me, and I learned early on to be selective. If a product or a campaign didn't align with my real life, I turned it down, no matter how lucrative the proposal.

It was always enticing when my agent called with big offers from the makers of detergents or appliances or other consumer goods. However, the product needed to clearly speak to my role as a working mom and never make the public question my endorsement of it. Looking back, I see how those early decisions shaped a new career path that was deeply fulfilling and that allowed me to make a meaningful impact.

EARLY MOMFLUENCER

This approach became my guiding principle throughout my career, extending far beyond my parenting years. As my life evolved, so did the companies and causes I aligned with—from health and fitness to cancer awareness and aging. Being intentional about my choices ensured that my endorsements remained authentic and credible. And that, I've learned, is the real secret to lasting influence.

Today, we live in a world where top influencers are making significant incomes, and, according to recent surveys, more than half of young people want to become an influencer—57 percent, to be exact. It's no surprise, since these days kids grow up on TikTok and YouTube. Interestingly, it's not just young kids who want to get in on the influencer business: Some of those same studies (by the influencer marketing agency IZEA) indicate that 54 percent of people in the US ages eighteen to sixty would quit their jobs if they could make a living as a full-time influencer.[1]

I'm not sure those survey respondents realize how demanding it is to make a living as an influencer. My Jamie is one of the successful ones in the wellness world, but it's a nonstop, seven-days-a-week effort. She and her husband, George, started by casually sharing their gym routines and motivational tips during early parenthood. As her platform grew, I watched—somewhat anxiously—as she left her PR job to become a full-time content creator.

Now she's a one-woman advertising agency, pitching campaigns and collaborating with brands to authentically showcase their products. She tells me she learned integrity and authenticity from watching me navigate brand partnerships back in the day, and that it's even harder today to earn and keep trust in an oversaturated space. Influencers have become so prevalent that social media platforms

---

[1] That's according to a 2023 Morning Consult survey of one thousand Gen Zers. And they're not alone; 41 percent of adults overall would choose the career as well, according to a similar Morning Consult survey of 2,204 US adults.

have ethics rules for them, and the Federal Trade Commission (FTC) plays a key role in ensuring that consumers aren't misled. I support this move toward transparency.

I have a front-row seat to Jamie's life as a top influencer with two podcasts, a roster of wellness clients and brand ambassadorships, and a range of products on QVC. She's constantly on the road shooting video and speaking at events. Sound familiar? I often worry about how she can sustain that schedule while raising two little boys.

When I voice my concerns by saying, "I'm worried about you, my love. This all feels a bit . . . ambitious . . .," she always has a comeback: "Well, you should know! It's how you lived your life!"

Touché.

Joan in Hasbro toy commercial, circa 1982

Chapter 27

CHANGING OF THE GUARD

The art of life is a constant readjustment to our surroundiings.

—Kakuzo Okakura, prominent Japanese scholar, author, and art educator

As 1986 came to a close, a monumental power shift was underway. ABC-TV had recently been purchased by Capital Cities—a business media group that had little patience for Hollywood-style demands. David was in contract negotiations, and the new execs seemingly felt he was asking for too much power and control over a network program; when they couldn't reach an agreement, David left the show.

At the same time, I was negotiating my own contract. I wasn't demanding equal pay, though I certainly felt I deserved it. Instead, I proposed something strategic: prime-time specials. The extra income from the specials would bring my salary closer to that of my male counterpart's, without directly challenging the show's pay disparity.

My agent, Jim, wasn't so sure about my plan. The network

already had enough "females with egos" competing for their own slots on the prime-time schedule. They were all doing sit-down interviews with celebrities and world leaders—two chairs, flattering lighting, and the biggest names they could get.

That wasn't what I had in mind. Not at all. "I have no desire to do a show like that, Jim. I want to show viewers what it's like to be a firefighter, a fighter pilot, or an FBI agent. I want to take part myself in those extraordinary careers so viewers can really see what they're really like."

"How are you gonna do that?"

"I used to watch a show as a kid called *Plimpton*. Remember it?"

Jim didn't remember the show, but he knew George Plimpton.

"On the show, Plimpton would immerse himself in different professions to show what it took to walk in someone else's shoes. He suited up with the Boston Celtics, threw passes with the Detroit Lions, even pitched to Willie Mays—and the guy wasn't even an athlete! He called himself a 'participatory journalist.' That's what I want to do."

I had fantasized about participatory journalism for years. Like Plimpton, I didn't just want to interview people—I wanted to step into their world. To feel the force of a race car going 160 mph around a track. To experience the gut-dropping intensity of an F/A-18 Hornet landing on an aircraft carrier. To deploy with the Navy SEAL team when they practiced warfare.

Jim was warming up, but agents never like a tough sell.

"It won't be easy to shoot. Who's gonna let you tag along on dangerous assignments? You're gonna have to get trained, right?"

Of course he was right. I would need to go through intensive training before I could even *think* about tagging along. "Yes—and we'd shoot it all. That's part of the allure!"

"All right. Lemme see if I can sell it."

Before he hung up, I added, "One last thing, Jim. Can you get them to *finally* call me the cohost of *GMA*? It's time."

To my surprise, the network said yes to both my prime-time special, later to be titled *Behind Closed Doors,* and my long-overdue cohost title. The catch? The title wouldn't kick in until February—the same month David's contract expired.

That's how I found out that David was leaving the show.

As the shift in power became more evident on the broadcast, the publishing world took notice, and I was approached to write a book about being a woman breaking barriers in television and raising kids while working in the spotlight. I had never written a book, but I was being offered a strong advance. So, I said yes—like I always do.

Writing about being a working mom in a high-profile job excited me. *GMA* contributor and humorist Erma Bombeck understood it immediately. She wrote on the back cover of *Good Morning, I'm Joan Lunden*:

> A Joan Lunden doll is every little girl's dream. Wind it up and it balances a daily network TV show, a cable show on mothers, lectures, public appearances, home, husband, and two children. . . . This book reveals what makes Joan run and how far she came to get there. She is a prototype for women of the eighties who want it all without sacrificing integrity and the importance of family life.

Oh, Erma, if only you knew the impostor syndrome I carried with me every day. At home, I was like every other parent—disciplining, guiding, second-guessing every decision. But as a public figure, I felt overwhelming pressure to be perfect, to never make a false move. Parenting is the ultimate crucible for your character. We tend to judge ourselves most harshly when thinking of ourselves as parents—constantly toeing the line and worrying about every choice.

And, like every working mom, I had *guilt*.

Not just for the *GMA* travel that pulled me away from my girls but for the little things too. The classroom parties where I showed up empty-handed while the other moms had spent the night baking Pinterest-worthy cookies. I noticed the occasional side-eye. "Don't worry, Joan; we've got this covered," they'd say. "We know you have a big job."

Did my daughters notice? Did it matter to them?

I've asked them as adults if it bothered them that I wasn't in the after-school pickup line. "No, Mom, we would just ask Bonnie if we could spend the afternoon at a friend's house" was their answer. But, unfortunately, their assurances did nothing to relieve my guilt.

As if that wasn't enough, my high-profile life added *another* layer of guilt—this time over the tremendous amount of public adulation that came with my persona. The girls grew up with a warped perspective of the human race. After all, the real world isn't populated only by nice people who stopped at your restaurant table to fawn over your mother and you. Jamie, Lindsay, and Sarah were experiencing *my* world. I was always cognizant of that. While I found it humorous at times, I often worried that it might leave them vulnerable as adults. Would my celebrity cachet, limos, and red carpets mess them up as adults?

By the time my book *Good Morning, I'm Joan Lunden* was released, I realized media writers weren't *really* that interested in my take on working motherhood. During my book tour, every male reporter skipped right past it. Instead, they all wanted to know how David was handling my growing role on the show.

Figures.  **GMA** *promo announcing Charlie as cohost*

Chapter 28

OUT OF THE SHADOW

Alone we can do so little; together we can do so much.
—Helen Keller, 1925 speech

David and I never discussed our power imbalance—likely because we both knew that the success of the show depended on maintaining a warm, friendly working relationship, at all costs. And I was also tremendously appreciative of how much I had been able to learn from him. He may have only *played* a teacher on *Lucas Tanner*, but to me he was always generous with his time as he mentored me in my early days at *GMA*. Now that his departure was growing near, *GMA*'s producers surprised me by asking who, in my opinion, should replace him.

Can you imagine that? *My* opinion on the new cohost?

Over the next few months, a parade of possible cohosts made their way through the studio, each sitting next to me for a week so the network could assess our chemistry. Among the contenders were sportscaster Frank Gifford, talk-show host Regis Philbin, New York news anchor Ernie Anastos, and even *Dynasty* star John Forsythe. They were all pros, but *GMA*'s format wasn't like anything they'd done before. It required quick thinking, precise timing, and an ability to pivot seamlessly from hard news to lighthearted banter.

For instance, if I had an interview scheduled to begin at 7:16, I knew that at exactly 7:22:55, I'd better be saying, "Thank you, we'll be right back." The show went to commercial at 7:23, even if I was still talking or my guest was still answering. Likewise, if a segment ran short, I couldn't just wrap early; the audience would see a still slide on the screen with our theme music. These were things that took time to master.

But there was one candidate who already had an edge: Charles Gibson.

Charlie had appeared on the show for years as a Capitol Hill correspondent, and when David went on vacation, he sometimes filled in with me. I liked him immediately. Charlie had a wonderful everyman's man quality. He was incredibly bright but never showy about it. He delivered the news with authority but didn't take himself too seriously. I was sure that America would relate to him.

Whenever a program changes hosts, there's always a concern about a ratings dip during the transition. Research showed that morning audiences especially liked consistency. They wanted to know that the same people would be in their home every day at 7:00 a.m.

That concern turned out to be unfounded.

In fact, some television critics suggested that our ratings held steady because of my growing popularity—yep, the momentum was shifting, and I was finally, *officially*, the actual cohost.

On February 20, 1987, we devoted the full two-hour show to celebrating David's tenure. And then, just like that, he was gone.

Three days later, we welcomed Charlie as the new cohost.

For his first show, we happened to be broadcasting live from Fisher Island, near Miami. Even at 6:30 a.m., it was already hot. I had dressed accordingly in a loose linen outfit—casual enough for the beach, polished enough for a live national news program.

Charlie, on the other hand, showed up in a dark navy suit, a starched white shirt, and a tie.

I couldn't resist.

As we opened the show, I turned to him and said, "Hey, Charlie, you're not on Capitol Hill anymore." Then I reached over and loosened his tie.

I'm pretty sure he was thinking, *Oh my God, what have I done to my career?*

The week before, Charlie had come by the studio to settle into his new office. After putting his books away (which, I assume, included a copy of the *Congressional Record*), he came into my office, shut the door, and sat across from me.

"I want us to make a deal," he said. "Let's promise each other that we'll work as a true team. Fifty-fifty. No one pulls rank on the bigger interviews. No one tries to overshadow the other. Let's show America that a man and a woman can work together as equals."

Hey, I *love* this guy.

Our new partnership kept *Good Morning America*'s early-morning ratings strong, and Charlie and I developed a close friendship in addition to being colleagues. The crew totally embraced Charlie, and for the next decade, Charlie, Spencer Christian, and I would traverse the planet together. Charlie was the kind of leader who didn't hold himself above others. He treated everyone on the staff as equally important as the two of us who fronted the show. And he always kept his word and treated me as an equal. I think his influence made a huge impact on my role and our ratings.

JOAN: LIFE BEYOND THE SCRIPT

* * * * *

Once I began interviewing presidents, I started getting invited to state dinners and other affairs at the White House. I covered five US presidents—Gerald Ford, Jimmy Carter, Ronald Reagan, George H. W. Bush, and Bill Clinton.

In 1987, I received an invitation to a state dinner the Reagans were hosting for the visiting president of Mexico. It was my first personal White House invite, not a *GMA* assignment. I was seated between Nancy Reagan and Ralph Lauren. Being in the middle, I couldn't help but overhear their conversation—Nancy quietly discussing her early-stage breast cancer, which had not yet been made public, and Ralph sharing his own experience with cancer. They seemed to speak without hesitation, despite having a network journalist sitting between them. Mrs. Reagan wouldn't have been so forthright if she thought she couldn't trust me as one of her invited guests. That kind of discretion was understood at the time; it was a very different world. My *GMA* bosses never asked if I'd gotten an inside scoop from my evening at the White House, since I had attended in a personal capacity—but that's the ethical tightrope journalists often walk.

In December 1992, I was invited to a Christmas party by President George H. W. Bush and his wife, Barbara, to honor their White House staff. It was, in effect, a farewell party, since he had just lost the election to Bill Clinton. I brought my mother along. I had lent Mom a glittering gold-beaded gown of mine, so she literally embodied her nickname, Glitzy Glady. As the evening drew to a close, we stood with the president and the first lady to listen to the United States Navy Band perform. Barbara leaned over and said, "We'd like to take you and your mom up to our private quarters. When the band finishes this song, we'll turn and walk to the elevator behind us. George will take your mom by the arm and lead her there."

Well—can you imagine what my mother must have thought when the president of the United States offered her his arm? Oh my God. She always loved being part of the extraordinary adventures this job made possible for me.

Once we were upstairs in the private residence, the president smiled at my mother and said, "I've always enjoyed your daughter. She asks the tough questions—as she should—but she's always been wonderful to my Babs. Anyone who's kind to my Babs is good with me."

Barbara offered to give us a tour, and as we moved from room to room, she told personal stories about their life in the White House. She showed us her office, which was already packed for the upcoming move to Houston. The president's office, however, remained untouched. "We really thought he was going to win," she said. "George feels he still has so much more to do; it's been hard for him to face the task of packing."

Passing what she called the door to the laundry room, Barbara recalled that after George had won the presidency, she wanted to check to see whether her living room furniture and rug would fit in the new space—and if she needed to bring her own washer and dryer. She laughed as she explained, "As you know, the Reagans were quite formal, so when I arrived for my visit I was ushered past a lineup of housekeepers, cooks, and other staff to say my hellos. When we sat down for lunch—cucumber and cream cheese finger sandwiches with the crusts cut off—I just kept wondering when I was going to see the laundry room. And I never did."

Barbara and Mom immediately connected. Mom was smiling ear to ear as she took it all in. Remembering the years that Mom worked nonstop to settle Dad's estate, ripping up those foreclosure notices and keeping her chin up, our being together at the White House felt like a quiet reward for all her sacrifices.

Barbara also told us that everything said in the presidential residence becomes part of the official presidential record—except for what's said in the bathroom. Knowing George would eventually write a memoir, she'd bought a tiny tape recorder. Each night, he would go into the bathroom and recount the day's events into it. Barbara would transcribe those recordings—and that became the foundation of his memoir. At the end of the evening, back at our hotel, Mom recounted all that had happened—the pageantry, President Bush's sincerity in thanking his staff, and, of course, the chance to see the warmth of their private quarters; such a stark contrast from the formal, public-facing rooms. "Barbara was so gracious and down-to-earth. And oh my, when the president spoke of his admiration for you and how professional you were, I couldn't have been more proud of you, Joni."

Then there was the time years later, long after I'd left *Good Morning America*, when my husband, Jeff, boarded a flight in Los Angeles. A member of the Secret Service approached him to ask if he would mind switching rows so President Gerald Ford could sit with security on either side. When Ford boarded, he shook Jeff's hand and thanked him for accommodating. Jeff replied that he'd always heard from his wife, Joan Lunden, what a kind and gracious man the president was.

President Ford brightened and said, "Oh, Betty and I have always loved Joan. We were big fans; please say hello."

A few minutes later, Jeff called to tell me about the friendly exchange. I happened to be in a store trying on swimsuits and had just removed one when the phone rang. When Ford heard Jeff on the phone, he asked, "Is that Joan? May I say hello?"

Jeff handed him the phone, and there I stood, completely naked and so flustered I could barely speak. "Hello, Mr. President. So good to hear your voice." Of course, he had no idea about my predicament (this was before FaceTime, thank God), but I was painfully aware of it. And that wasn't exactly the kind of story I could share with anyone back then.

Until now.

That funny—albeit embarrassing—moment happened only because of the genuine relationships I was able to build over years of interviewing President Ford and other heads of state. I began to notice a shift. I was stepping into rooms—and roles—that had once seemed reserved for others. That realization struck me shortly after Charlie joined the show and we traveled to Sweden in 1988.

International assignments always carried a thrill—new places, new faces, the chance to bring the world a little closer to our viewers back home. But nothing could have prepared me for what I found waiting in my hotel room. After unpacking, I settled in and flipped through the stack of research packets that had been delivered. My eyes skimmed the names on the top pages, and then there it was: King Carl XVI Gustaf and Queen Silvia of Sweden. I blinked and read it again.

A sit-down with the king. A private tour through the royal halls of Drottningholm Palace with the queen. I almost laughed at the sheer magnitude of it. When David had been my partner, there wouldn't have even been a question—he would have been the one shaking hands with royalty.

The next day, as I stepped onto the palace grounds, I felt the weight of history beneath my feet. Inside, I sat across from the king, taking in his measured, deliberate presence as we spoke.

Then, Queen Silvia took me through the grand, gilded rooms, her voice soft but assured as she shared the stories held within the walls. For years, I had watched powerful men claim these kinds of interviews as their own. But here I was, walking beside a queen. And for the first time, I wasn't just reporting on power—I was stepping into my own.

Speaking of stepping into one's own power, Mary Tyler Moore was someone I'd always admired and perhaps modeled my career after. In the 1960s, I never missed watching her as Laura Petrie on *The Dick Van Dyke Show*, where Dick was, of course, the star. But Mary finally showed what she was made of in the '70s when she got her own *Mary Tyler Moore Show* and her character, Mary Richards, embodied independence and ambition in the WJM-TV newsroom.

When I heard that I would be interviewing Mary Tyler Moore on our show, I could hardly believe it!

That morning, as the *GMA* theme music played and Charlie and I opened the last half hour of the show, I spotted her entering the studio. She moved quietly in her flats, taking in every aspect of our studio as if she'd never been on a TV set before. It struck me then that she was just as in awe of this moment as I was.

When the news segment and weather wrapped, it was time for me to walk across the set to meet her. My nerves kicked in. This was *Mary Tyler Moore*. A woman who had established a blueprint for so many of us.

To my surprise, before I could even say a word, she broke into that effusive Mary Tyler Moore smile and said, "I'm a little nervous. This is so fabulous—actually being here in this studio. I watch you guys every morning; I feel like I know you."

Her words stopped me in my tracks. *She* felt like she knew *me*? I'd spent years watching her redefine what a woman in television could be, and yet in that moment, we were just two professionals meeting on equal ground, each admiring the other.

When the show broadcast from Holland in 1989, I was given the opportunity to interview another one of my all-time favorite movie stars: Audrey Hepburn. Even after I'd spent years in the business, sitting across from certain people still felt surreal, and Audrey was one of them.

It was easy to admire her effortless beauty, which was even more striking in person than on the screen, but in her presence, I was struck by the quiet grace with which she carried herself. Unlike so many Hollywood legends, she had never clung to fame. Instead, she'd devoted herself to something far greater. She was on our show to speak about her humanitarian work with UNICEF, a cause she championed with relentless passion. As we spoke, her elegance came out not in the way she looked but in the way she *cared*. "Doing something that makes a difference in people's lives," she told me, "that's what keeps me inspired. That's what gives my life purpose—and joy."

Her words stayed with me long after the cameras stopped rolling. Here was a woman who had spent decades in the spotlight, yet found her greatest fulfillment not in being adored but in serving others. It made me wonder how I defined purpose. Was it in the power of the interviews I had claimed? Or was it in the impact they left behind?

Joan and Charlie Gibson covering presidential inagurations

Chapter 29

LIFE IN A FISHBOWL

*Showing your emotions to toxic people
is like bleeding next to a shark.*

—Coral Anika Theill,
author of *Bonshea: Making Light of the Dark*

For all the glamour and excitement of hosting a network television show, there's a side to celebrity that few people truly understand—a darker side that exposes you to relentless scrutiny, invasive comments, and outright fabrications about your personal life.

I often wonder how most people would react if they saw the letters I received daily over the years. Every detail of my existence was fair game—my hair, my makeup, my clothes, my shoes, the way I spoke, the way I raised my children, the way I navigated my marriage, and, later, my divorce. Some letters came from well-meaning viewers offering unsolicited advice ("You should really try bangs"; "That shade of lipstick washes you out"). Others were more biting, laced with a kind of casual cruelty that made me wonder how people could be so bold when hiding behind a piece of paper or a keyboard.

Yet I've always believed that if I were in a room with many of these same people—the ones who'd had no hesitation about sending a scathing letter—they would probably be perfectly nice to my face, and maybe even ask for a selfie.

In the age of social media, however, that anonymous boldness only intensified. Now the criticism came instantly, publicly, and often relentlessly. It was around this time that my daughter Lindsay, who later ran my production company for eleven years, gave me some of the best advice I've ever received: "Don't engage with these people. Ever." And for the most part, I've followed her guidance. Still, I'll admit that every now and then, when a comment is especially cruel or blatantly false, I can't help but respond—not face-to-face, because I'm not confrontational, but with a carefully worded reply online.

One of the most relentless topics of public commentary is my weight. It seems there's nothing the media enjoys more than tracking every pound a woman gains or loses. Over the years, I've watched as the press and the public tore apart actresses, singers, and other women in the spotlight for something as natural as fluctuations in their weight. And while the focus has traditionally been on women, lately even men are subjected to public body shaming for having what the tabloids refer to as a "dad bod."

Why should anyone have to deal with this level of scrutiny over their body? And yet the conversation around weight seems to have only gotten worse. Now, with the rise of new weight-loss drugs like Ozempic and Mounjaro, the latest media obsession is speculating about who's taking them. If someone loses weight with the help of these drugs, they're accused of cheating. If they don't, they're criticized for not taking control of their health.

My own reckoning with weight and wellness came in 1989 when I interviewed a representative from the American Heart

Association, who had brought along a simple quiz to help our viewers assess their risk for cardiovascular disease. As I read through the questions, I instinctively started answering them in my head: Are you getting an adequate amount of exercise? *Hey, I'm always on the run as a working mom—does that count?* Are you eating healthy? *Come on, there were donuts in the greenroom this morning.* Are you getting enough sleep? *Are you crazy? I'm lucky if I get five hours.*

As we went through the list, I felt myself sinking lower and lower into my chair. I was failing the test—and failing it badly. I wasn't just carrying extra baby weight from three pregnancies, I was putting myself at risk. My lifestyle wasn't just demanding—it was unsustainable.

Something had to change. I began working regularly with a fitness trainer and a nutritionist and committed to my health as if it were a second job. I treated workouts like I would major interviews: They were nonnegotiable and part of my daily routine. No excuses.

Over the next year, I transformed—not just physically but mentally and emotionally. I was no longer just trying to keep up; I was taking control. And just in time, because I was about to face the most public, scrutinized, and challenging transition of my life.

By the time my youngest daughter, Sarah, was five, I knew I couldn't put it off any longer. It was time to leave my marriage. When I first met with my attorney, Marc Chamlin, he was blunt: With my public image as "America's Mom," he was concerned that a divorce would likely shock people, and they would question my judgment.

Although I couldn't see how anything was going to change my mind, Marc had always given me good advice—this time, he recommended marriage counseling. What followed was six months of torturous sessions with a couples therapist. Six months of listening to my now ex-husband rationalize how he had always been right and how I was wrong for wanting to leave. Six months of reinforcing exactly why I needed to go.

Once I finally pulled the trigger and filed for divorce, I braced myself for the media storm.

It was still shocking when it actually hit.

In divorce cases, the spouse with the higher income is often required to provide financial support to the other while the case is pending. That meant I was responsible for temporary alimony payments to my soon-to-be ex-husband. When the court ruled that I would have to pay $18,000 a month in alimony, the press pounced. Since I was one of the first high-profile women to have to pay support to her husband, this was big news.

I had just finished *Good Morning America* for the day and was now on my way to shoot a location interview. As I took a moment to relax in the back seat of the car, my field producer picked up his ringing phone. He looked over at me. "It's the ABC operator, but they're looking for you."

With that, he handed me the phone. I heard "Hi, Joan, I'm a reporter with the *Daily News*. Just calling to get a response from you about the news of the morning."

"Hi?"

"What do you think about having to pay your husband eighteen thousand dollars a month?"

I hadn't even processed the ruling myself. The reporter didn't know the half of it; I would also still be paying my ex-husband's mortgage, property taxes, electricity, fuel, insurance, and cable television bill, as well as every other service that I had set up in my name.

Before I could filter my response, I blurted out: "The judge should have told my ex to get a job."

That was all they needed. The call ended.

Uh-oh. I'd just experienced ambush journalism.

The next day, splashed across the front page of the *New York Post*, was the headline "GET A JOB."

Gulp.

Sure, I lost my cool for a moment. Who wouldn't have under the circumstances? But now I had to deal with the consequences. The very next day, the *New York Daily News* entered the fray with its own headline: "PAY UP OR SHUT UP."

This wasn't just about me anymore. The entire conversation around women paying alimony was shifting, and my case became part of the national debate. For decades, men had been the ones who were required to pay spousal support after a divorce. But now, women—many of whom had built successful careers—were finding themselves in the same position. I had just stepped on a cultural land mine.

The media ran with it. Articles popped up everywhere, speculating about the future of alimony and whether women should have to pay. "Men are popping champagne bottles all over the country," one article declared.

Great. So my divorce had become a national celebration for disgruntled ex-husbands everywhere.

The alimony ruling was only the beginning. Once the press had a taste of the drama, they wanted more. Every week, a new headline. Who cheated? (Neither of us did.) Who would get custody of the kids? (We settled on joint custody.) How much was I going to have to pay? (More than I wanted to, but that was beside the point. As their mother, I wanted to make sure my daughters wouldn't be suffering any more than they already were because their parents were getting divorced and the details were being splattered all over the newspapers.)

And then came the worst headline of all. One morning I walked into a grocery store and froze. There, staring back at me from the checkout aisle, was a *National Enquirer* headline in big, bold letters: "LUNDEN COMMITS ADULTERY."

I nearly fell over.

Not only was this completely untrue but the article claimed I was leaving my husband for Alan Thicke.

Wait, what? Alan Thicke?

I had interviewed him a few times about *Growing Pains* and we had cohosted the Walt Disney World Christmas and Easter Parades together, but I'd never even had a phone conversation with Alan Thicke, let alone a romantic relationship.

The magazine had doctored a photo of us from one of the Disney parades, cutting out Mr. and Mrs. Easter Bunny from the group shot. If you looked closely, you could still see a bunny paw on my shoulder. But a cropped Disney promo photo couldn't possibly be the basis of their scandalous affair story.

It was unbelievable. I couldn't let this slide. I hired a libel lawyer and prepared to sue the *National Enquirer*. Once the lawsuit was in motion, the tabloid was required to reveal their source. It turned out the tip had come from someone who worked in the *Growing Pains* production office. This "source" had overheard Alan's assistant say "Joan's on the phone" and assumed that meant me.

Except . . . it wasn't me. It was another celebrity with a name that sounded like Joan who was also going through a divorce and had three kids.

When the *Enquirer* realized they had gotten the story wrong, they made a substantial offer to settle—but no dollar amount could touch the damage they'd done to my mental health and reputation. They also promised a printed retraction, but of course it was buried on page three in tiny print. While most of the scandalous headlines were only in the tabloids, and kids don't read them, I worried that parents from school might see those headlines in the grocery line and wonder if I had done all the things the rags accused me of. Would that get back to the kids, including mine?

Once those headlines were out there, people didn't know that I got a tiny retraction on page three or that I'd received damages for their scandalous and false claims about me. The damage was done. To this day, it continues to trouble me that people might still think I did those things. In fact, I feel the angst as I write these words.

Settling the lawsuit didn't stop the tabloids. For a full year, there was a new article about me every week. I had to hire a PR specialist, Stan Rosenfield, not to get me more publicity but to keep me *out* of the papers.

The damage control was exhausting. The financial cost was infuriating.

But the worst part? It wasn't over yet.

Chapter 30

FIELD OF LAND MINES

*Do not judge my story by
the chapter you walked in on.*

—T. L. Martin

For the first time in years, I had space to focus on myself, my children (then ages eight, twelve, and fifteen), and my career without the weight of a failing marriage hanging over me—or that fifty pounds of baby weight.

As that weight had come off, people had started noticing. Colleagues, friends, and even viewers would stop me and ask, "How did you do it?" Before long, I was approached by a company called Republic Pictures with an unexpected offer: to make an exercise video.

I laughed at first. *Me? Leading a workout video? I'm not Jane Fonda!* But as I thought about it, I realized something: This wasn't about being a fitness expert, it was about sharing my journey in a way that could inspire others.

And that's how *Workout America* was born in 1995.

The producer of that video was Laura Morton, who became my longtime friend and collaborator. She helped pioneer the celebrity exercise video market, so I knew that I was in very good hands with her. I even roped my assistant Samantha Berg into joining me as one of my backup dancers in the video. When we wrapped production, Laura and I went to dinner to celebrate. Laura felt the video told only part of my story, however. And she was right. At that time, 50 percent of married American women were divorcing and in the same boat as I was. Laura reminded me that I could use my voice to educate and inspire these women, and that's when the idea of the book was hatched.

Writing a book about healthy eating and exercise? Really? The prospect was intimidating. But the more I thought about it, the more I realized that my journey wasn't just about weight loss—it was about taking control of my life.

The next day we went to see my agent, Jim Griffin, to share our plan, and Jim told us it was the worst idea he'd ever heard. When we asked why, he said, "Because Joan doesn't cook." Jim just couldn't imagine me in my kitchen cooking up dinner for my family. Laura reminded him that every morning I was in the *GMA* kitchen with the likes of Julia Child, Emeril Lagasse, and Daniel Boulud. Surely I had learned something from them by osmosis!

Despite Jim's reservations, Laura and I dove in, completely unaware of how the publishing world worked. We had no grand plan, no connections in the industry—just a story we believed in. And, thankfully, so did the iconic literary agent Al Lowman, who ended up selling the book at auction for a lot of money. Over time, the book shaped up to be a combination of memoir and cookbook.

FIELD OF LAND MINES

When *Joan Lunden's Healthy Cooking* was released, it instantly became a *New York Times* bestseller. I couldn't believe it. My personal journey had turned into something that was helping others—something that felt more rewarding than anything I could have imagined.

Somewhere in the concluding pages, I wrote: "I hope you find this book helpful on your journey to fitness, and that in the end, you too will believe anything is possible. After all, I wrote a cookbook!"

Looking back now, I can see that my career as an author didn't happen because of a strategic plan; it happened because I was living my life, learning, and sharing my journey along the way. One step at a time, I turned personal transformation into public inspiration.

Now I just had to transform my personal life. I was single again, happily, but awkwardly. At first, I just stayed home; but in time, I realized that wasn't fair to me. I'd put my life on pause. Everyone had an opinion on what I should do next. Friends, colleagues, and even strangers had the same advice:

"You need to get out there!"

"It's the only way you'll meet someone!"

"You're not going to find love sitting at home!"

I appreciated their enthusiasm, but my experience with what the tabloids had done during the divorce made me wary of what they would do if I started dating again. I couldn't put the girls through that, much less myself.

When you're a well-known public figure, dating is simply not normal dating. Once I finally agreed to try—it must have been two or three years after the divorce—some of my friends and colleagues took it upon themselves to find me the perfect match. The setups followed the same script; either "Joan, you have to meet this guy. He's really smart" or "He's brilliant. He's powerful. He's fabulously wealthy."

Wealth? Power? Those weren't necessarily the qualities I required in a partner. But I figured, what could it hurt to at least go on the date? One man was, as advertised, extremely bright and successful, and the conversation was interesting—so far, so good.

Then, on our third date, he dropped a bombshell: "I feel like I'm running out of time. I should really think about getting married."

I barely had a minute to process that statement before he continued: "Actually, you're just the kind of woman I've been looking for—smart, ambitious, successful. And best of all, you already have kids, so I don't have to worry about that."

Excuse me? Was this man looking for a wife like he ordered a Chinese meal? One from each category?

Smart? Check. Ambitious? Check. Doesn't require fatherhood? Check.

Before I could wrap my head around what was happening, he made one final pitch. "I want you to come with me to Cuba this weekend. I have a dinner meeting with Fidel Castro, and I'd love to have you by my side. I'll send a car for you and meet you at my plane at Teterboro."

Wait, what? Cuba? Castro? How did we get here?

I stared at him, utterly speechless. I tried to be polite, but my answer was firm: "I won't be able to do that with you this weekend."

He received the rejection with grace—but, not surprisingly, I never heard from him again.

And why did people think the only men who qualified for dates were celebrities or financial moguls? Sure, they might understand my demanding lifestyle better, but maybe the person I really needed wasn't "in the biz."

Regardless of who I dated, I felt like I was under surveillance now. I was navigating a field of land mines. Would I end up in the

FIELD OF LAND MINES

tabloids tomorrow? Would my date be scared off by the attention?

I didn't want my persona to morph from "America's Mom" to "Who's Joan Got on Her Arm Today?" I knew in my heart of hearts that the execs at ABC wouldn't like that change either. I didn't want the frenzy to affect how the public saw me or to jeopardize my job. But what could I do about it? One half of me knew I had to get out there and socialize to move forward in my life, but the other half felt selfish and maybe even reckless for pursuing a personal life.

One of the saddest parts of this heavy scrutiny of my love life was that it often affected whether I gave someone a second glance—and it likely caused some men to not want to date me because they would end up on the cover of a tabloid. Of course, I couldn't blame them, since I was constantly worried about my privacy and reputation too.

Even when I went out to a club with a bunch of my younger girlfriends (and left with them), I would invariably be labeled a "party girl" in the tabloids. This greatly amused my teenage daughters, who knew me as the complete opposite, but what if Mr. Right was out there reading these stories? Would that dissuade him from wanting to meet me when he had thought I was a nice, respectable woman?

One week I was supposedly dating a famous businessman. The next week I was linked to a Hollywood star I had never even met. The *New York Post* ran a story claiming I had been seen leaving a Los Angeles party with LL Cool J in his limo. Come on—I was obviously in New York, hosting *Good Morning America*. When I showed the headline to my daughters, they burst out laughing. "Mom, don't worry. No one will believe it. You're not *that* cool." Okay, fair. But still—how was this my life? At one point, I even joked with my friends: "My New Year's resolution this year is to have *half* as much fun as the tabloids say I'm having!" But the truth is, it wasn't funny at all.

I had a morals clause in my contract; calling me a party girl or falsely portraying my behavior could seriously risk my position at ABC. I basically had a libel lawyer on speed dial in the event of such concocted stories. The financial toll was one thing; the emotional toll was another.

Still, even with all the false headlines, the paparazzi, and the intrusions into my personal life, nothing prepared me for the real danger of celebrity. The danger that wasn't just about reputation. The danger that could actually threaten my life.

For all the frustration, humiliation, and outright absurdity of dealing with the tabloids, at the end of the day, those stories—no matter how infuriating—weren't life-threatening. But some aspects of fame were.

I had always thought of *Good Morning America* as a safe space—a show that families watched together while getting ready for work and school. It was comforting to imagine millions of viewers starting their day with us, sipping their coffee, listening to the news, and sharing a moment before rushing out the door.

But there was also another group watching us every morning: prisoners.

What I hadn't considered—until I started receiving frightening, deeply personal letters—was that *GMA* was also being broadcast into prisons across the country. For some of these incarcerated men, I became a fixation. Some were harmless admirers, writing letters filled with flattery and longing. Some proclaimed their innocence and requested my help. They sent thick dossiers containing long court transcripts. Others were far more disturbing. I received letters detailing violent fantasies about me. Some included chilling threats.

One inmate up for parole casually mentioned that he was planning to visit New York after his release—and looked forward to

FIELD OF LAND MINES

finally meeting me in person.

I tried to brush these things off. *They're just letters. These men are locked away.* But then one of my colleagues at ABC reminded me of something terrifying: "Not all of them stay in prison, Joan. Some of them get out."

That's when I started keeping a file labeled "IF YOU NEVER SEE ME AGAIN."

I wasn't being dramatic. If something happened to me, I wanted law enforcement to know exactly where to start looking.

Eventually, things escalated to the point where I had to hire attorneys to attend parole hearings on my behalf, arguing that certain prisoners should not be released because of the threats they had made against me.

It was terrifying to learn that I wasn't the only public figure who was dealing with this. My lawyer returned from one hearing and casually mentioned, "Oh, by the way, I ran into so-and-so's attorney. She was there fighting against the same guy."

Celebrities don't just dodge paparazzi and fight off tabloid rumors; some of us have had to actively try to prevent dangerous men from being released back into society because of the concern that they might come after us.

People assume that fame is glamorous. And, in many ways, it is. I've had incredible experiences interviewing some of the most fascinating people on the planet and building a career that I'm deeply proud of. But fame also steals things from you. It steals your privacy. It steals your sense of safety. And sometimes it even steals your peace of mind. I became hyperaware of my surroundings, and I reassessed security measures at home and in my workplace.

At the end of the day, the most important lesson I've learned from dealing with this aspect of my career—and from life—is this:

You can't control what people say about you. You can't control what the tabloids print. You can't control the actions of strangers. But you can control how you respond.

I refused to let fear—whether of the press, the public, or anyone else—preoccupy me. I had worked too hard to become the strongest, healthiest, happiest version of myself. And I wasn't about to let anyone take that away.

Chapter 31

THE FLYING INFERNO

It's hard to turn the page when you know someone won't be in the next chapter, but the story must go on.

—Thomas Wilder

July 17, 1996, started like any other morning. After *GMA*'s opening sequence, Charlie and I said our good mornings and bantered a bit, and then Eddie Luisi, our stage manager, cued Charlie to camera one.

"A lot is going on today," Charlie began. Yasser Arafat had been reelected president of the Palestinian National Authority, becoming the first democratically elected leader of the Palestinian people. We would also be going live to Atlanta, Georgia, where the Summer Olympics were getting underway.

Then Eddie cued me to camera two. "The Midwest is getting hit with some treacherous weather, the Illinois and Mississippi Rivers have both risen to above flood stage, and a record-breaking twenty-four-hour rainstorm in Chicago has resulted in dangerous flash flooding in that area. Spencer Christian will have all the details on the weather coming up, but first, with so much news going on, let's go right to it."

Once we were in the news break, Charlie and I looked over our upcoming spots. Mine was a simple throw to Atlanta for a report on the Olympics, while Charlie had an interview with a senator about the UN's approval of an Iraqi aid distribution plan, a major step toward allowing Iraq to sell oil under UN Resolution 986. I was glad he was doing that interview.

Then, about twenty minutes into the show, a producer ran into the studio and, with controlled panic, said, "Everyone, listen up. There's been a terrible plane crash off Long Island. It's bad, you guys. Really bad. It sounds like the plane exploded in the air not long after it took off from JFK and then fell into the ocean. We're just starting to get pictures coming in."

He handed Charlie and me the wire copy he was holding. "This is all I have for you now; we're in the process of trying to line up guests. We'll get you more information as it comes in. This is going to take over the rest of the show. There were two hundred thirty people on that plane, and it doesn't sound like anyone could have survived."

Charlie and I began reading the wire copy: *Tragedy struck TWA Flight 800, a Boeing 747, which has seemingly exploded in the air twelve minutes after taking off from JFK, then fell into the Atlantic Ocean off the shores of Long Island. Rescue boats are racing to the wreckage ten miles offshore in hopes that there might be survivors . . .*

As networks started to get choppers in the air and pictures of the wreckage began to come in, it soon became evident that everyone on board had perished. Then, as television satellite trucks

THE FLYING INFERNO

arrived along the shores of the Hamptons and began setting up their cameras, we started getting more details from the scene and hearing onlookers' questions. "Was it shot down by a missile?" "Had an explosion onboard the plane blown it apart?"

It was an unthinkable tragedy.

As journalists, we are expected, when reporting live on an unspeakable event, to remain focused on obtaining the facts and being able to speak to the moment. I must say, it was difficult not to imagine what it must have been like for those passengers who weren't killed immediately in the explosion—the ones who endured a fall of thirty-five thousand feet into the ocean. But in those momentary flashes, I'd learned quickly to pull myself back, lest they bring me to tears.

We were 100 percent focused on the live coverage of the crash. The lineup changed to interviews with members of the Coast Guard and the navy who were on the scene in the waters off the shore of Long Island, where the wreckage covered a huge area; representatives from the National Transportation Safety Board (NTSB) who would be responsible for determining the cause of the crash; eyewitnesses who described a huge explosion in the air before the plane fell into the ocean; and FBI agents who were being besieged with questions about whether the plane had actually been shot out of the sky (a theory that was later disproven).

I had just finished an interview with one of those FBI agents when Eddie motioned to me. "Joan, the producers want you in the control room."

That was odd. Was it about the interview I'd just done? I'd thought it went well.

As I walked into the control room, I immediately knew something was wrong. It seemed like all eyes were on me. What was going on?

The producer said, "Joan, we have someone on the phone who says he's a friend of yours, and he thinks his twin brother was on the TWA flight. His name is Jay Johnson." And with that, he handed me the phone.

A chill literally passed through my body as my mind drifted back to our swimming pool, in which Jed, Jay, my brother, and I played Marco Polo after school. Jay's frantic voice interrupted that flashback to our happy childhood.

"Oh my God, Joan; I think Jed might have been on that plane. He was going to Paris on a later flight, but he called me from the airport—he'd gotten there and had caught an earlier plane. I'm afraid it was this one." His voice cracked. "I didn't know who else to turn to. Can you help me find out if he was on it?"

What could I say? "Oh my God, Jay—not Jed, no, no, not sweet Jed." I saw someone waving a sheaf of papers in the air. "Wait, my producer is motioning to me that he has someone on the phone right now from TWA and he's asking for the names on the manifest. So let's just hold tight for a minute and hope to God they don't find Jed's name." For a moment I could literally hear the silence in that control room. "Wait, Jay, it sounds like they're reading through the manifest for our producer, so I think they're going to get an answer for you."

The show was in commercial at that moment, so every person in the control room was focused on the producer who was on the phone with the airline rep. And then the moment came when he looked up at me. I only had to see his face to know the answer to the question: Jed's name was on the list.

I sat there, trying to figure out how I was going to tell Jay that his twin brother was on that plane. Seeing the shock and disbelief on my face, one of the producers gently took the phone from my hand and delivered the horrible news to Jay.

THE FLYING INFERNO

And just like that, I was thirteen years old again.

I could see the tension in Mom's face when she picked us up from school. "Let's try to catch your dad before he takes off. I've packed our bags so we can go to Squaw Valley from Los Angeles after his conference is over." When we got home, she didn't even park—she drove straight out to the edge of the runway, where Dad's Cessna 310 was preparing for takeoff. We jumped out of the car, waving wildly, trying to get his attention.

Dad thought we were just sending him off on his maiden flight in the new plane. He smiled and waved back as his plane lifted off the runway and disappeared into the sky.

We had missed him by minutes; otherwise, we would have been on that flight with him.

That was the last time I ever saw my father alive.

Now, decades later, standing in the control room, watching the live shot of the wreckage floating in the Atlantic, I realized I had been holding my breath. My father's plane had gone down in the mountains of Malibu; Jed's had gone down in the ocean. Different crashes, different decades—but the same sickening, hollow feeling in my chest.

No chance to say goodbye.

As the producer hung up, everyone in the control room had to spring back into action. The director cued Charlie in the studio, who introduced an NTSB official and once again we were all glued to the ten screens in the room showing the oil-streaked Atlantic Ocean where the plane had come down, its component parts dotting the surface. This was now "Jed's flight," and it was painfully evident that no one could possibly have survived.

I couldn't stop my brain from thinking about what Jed must have gone through in those horrific moments—my sweet, soft-spoken

Jed, who'd been a lifetime buddy since we'd learned to ride bikes together. I just hoped that his death was instant and painless.

Meanwhile, we were on the air and in the middle of live coverage of a major news event. I tried to pull myself back into reporter mode. We were supposed to be able to speak of life's tragedies with calmness and objectivity, remember? But this felt like losing a family member.

I slowly walked back into the studio to take my seat next to Charlie. The producers had already told him what happened in the control room, and he motioned to me to take five. "Go splash some water on your face or get a drink of water—whatever might help you catch your breath. I got this, and when you're ready to come sit back down next to me, I'll be here. I've got your back."

"Thanks, Charlie."

I walked to the back of the set where there was a touch-up mirror. As I stood there looking at my reflection, I could see that my makeup was okay, but the light had gone out of my eyes. I thought about the last time I'd seen Jed; it had been far too long. He and Andy Warhol had grown apart, and Jed had found happiness in his business and personal life with his partner Alan Wanzenberg. I'd been to their apartment across from ABC's studio, and it thrilled me to see Jed so happy. He was now a renowned interior designer, catering to the likes of Mick Jagger, Barbra Streisand, and Yves Saint Laurent. He'd come such a long way since helping me find my little one-bedroom apartment at the Beekman. My thoughts were interrupted by our hairdresser and makeup artist, who'd also heard the news about Jed and were coming to see if a touch-up might possibly brighten my spirits. As they applied lipstick and powder and hairspray, we all remained silent, afraid to say anything for fear I would burst into tears.

When I finally settled down into my seat next to Charlie, he

THE FLYING INFERNO

put his arm around me, gave me a hug, and said, "When we come out of this commercial, I've asked for a two shot and I'm going to tell the viewers what just happened, okay? Just let me take care of it; I think it will help you be able to go on this morning."

Eddie counted down—three, two, one—and cued Charlie to camera one, which was the two shot he'd asked for. "I want to share with you all what has happened here in our studio this morning. A few minutes ago, Joan learned that a close friend of hers was on board the TWA plane. He was a childhood friend, and so . . ." Charlie turned to me, with the most compassionate look he could possibly give. "It's not often while reporting on an unthinkable tragedy that we find it's touched us personally. So whenever you need a little help this morning, it's understandable, and I'm here for that."

I could only acknowledge his incredibly compassionate support by nodding my head in thanks, because the lump in my throat wouldn't allow me to speak. But after what Charlie had told the audience, I assumed they would all understand.

Charlie kept a close eye on me to see if I could swallow that huge lump and carry on. It wasn't easy. One minute it was just a tragic story I was reporting on; the next minute I felt like I was part of it. We'd covered tragic events many times in the past, but I can't think of another time when someone in our studio—much less the host—became part of the story while broadcasting.

When Eddie called out "It's a wrap" at the end of the show, the entire crew let out a sigh, as if we had all been holding our breath. I was immediately surrounded by my TV family and was both comforted and overwhelmed as everyone repeatedly asked if I was okay. I couldn't fathom how to answer that question, unaccustomed as I'd always been to airing my personal burdens outside my tight circle of friends and family.

Once home, I called my mom in California right away, since I knew she'd be waking up at seven o'clock California time and turning on our show as she did every day. I got to her in time to softly deliver the horrible news about Jed before she saw Charlie announce it on the show. Mom had treated Jed like a son as we grew up, and I knew this would be terribly upsetting for her, so I tried my best not to get too emotional. That was pretty futile, so we cried together and shared stories about what a sweet young boy he'd been and how he'd been such a good friend to me over the years.

I knew that when my daughters came home from school later, I would have to tell them what had happened. They had never gotten to know Jed well, but I think we all want to remain strong for our children, so I needed them to understand why I was feeling so emotional.

For the ensuing weeks our show was consumed with coverage of the horrific crash, interviewing flight experts and distraught family members of the victims of Flight 800. Every day was an emotional challenge for me. One morning I was interviewing a woman whose husband had been on the flight. She stood with dozens of other families in a huge hangar where authorities had collected all the pieces of the wreckage, including suitcases and the personal belongings of the passengers. The airline offered grief counseling at the location to help the families with the dreadful task of identifying their loved ones' effects and to mourn.

I couldn't help but think of my mom the day she received Dad's personal effects weeks after his crash. In. The. Mail.

I don't remember what entity had sent the package, which was the size of a shoebox. I was with her as she unwrapped the brown paper and, after opening the lid, found his wallet. They had tried to clean it up, but it was still bloodstained. Mom recognized Dad's mangled glasses and his silver watch. I remembered that watch from our hospital visits; he'd always consult it when checking a patient's pulse.

I found myself consumed with grief for weeks as the crash coverage continued. It was hard to fathom that this was the second time I was losing someone in my life in a horrific plane crash—only this time I had to deal with it in front of millions of viewers.

Several weeks later, as part of our continuing crash coverage, I was interviewing Ellen McGrath, a psychologist whom we often had on the show, about the process of dealing with grief. When our segment was over, she asked if I would meet her later to talk about my own sadness and grief, an offer I welcomed.

When we met, I explained to her that I was confused by the intensity of my grief—that it seemed to me to be far more than when I'd lost my dad. She helped me to understand that I was likely processing not only Jed's death but grief from my father's death as well. I was so young when my father died in his plane crash that I don't think I could fully grasp the reality. But now, as an adult, seeing the constant coverage of the rescue teams retrieving the parts of the TWA plane strewn all over the ocean's surface had brought the gravity of that loss full circle. I told her that I'd had moments when my brain was literally flashing between that crash site and the grainy black-and-white newspaper image of my dad's crash site. She explained to me that when grief from a tragedy isn't fully processed, it can remain with us like a smoldering ember that can then be reignited later by another tragedy.

At Jed's funeral, his younger sister, Susie, ran up to me and threw her arms around me. Through her tears she shared something with me that I had never known. "It means so much to all of us that you're here. Going through this today reminded me of all those years ago when your dad died. And if you don't already know this, Jed stayed in his bedroom for four days grieving and refused to come out." I'd always known Jed was sensitive, but I never understood the depth of his admiration and connection to Dad until that moment. Thank you, Susie.

A few years after the crash, I drove to the beach on Long Island where there had once been countless news cameras set up to capture the aftermath of the horror that had taken place a few miles out in the water. They'd stayed for weeks as the pieces of aircraft, along with the 230 bodies, were pulled from the ocean. I took off my shoes and, along with my good friend Laura Morton, walked quietly in the sand as the sun slipped beneath the horizon of the ocean. I thought of that little boy I saw on the first day of fifth grade. That kind, sweet, quiet soul who had always seemed so unassuming, who had turned out to be someone who dared to dream big, who would show courage in living out his dreams, and who would so generously share that strength with me on my journey. And I said a private goodbye to my sweet, quiet, good friend.

Chapter 32

HE HAD ME AT HELLO

Fight for the fairy tale. It exists.
—Katie Reus, author of *Covert Games* (2019)

Just as my career has gone through many incarnations over the years, so has my personal life, and it has become abundantly clear to me that it's our personal redesigns that are the most important.

It happened for me one ordinary Saturday afternoon in November 1996. I was having lunch at one of my favorite local spots, the Rye Ridge Deli, with my daughter Sarah and my friend Laura Morton. Laura and I were working on editing one of my books at the time, but we'd taken a break to take Sarah to lunch. I suddenly looked up and saw this tall, handsome, athletic-looking guy standing at the front of the restaurant, looking around. His eyes landed on me, and he broke into an irresistible smile. I reflexively smiled back.

I said to Laura and my daughter, "Why can't I meet a nice guy like that?"

Nine-year-old Sarah replied, "How do you know he's nice?"

I looked back at him, and at that moment I realized that he, too, was taking another glance at me. Now I blushed as I answered, "He just seems confident but not cocky, and that smile of his could light up the Empire State Building."

"Then why don't you go say hi to him?" Sarah asked in her young, naive, and incredulous voice.

"It doesn't work that way, Sarah. Girls don't just walk up to men and introduce themselves," I explained.

"Well, then you won't meet him. That's pretty stupid," she countered. I couldn't argue with her. Maybe her remark was enlightened, not naive. Sarah wouldn't let it go. "Mom, he's looking at you!"

I took a glance, but he was walking toward another table a few feet away, obviously saying hello to friends. I later learned that he kept sneaking glances at me from there, and his friends asked, "Do you know who that is?" He said, "Sure I do. It's Joan Lunden, and I'm gonna go ask her out."

A chorus erupted. "No way!"

"Watch me. I can handle rejection; I just can't handle not knowing. When I put my head on my pillow tonight, I'd rather know whether I had a chance with her than not know at all."

Sarah leaned in and whispered, "Mom, he's headed this way!"

Jeff Konigsberg introduced himself and said he had coincidentally been invited by a date to attend a party at my house in the Hamptons the prior summer. Laura personally knew the date, so this de-escalated any stalker vibes right away. He explained that he hadn't been able to attend the dinner party because he owned children's summer camps in Maine, and he never left the grounds when camp was in session.

After a bit of banter, he turned to me and said, "Well, since I wasn't able to join you last summer, maybe you'd let me take you to dinner sometime."

Pretty smooth line, don't you think?

Laura, knowing that I would be reluctant to hand over my phone number even though she could tell I was smitten with this guy, pulled out a piece of paper and a pen and wrote down my office number at ABC and handed it to him. That same night, I called a man I had been casually dating and broke it off, then called Laura to tell her that news.

"Wait, what?! How do you know this Jeff guy from the deli is really going to call you?"

"If he does and he asks me if I'm dating someone, I wouldn't want to start a relationship with a lie."

Two days later, on Monday, we signed off from the show and I turned to my assistant, Jill Seigerman, who stood off camera ready to help me transition to the next part of my day, be it meetings, more interviews, or hopping into a car to make a flight. I can't say enough about the assistants with whom I worked. Jill had been referred to me about a year prior by her predecessor, Samantha Berg, and like an Olympic relay team, Samantha smoothly handed the baton to Jill as they raced with me through my tabloid years. As a result, Jill had become my champion—very protective and always two jumps ahead of anything that might come my way. That morning, as we walked from the studio to our office, I interrupted her with what was top of mind for me. "I met a guy."

By the time we got to our office at 9:30, Jeff was on the phone, but Jill told him I was on another line. That gave her leeway to ask him enough questions to start a background check on him. By the time we went out on Tuesday night, Jill had built a dossier!

I know it sounds schmaltzy to say it was love at first sight, but

I felt like I instantly knew that this was the man I wanted to spend the rest of my life with. As we began dating, I tried to keep our relationship under wraps, since Jeff wasn't the flamboyant type looking to get his name in the papers. In fact, I was petrified that he might be scared off once the tabloids got wind of my "new guy."

But we managed to keep it quiet for a few months. Then one day when I was booked as a guest on *The Rosie O'Donnell Show*, we decided it would be fun for him to tag along and watch. As we got off the elevator on the eighth floor of NBC's Rockefeller Center headquarters, Rosie was standing there. As I said hello, she literally looked Jeff up and down and said, "Joan, who's the hunk you brought with you?" Yep, that's Rosie.

When the time came for Rosie to introduce me as her next guest, I took my seat on the set, and she barely got a hello out before she looked at the camera and said, "I gotta tell you all, Joan came to the studio today with quite the hunk, Jeff Konigsberg. Let's say hi to Jeff." With that, a camera panned across the audience to get a close-up shot of Jeff. This was a live broadcast, so you might say the cat was out of the bag.

The tabloids went on high alert. Jeff immediately had a bounty on his head, and soon found photographers lurking outside his apartment building. I put a call in to "Stan, Stan, the PR Man" (as many of his clients refered to him). He called each tabloid and made deals to end the bounty. Here's how it was to work: Jeff and I were to meet at a prearranged location with one of the tabloids, and we would allow them to get a photo of us and ask a few questions. So, the next day, after *GMA* signed off, a limo took us into Central Park. We got out in front of Tavern on the Green, held hands, smiled, and gushed for a few minutes. The reporter asked for a kiss; we did not oblige. Come on.

Then we went back to my dressing room and changed into other clothes. Thirty minutes later, our limo pulled up in front of the Plaza Hotel, where we got out and met another tabloid; photo op repeated. And on and on it went, until they all had their exclusive pictures ("exclusive" because each one had us in different clothing in a different location) and they printed their stories. "Lunden sets up camp" with summer camp owner Jeff Konigsberg. Jeff's family still teases him to this day for the headline "Joan's New Beefcake."

As Jeff saw the tabloid articles, I held my breath. I was used to this kind of intrusion and sensationalizing of my personal life, but he wasn't. Thankfully, they'd all gotten their stories and seemed to back off. Jeff didn't bolt; we laid low and life went on, both of us knowing we had found something special in each other.

As Jeff became part of the fabric of our family, he showed himself to be an incredible father figure in the lives of my three daughters. In the beginning, they called him "the new sheriff in town." As the teenage boys began coming through the front door, Jeff had a way of patting them on the back while saying hello—or should I say patting their backpacks? He would quickly confiscate any cans of beer. I never would have thought to do that, and if I had, I don't think I would have been bold enough to take action. Actually, if I'd done it, my girls would have been mortified and angry with me. In time they came to understand that Jeff was protecting them, and they respected him for it.

Soon, Jeff's protective nature would provide me with calm in the storm of my professional life.

Chapter 33

TROUBLE ON THE HORIZON

*When you can't control what's happening,
control the way you respond to what's happening—
for that is where your power lies.*

—Lisa Nichols, Motivational speaker

On May 7, 1997, I awoke with a start and looked at the alarm clock. 3:30 a.m.

For almost twenty years my mornings had begun this way. Why, after all these years, could my body never get used to this schedule?

This would be an exceptionally hectic and trying week. For the first time since I'd joined *GMA*, our ratings were slipping. Rumors were rampant that one or all of us would be replaced. Each morning, along with our scripts, there was at least one news article predicting who would be taking our jobs. Meanwhile, our lives had to go on as usual.

For me, that entailed a photo shoot for an upcoming *TV Guide* cover after the show and an interview for the same magazine to follow. In the darkness, I pulled myself out of my warm bed and shuffled across the carpet to the bathroom. The early-morning wake-ups seemed even more difficult these days. I didn't know whether it stemmed from staying up late and trying to have more normalcy with Jeff in my life, or wrangling my now teenage daughters at night, or just the inevitable toll of years of constant sleep deprivation.

As I turned on the shower, I quietly sighed and thought to myself, *God, I wish these early mornings could end.* There was no denying the wear and tear a schedule that pulls you out of your sleep before daybreak has on your body and brain. Somehow, though, the water beating down on me could always wash away enough of the exhaustion to get me through another day.

When the time came for my interview with *TV Guide*, I ran through the list of questions I'd likely be asked one more time. The writer, Janice Kaplan, was someone I'd worked with over the years at *GMA* when she'd been a writer and producer for the show. I considered her a friend, but she knew where all the bodies were buried in the TV industry. It wasn't her job to be my friend in the interview; it was her job to extract as much information about my fate at *Good Morning America* as possible.

Were any of the rumors true?

Was I leaving or being pushed out?

How was I dealing with that prospect?

How would I feel about their grooming somebody to take my place?

Then there would be the questions about every aspect of my personal life. Janice had asked that Jeff take part in the interview, and I was nervous about how he would feel when she posed personal questions about our relationship or about his being ten years younger than me. (That was a guaranteed question.) He agreed to come along because he felt protective of me amid the swirling speculation, but still, I didn't want him to feel that I was pressuring him. He's so self-assured (which is one of the things I love about him) that when I asked if he was truly okay with being interviewed, he replied, "Don't worry about me, my love. I'll be fine." That was Jeff—unshakable, steady, and always ready with a reassuring word. His confidence was something I'd come to admire, especially in contrast to the uncertainty I'd been feeling around my career.

Before the interview, I called my agent, Jim Griffin. "I've got a *TV Guide* interview today. Have the ABC executives made any decisions about my future with the show? Are they close to making a move yet? You know the *TV Guide* writer is going to ask me all the hard questions," I reminded him. "If the ABC executives know anything at all, I wish they would please help me out here."

Jim sensed my frustration. "I can't get anything out of them, Joan. I tried and tried."

Just three months earlier, when we were negotiating my last contract, I remembered telling Jim, "You know, I'm not sure if I feel good about signing this. It's getting harder and harder to commit to the grind for another three years."

I've long kept a postcard that reminds me of that contract negotiation propped up on my desk. It has a black-and-white drawing of a man and a dog. The man has a stick in his hand that he's getting ready to throw for the dog to fetch. The caption above the dog says, *OK, just one more, and then I've got to get on with my life.*

I felt like that dog. The network executives had made the stick look so appealing; how could I possibly not go for it? I had agreed to stay on, but part of me was thinking, *Okay, throw the stick for one more contract and I'll play, but then I have to get on with my life.* Even more unsettling would be to have the stick thrown and then taken away.

During those last contract negotiations, Jim had also asked them to put to bed the rumors about replacing me with the thirty-five-year-old newcomer, Elizabeth Vargas. Media reports indicated that I might be pulled from the show, and *TV Guide* even ran a Lunden versus Vargas story entitled "Showdown at Sunrise."

Since the network wouldn't commit one way or the other, Jim had asked them to just move me out of the early-morning slot, but they insisted that they were keeping their options open and hadn't yet decided to make a host change. I'd agreed to sign for another three years, and then, almost before the ink dried on the contract, they started talking to other candidates to replace me. Viewers were unaware that I'd just negotiated a new three-year deal, so the network had created a situation where it clearly looked like I was being pushed out. It was not a comfortable place to be, and there was nothing I could do about it.

"Sorry, Joan," Jim said. "They're just not sure what they're going to do yet."

I knew what *I* had to do—get myself prepared. I conferred with the executive director of publicity for ABC, Anne Marie Riccitelli, as we always did before big interviews. She had conjured up two pages of questions I might be asked, making them as tough and cutting as she could. "Don't let her get your hackles up," she reminded me. "No matter what she asks, play it cool."

I'd done many interviews with *TV Guide* over the years, and this one had originally been booked for their issue devoted to spring fitness and the people on television who inspired it. During the cover photo session, they had requested that I wear workout clothes while flexing my biceps with ten-pound free weights. Trying to be a good sport, I'd chosen one of the spandex outfits their stylist had brought along, picked up the weights, flexed, and flashed a warm smile at the photographer's lens. Now, with all the juicy *Good Morning America* rumors going around, I was already imagining the headline: LUNDEN FLEXES HER MUSCLES IN THE MORNING BATTLE FOR RATINGS. The rumors also meant that this interview would be laden with professional and personal traps, including the inevitable question "Do you have any wedding plans?"

As predicted, Janice asked all the hard questions. "Joan, you've hosted *Good Morning America* for seventeen years. How will you feel if they take you off the program?"

"Janice, I'm sure it wouldn't be that easy," I said, "since I'd be leaving my security blanket where I know what I'm doing. But I'd also welcome the opportunity in a new arena."

"But wouldn't you be resentful if you still had to prove yourself after two decades with the network?"

"It would be up to me to be creative and tenacious," I said. "When I first got to *GMA*, I was always given small stories, but instead of being discouraged, I was able to grow my role there. I can still use that philosophy. I just want a venue in which to flourish." Whew; I'd rehearsed that answer and stuck the landing.

"The network hired Elizabeth Vargas to do the news segments, and it's rumored that they've talked to several other young anchors around the country. It appears that ABC wants to find a younger host."

"I can't tell you what's on the minds of the ABC executives or what their plan is. You can dissect it and analyze it all you want, but I plan to focus on the good part, which would be an opportunity in a new time period." I'm proud to say my voice didn't shake despite her cutting so close to the bone.

"But aren't you going through some moments of self-doubt? Isn't it natural to feel some hurt when you consider the possibility of being replaced?"

Jeff leaned forward slightly. I could feel the shift in his energy—he wasn't just answering, he was standing up for me. As he spoke in a firm but calm voice, he rested his hand lightly on my knee under the table, a quiet but steady reassurance.

"Absolutely not," he said. "Whatever happens, there will be no sense of failure here. I've seen the impact Joan has on people, and that wouldn't change. Joan would just go on."

I glanced at her to gauge her reaction to his jumping into the conversation. She seemed to take it in stride. Well, she should have; she'd invited him to be part of the conversation. How long was he supposed to sit there as I stoically took missile shots?

Without skipping a beat, Janice turned back to me like the hard-nosed journalist she was and asked, "After years of insisting you have the best job in the world, how would you adjust to not being on TV every morning?"

"If I left *GMA* tomorrow, if I never worked another day on TV and just spent my time writing and doing all the other things I enjoy, it would be okay. Plus, I have another life at home with my daughters that's full and a top priority. People think that as children get older, they need us less. That may be true in terms of watching over them, but otherwise it gets much harder. It's not just lip service to say that I really want a chance to live a more normal life and be around home more with my family."

"What would you do next?"

"The fact is that I've never been so open-minded about my future." I looked at Jeff and smiled. "Maybe it's because I've really enjoyed my life in the last year."

"Yes. What's it like being with a younger man?"

There it was—the question we knew would be coming at some point. So, here we go . . .

"Our philosophies and moral fiber are the same. We're really happy, and we spend a lot of time together. People say we're very similar, and that's important when you're talking about a lifetime mate. We talk about the future, but we have to let that happen."

Janice kept on plugging away. "What if they actually do hire somebody younger than you to take your seat after you've been there for so long?"

"You know, Janice, who will come after me is not for me to figure out, but I would hope they'd make a good choice. Even if I wasn't there, I wouldn't want to see the show fail. I have twenty years invested in this franchise."

As we were leaving the interview, Jeff caught my glance and winced as if questioning how I put up with this. Once we were outside, he asked, "Do they always go that hard?" I laughed, shrugging. "Pretty much." He squeezed my hand and grinned. "Well, you handled it like a champ and like a lady, as always."

Chapter 34

THE TAKEOVER AND THE TAKEDOWN

No matter the situation, never let your emotions overpower your intelligence.

—Jean Houston, American author

The phone was ringing as I stepped into the house. I dropped my bag by the door and rushed into my bedroom to answer it.

"Joan," came the voice on the other end. It was my attorney, Marc Chamlin. My agent, Jim Griffin, was on the line too.

I froze. The two of them? Together? This wasn't going to be good. I should sit down for this one.

"We have something to talk to you about," Marc said. His voice was steady, but something in it felt practiced. Measured.

I braced myself.

"ABC has finally decided to make the change," he continued. "They think it's time to revamp the show. We need to talk about what your role will be with the network, since they're hiring another host to take your place in September."

The words landed in slow motion.

T-h-e-y-'r-e h-i-r-i-n-g s-o-m-e-o-n-e t-o t-a-k-e y-o-u-r p-l-a-c-e.

I gripped the phone tighter.

I had known this moment was coming. The rumors, the whispers, even my own restless thoughts over the past year; of course, knowing something is possible and hearing it said out loud are two entirely different things.

I swallowed hard. My life was about to change.

Forever.

For months I had been saying that I was ready for change. The brutal early mornings, the exhaustion, the gnawing feeling that I was missing out on time with my girls and with Jeff—it had all weighed on me. I had even suggested to ABC that they consider moving me into a new role on one of the evening news programs. But now that the decision had been made—without me—it wasn't my choice. It was being taken away.

My mind was jumping from one thought to the next without landing anywhere.

I was so glad Jeff was there, sitting by my side as I took it all in. While he heard enough of the conversation to understand what I was facing, he didn't interrupt—he just supported me with his calm presence.

I tried to refocus and find out more about how the situation was going to develop. "Why September?" I asked quickly. "Why don't they just go ahead and make the change now?" It was May, and I didn't want to be on the air through the entire summer knowing I would be leaving in the fall. "Couldn't we just go ahead and get it over with?"

"They're still not ready for you to go yet," Jim said. "They don't even know who your replacement is going to be. They're just letting you know that they're committed to making the change." He dropped his voice to make it more soothing on my ears. "Remember, though, you're secure at the network. You signed a three-year contract two months ago, and while they have the right to take you off the show, they still have to pay you for the duration of the contract."

But what would my opportunities be once I was off *GMA*? Would all those years of early mornings pay off? If I tried something else, would I be good at it? Would I like my new life?

Marc reeled me back in. "This is the call you've been waiting for, Joan. Are you forgetting that last year we were badgering them to let you off this early schedule and move you to prime time? You're the one who asked for this, and now you're getting exactly what you wanted, exactly what you've been wishing for."

They were right; I had wanted more time for my family, more balance in my life. But even if I'd secretly been hoping for this, it still didn't take the sting away. You know the adage *Be careful what you wish for, because you might get it*—it's also often said that not getting what you desire and getting what you desire can be equally disappointing.

Change never really happens overnight. In hindsight, the writing had been on the wall for years—I just hadn't wanted to read it.

It started in 1993 when ABC News took control of *Good Morning America*. The show had always been part of the entertainment division, which made sense because it was more than just news—it had warmth, energy, personality. It had heart. Shortly after the takeover, news executives, along with ABC president Bob Iger, gathered us all together to tell us that the show would remain the same. Bob reassured us, "If it ain't broke, don't fix it."

I remember sitting in that meeting, nodding along, trying to believe it.

Charlie Gibson leaned over and whispered, "So, what do you think will go first—us or the set?" We had laughed then, but deep down, we both knew the news department would invariably want to put their own thumbprint on the program.

One news executive commented, "We don't really understand this program—it has celebrities, bands, cooking spots . . ." He was right, and that's what had separated us all these years from other morning shows, and was likely why the network programmers placed it in the entertainment division back in the seventies.

The changes came slowly in the beginning. First up was a new show logo, then new music, new graphics, new colors, new contributors, and finally a new set. With each change, we all began to feel a little more vulnerable. We'd never felt that way before.

I think I'd known from the day we attended that meeting that they would get around to me. I wasn't so sure they would target Charlie, since ABC had brought him over to *GMA* from ABC News.

When I hung up the phone, Jeff embraced me with his long arms, intuiting that words were unnecessary. Eventually, he came up with the best ones: "C'mon—for starters, you're one of the most amazing people on the air, sweetheart. You don't have to worry about your future. You'll be fine. But that's not to say that this isn't hard. Really hard."

I could only nod into his shoulder.

"You know I'm here if you feel like talking. And if you don't, that's okay too. I'll be here for whatever you need."

I was actually afraid to talk about it because I didn't want to break down. The reality of the change crystallized and seemed so real, so big, so fast, and so sad.

I hadn't thought it would feel so sad.

I could fall apart in private, but not in front of my daughters.

THE TAKEOVER AND THE TAKEDOWN

They were teenagers, old enough to sense when something was wrong but too young to carry the weight of my fears. I couldn't let them see me unravel—not when their own lives were so shaped by my stability.

That night, over dinner, I put on my best performance yet. I smiled as I passed the salad bowl, asked about their day, laughed at a joke I barely registered. I nodded along as they talked about school, friends, and weekend plans, and even made a comment about a math teacher's impossible quizzes. Jeff caught my eye across the table with a look that said "You're doing fine." I quickly looked away, though, reaching for my water glass to busy my hands.

As I twirled my pasta with my fork, I thought about how many times I'd done this before—on camera, in meetings, in interviews—slipping into the role people expected of me, even when my mind was a million miles away. But this wasn't a segment on our show; this was my family. And if they saw even a flicker of uncertainty in me, they might wonder what was up.

So I kept going, kept talking, kept smiling. I made a mental note to remember what they were saying, as if committing the details to memory could make up for how distracted I felt. I had no idea what the future looked like, but at least for tonight I could give them this: a dinner with a mother who was present, even if she was only pretending to be.

That night, after the girls had gone to their bedrooms, Jeff and I sat, supposedly watching TV. I could feel tears burning in my eyes, but I didn't let them fall. Why did I feel like I always needed to be strong?

The next morning, I was unusually quiet as I sat in the makeup chair, and I worried that my colleagues might suspect something was wrong. There was one person I would tell almost immediately:

Charlie Gibson, my ten-year cohost on *GMA* and my good friend. We were like brother and sister, and it didn't feel right keeping this information from him, since it would be affecting him as well.

"Charlie, I need to talk to you," I said, keeping my voice low. "In private."

He nodded, sensing the weight in my tone, and led me down the hall to his dressing room. The door closed behind us with a loud, final-sounding thump.

I took a breath, steadying myself. "It's happening," I said. "ABC is redesigning the show. They're making the change. I'll be leaving *GMA* on September fifth."

Charlie stared at me, and I couldn't quite figure out his expression. Did he already know this was coming, as I'd known when David left the show? Then, softly: "Oh, I'm so sorry, kiddo. I guess we were right. They just couldn't help themselves. The changes have been coming one after another, but this one . . . this one feels the most shocking."

I nodded. "They called me yesterday."

Before I could say anything else, he pulled me into a hug. We stayed like that for a long time. No cameras, no scripts, just the quiet understanding of two people who had shared the weight of this job—and, now, the pain of one of us saying goodbye to it. I'd be lying if I said there weren't tears. I'm so grateful to have had Charlie as my partner all those years at *GMA*. I thank you, Charlie Gibson, for your part in my journey.

The moment I walked out of Charlie's dressing room, the reality of it all hit me like a wave. This was really happening. It wasn't just my job that was changing—it was my entire life, my daily routine, and my identity.

I couldn't help asking myself, *Who am I without my role at* GMA*?*

THE TAKEOVER AND THE TAKEDOWN

For twenty years, I had been the first face that many Americans saw when they woke up. I had set the tone for their mornings, welcomed them into their day. I had been part of their ritual, their comfort, their home. Now I would disappear from their screens. And in a world before Facebook, before Instagram, before Twitter, I wouldn't be able to reach them at all. For me, that was one of the saddest parts of leaving the morning show.

I tried to push away the creeping thoughts about what this meant.

Would my career survive this?

Would I still be relevant?

Weeks before, I had sat across from Charlie Rose on his show as he asked me a question that now felt eerily prophetic: "What will it mean to you if some ABC executive comes to you and says, 'Joan, you've made a huge contribution to *Good Morning America*, but we want to make a change'?"

I had smiled then, confident. Certain.

"When one door closes, another opens," I had said. "That's the secret to happiness—embracing change. I'd write them a thank-you letter and move on."

"So, in a way," he said, "if somebody would come to you and say 'No *GMA* anymore,' they might be doing you a favor?"

I'd answered, "You couldn't have said it better." It had been so easy to say then, so easy to believe—when the door was still open. But now, faced with the reality of the change, a certain kind of immobility seemed to be taking over.

Maybe you've felt it when you've gone through some uncomfortable change or challenge in your life. It can be anything from a change in jobs to a breakup with a boyfriend. Even if you orchestrated the change, there's still that scary feeling that your entire life will be different or empty because it will no longer be consumed with that person or that job anymore. That's how I was feeling. Getting the word that the execs were finally moving forward with this change meant that now I was going to have to deal with it.

So I decided to allow myself twenty-four hours to agonize, and then I needed to let it go and begin to think about moving on. Okay, that sounded good—on paper.

Fortunately, I didn't have much time to indulge in despair, because I was scheduled to leave in two days for a weeklong Scandinavian tour with the show. After that, I would begin to plan for my future.

Chapter 35

HEAD UP, STAY STRONG, SMILE, AND MOVE ON

*Smiling doesn't necessarily mean you're happy.
Sometimes it just means you're strong.*

—Nishan Panwar, author and motivational thinker

During the forty-eight hours leading up to our departure for Scandinavia, I was preoccupied with developing my strategy for dealing with the ABC executives. Since my morning viewers were loyal, ABC had to realize that they could have a public-relations disaster on their hands if it appeared as though they were kicking me out for a younger woman. Everyone remembered the negative press that NBC's *Today* show received when they moved Deborah Norville into Jane Pauley's seat.

Fortunately, I didn't have to give trip prep my full attention. I'd packed for sweeps travel for seventeen years, and thanks to my assistant, Jill, I knew the itinerary and expected weather conditions. Stockholm, Sweden, was expected to be gorgeous, full of sunshine and colorful tulips, while for Norway I'd have to pack something I wouldn't mind smelling like fish for the rest of the trip, since we'd be broadcasting from the center of Oslo's fishing industry. Iceland was a wild card—the itinerary read "Dress in layers and pack a waterproof jacket," so I added some thermals.

As I laid my capsule wardrobe out on my bed, a thought kept running through my head like a mantra: *It's in my best interest to find a way to ensure a smooth departure so I come out looking strong, my head held high.*

For years I'd felt as if I had been straddling a line—the line between being an assertive and professional female journalist and not being seen as *too* assertive. Early on, I'd endured years of female viewers writing in to complain, "You aren't getting fair time or billing, and it makes us mad to watch. For the sake of women and equality, you should demand equal time and stories."

With my eye on the bigger picture, my answer had been, "While I understand your frustration, I happen to have one of the best jobs in television. If I take what they're willing to give me and do my best with that, I'm confident that my role will grow."

And it did.

However, I do sometimes wonder how life would have unfolded if I'd just been inclined to lean in more and speak up for myself. I once read "Closed mouths don't get fed," and I think this is a quandary for a lot of us—women especially, even today. We're not always so comfortable with asserting ourselves and tooting our own horns.

David Westin, the president of ABC News, would be the one approving my future role and answering to the press, so I decided I

HEAD UP, STAY STRONG, SMILE, AND MOVE ON

should speak with him about my plan. It was the kind of conversation that required some preparation and the input of a clear head—namely Jeff's.

We went to the Old Oaks Country Club for lunch. The Oak Room there was a wood-paneled dining room that lent itself to quiet negotiations. Since it was almost empty now, Jeff and I lingered and formulated my plan. We had asked for a table in a back corner so we could strategize without being overheard. Sunlight slanted through the tall windows, casting long golden streaks across the polished mahogany walls.

"There's a part of me that wants the network to own the fact that they're replacing a host who has been a loyal, hardworking soldier," I told Jeff. "But they can easily point to the recent softening in the ratings as the reason, and I don't want to get into an argument with the network right now. I just want to come out of this with my head held high, like a class act."

Jeff reached across the table, taking my hand. "You've always been a class act, my love."

I knew what I had to say, so I pushed back my chair and made my way to the corner of the room where I knew there was a phone. I could feel my pulse quicken as the ABC operator transferred the call to David Westin's office. As soon as David picked up, I launched in.

"David, I've thought a lot about how we can handle my departure, and basically, we have two choices. We can choose the wrong way, which could easily alienate viewers. Or we can take the high road, which will serve us both well."

I kept going, my voice smooth and unwavering.

"I'm hoping that we can find a way to announce my departure that will be comfortable for both of us. If our viewers feel the network is pushing me out after all these years, then whoever takes my place could have a very tough time. But if we join hands in this transition, I think we can avoid a lot of those problems. I'll say that I'm choosing to leave."

I pushed forward. I needed to frame this as the network's best option, not just mine. "I'll still be doing my *Behind Closed Doors* specials. Anyone doing specials on the network would be an idiot not to promote them on *GMA*. So, I'll sit next to whoever takes my seat, embrace her, and promote my special. That's just good business— good business for me, for you, and for the audience. It tells them this is a transition I support."

David seemed relieved to hear my proposed plan and quickly agreed that it was the best way forward.

With the strategy in place, I turned my focus to the final weeks on the road—trying to carry on as if nothing had changed, even though everything had. The Scandinavian trip was expected to be grueling, and I had no intention of making it harder. So I kept my torturous secret to myself. Five countries in five days— *Planes, Trains, and Automobiles* in real life. Each day brought a new language, a new currency, a new electrical adapter. It was exhausting.

Keeping the secret from my team was equally tough. We weren't just colleagues; we had traveled the world together, built something remarkable together. And right now, with the ratings slipping and morale at the show in a bit of a freefall, this news would feel like the final blow.

Our final stop was Reykjavík, Iceland. We gathered at a volcanic lava field that surrounds the city. To us, it looked like the surface of the moon. We braced ourselves against the worst weather we'd seen all week—rain slamming sideways, wind gusts so fierce that they knocked us off balance. By the time we wrapped, we were drenched to the bone, our clothes clinging to us; even our underwear was soaked through. Teeth chattering, we collapsed onto the bus, too drained to speak. For me, the silence was welcome.

When we returned to the States, I would finally have to share the news of the transition with my colleagues... and then the world.

I had been through turbulent transitions before. My painful, very public divorce six years earlier had taught me one thing: In the most stressful situations, *staying* even is almost always better than *getting* even.

This transition would require careful execution. I needed to project excitement for my future and gratitude for two extraordinary decades at *GMA*. I wanted my audience—my morning family—to feel comfortable and confident in my move, to follow me wherever I went next. But as I was embracing this idea of looking forward, I also couldn't help looking back. Would things have turned out differently if I had fought harder behind the scenes? While the men huddled in post-show meetings, shaping the future of *GMA*, I was heading home to my daughters. No one was in those meetings speaking up for me.

Would I still be sitting in that anchor chair if I had muscled my way into those rooms?

Or had I lasted two decades *because* I wasn't confrontational—*because* I had learned to navigate power with positivity instead of force?

It was too late to rewrite that history. But the next chapter? That was still mine to shape.

* * * * *

My viewers learned of my departure on May 28, 1997—the morning I steeled myself for one of the hardest days of my career.

At 7:00 a.m., Charlie opened the show. "Good morning, America. I'm Charles Gibson here with Joan Lunden, who has some news to share this morning—and I must say, I don't like this news." He turned to me with that adorable, boyish wink, the one that had carried us through countless tough moments.

That wink saved me from choking on the lump in my throat.

I turned to the camera, forcing a smile. "I do have news to share, Charlie. And it's with a heavy heart that I'm announcing that after almost two decades of sharing my mornings with all of you, I will be leaving this seat in September. But for the first time, I'll have the chance to share my mornings with my daughters."

I wanted to stay strong, composed. I wanted the audience to feel my sincerity—how much I would miss them. And, most of all, I wanted them to see that I was leaving on my own terms. Whether that was the whole story . . . well, I hoped they wouldn't look too closely. In a way, I felt like I was doing it for them too, leaving my seat with integrity.

As I finished my final line—"I will miss my connection with all of you terribly—but again, I'm not going anywhere until September"—the entire studio exhaled. I threw it to the news, flashing a confident smile. Mission accomplished.

By the time I walked off set, the phone was already ringing.

The press wanted the *real* story. Friends were calling—*Was it really your decision?* My assistant, Jill Seigerman, and of course Jeff ran interference while I slipped out of Manhattan to watch Sarah's spring play, as if this were just another ordinary day.

The next morning, when I was scheduled to deliver a keynote speech for the National Down Syndrome Society in Manhattan, the press swarmed. It was clear that this would be my life for months. No

HEAD UP, STAY STRONG, SMILE, AND MOVE ON

matter how much I wanted to move forward quietly, I had to keep showing up at all my planned appearances, pretending like a grenade hadn't just been thrown in my path.

At the ABC affiliates meeting in Orlando, I played the role of the good soldier, standing before station execs, selling the storyline I had created: *I've had an extraordinary run, but I'm stepping away to spend more time with my family. I want a more manageable schedule.*

Half-truths, yes, but not falsehoods. I did want more time with my family, especially now that Jeff was in my life. Yes, I wanted a better work-life balance, but I didn't want to be pushed out.

Soon after, *Time* magazine ran a piece listing my potential replacements: Elizabeth Vargas, Deborah Roberts, Willow Bay, Cynthia McFadden, Connie Chung. That same day, *The Hollywood Reporter* printed that ABC was courting Lisa McRee—though she initially denied interest, refusing to move from LA to New York. (Obviously, they convinced her.)

Then, the *New York Post* unearthed a Lifetime TV promo for *Intimate Portrait*, which I had filmed months earlier. They had me on tape saying, "Even though we don't like change, it's almost good to get a little nudge and get pushed through the door."

At the time? A harmless, theoretical comment. Now? A front-page headline: "Joan Admits ABC Pushed Her Out."

Not surprisingly, *TV Guide* jumped in. A few weeks later, their cover blared: JOAN ON HER OWN. Inside, the article read:

> Rumors swirl that she was sidelined due to NBC's Today show gaining the ratings edge. ABC insists the choice was hers. But as Lunden's many interviews—and hairstyles—fade into memory, speculation over her replacement takes center stage.

Hairstyles? Really?

The speculation dragged on for weeks, with auditions happening in secret after we went off the air. Of course the studio crew I had worked with for years kept me informed.

Admittedly, reading headline after headline about who would replace me was a hard pill to swallow. Then again, after decades in the business, I did allow myself one private moment of satisfaction:

"*Well, boys, good luck finding another me.*"

On June 27, it was official: Lisa McRee would get the job.

On July 2, I released my own statement: "I'm thrilled for Lisa. This is the best job in the world. I know she'll be terrific. I wish her great success."

Joan announces she's leaving GMA.

Chapter 36

FINDING THE GOOD IN GOODBYE

*How lucky I am to have something
that makes saying goodbye so hard.*

—From the movie *The Other Side of the Mountain*

You might think that someone who parachutes out of planes and bungee jumps off bridges would welcome change as an adventure. Yeah, right.

I was just as uncomfortable as anyone else when it came to leaping into the unknown. I kept reminding myself that I was ready, but I also knew from experience that major life transitions were slow burns.

Years earlier, I had interviewed a psychologist who'd written a book about dealing with change. He told me that it takes *three to five years* to recover from a major life change. I had just gone through my divorce at the time and thought, *Three years? Please. I'll be fine in six months.*

I wasn't.

In the months leading up to and beyond this latest massive shift, I wondered how long it would take this time. Would I land on my feet like everyone assumed? Or was I just really good at faking the landing?

All the while, the media had a field day.

"How will you handle your last day?"

"Will you cry?"

"This isn't just a job change—it's a shift in your national identity."

It became evident that I would need to curate my responses and take control of the narrative.

For *The Late Show with David Letterman*, I called ahead. "There's nothing I won't answer," I told them. "But I want to do one thing—I want to smash my alarm clock on air." They loved it. When that night came, I wore safety glasses and took a sledgehammer to that clock, symbolically destroying twenty years of predawn wake-ups.

For every other interview, I tried to convey how much I appreciated my time on *GMA*. I wasn't bitter. I was grateful, optimistic, and moving forward.

For almost twenty years I had always known what was on the upcoming show, but that wasn't the case for my send-off show. For the first time in my career I would walk onto set with no script, no rundown, no control. The only thing I could manage was my own attitude. There was no way I was going to let myself cry at any point on my last show. It had to feel like a celebration.

In the early-morning hours of September 5, 1997, I stepped into the shower with a mission. I had one job: Set the tone. If I broke down, everyone else would follow. If I smiled, they would take their cues from me. So, as the hot water hit my skin, I repeated over and over: *Today is a celebration. Today is a celebration.*

Ironically, just like my first day at *GMA*, there was a mishap with the car. While it broke down on the first day, this time it didn't show up. In the chaos of keeping everything under wraps, the producers forgot to book my ride. Jeff jumped out of bed, threw on clothes, and drove me there himself.

That was fitting. After all, through every moment of this transition, Jeff had been my safety net. He had seen me—not the TV version of me, but the real me. When I struggled to take stock of my career, he reminded me, "You've been so busy doing it all, it seems ordinary to you. But what you've done in your career is anything but ordinary." He made sure I saw myself the way the world saw me—which, for someone used to running at full speed, was harder than it should have been.

Walking into the studio that last morning was surreal. Colleagues stopped me in the halls, already tearing up. "I just wanted to say goodbye before the show started." They'd kiss me, then burst into tears. I absorbed it all but refused to let it shake me.

Naturally, Mom had flown in for the occasion. Before I took my chair, I gave her a kiss and she whispered, "Just keep that beautiful smile on your face, baby doll. Remember what I've always said: 'Never give them the satisfaction of knowing you're upset.'"

That would be my strategy. Grace, gratitude, a big smile, and a clean break. Thanks, Mom.

Then, at 7:00 a.m., the show began.

For the next two hours, I was hit with a tidal wave of love. Bill Clinton, the Bushes, the Fords, Michael Douglas, George Clooney, Billy Joel, Bruce Willis, Demi Moore, John Travolta, and Michael Bolton—they all appeared with videotaped messages wishing me well.

The producers had hidden surprise guests all over the studio. Nostalgic clips rolled, including a montage of my hairstyles over the years—which got the biggest laughs of the morning.

At one point, I caught myself watching my own life flash before my eyes. *Who gets a send-off like this?*

I held it together—until Celine Dion walked in.

I had been one of the first journalists to interview her when she started her US career. She had been terrified, struggling with her English. Before we went on air, I had sat with her in the greenroom, coaching her through her nerves.

She never forgot.

Years later, she had let me travel with her on tour for *Behind Closed Doors*. I had seen every part of her world—her intense preshow rituals, her backstage routine, the silent days she enforced to protect her voice. And now, here she was—for me.

I've heard from so many people over the years who told me they cried watching that final show. They had been, as I've so often called them, my morning family. And I knew, as I walked out of that studio for the last time, that I would miss them.

But my future was waiting.

There was no looking back now.

Joan's final **GMA** *show*

Chapter 37

WHEN A DOOR CLOSES . . .

The shift inside shifts the outside.

NADIRA RAMAUTARSING,
AUTHOR OF BEYOND INFLUENCE:
REMEMBER WHO YOU ARE (2021)

When I left the *Good Morning America* studio on my last day, Charlie said, "We may not see you Monday morning, but don't you worry, I'll call."

When the weekend had passed, for the first time in two decades, I was sound asleep at 6:30 a.m. *on a weekday*. Jamie tiptoed into my room and whispered in my ear, "Mom, I told him you were still asleep, but he told me to wake you."

In a blur I took the phone from her. A much-too-cheery voice was on the other end. "Good morning, JL." It was Charlie, using his nickname for me.

"Good morning, Joan," a chorus of all the voices in the studio rang out in the background.

"Good one, Charlie," I said. As I stretched and turned over, I smiled; it was nice knowing that someone I'd worked with for so many years was thinking about me. I think I would have been disappointed if he hadn't called.

When we hung up and the line went quiet, my morning unfolded without makeup, wardrobe, producers, or a countdown. For the first time in twenty years, no one needed me to be "on." That release from routine, once so coveted, now felt strange—spacious in a way I hadn't prepared for.

It was now time to get serious about the task of reinventing my life. I remembered once hearing "If you are brave enough to say goodbye, life will reward you with a new hello." It's a great line, but will life really do that? The problem with this wonderfully optimistic life prediction is that you must be able to hear the "new hello"—and that's hard when all your mind can register is the dull echo of "Goodbye . . . goodbye . . . goodbye . . . goodbye . . . goodbye."

I had to keep telling myself, *You can get fired from a job, but you can't get fired from your gift. So, know your gift, and you will always have work.* That was one of the life gems from my collection of favorite quotes. Some people collect autographs; others collect stamps, coins, and comic books. I've always collected quotes. When I see one that moves me, I just have to save it. I have pages and pages of them, but only a few are bolded—those that inspire me, motivate me, comfort me.

And thank goodness, some of them just make me laugh.

For instance: "Brain cells, hair cells, and skin cells—they all die constantly, but freaking fat cells seem to have eternal life." Or, "I didn't know I had OCD until I watched my kids hang ornaments on the tree wherever they wanted." And this one: "A recent study has found that women who carry a little extra weight live longer than the men who mention it."

WHEN A DOOR CLOSES...

Come on, I made you smile, didn't I? I needed that too.

But in this moment, the quote I wanted emblazoned on my brain was: "You can't get fired from your gift." The other part—"Know your gift, and you will always have work"—is what I want to pause over today. Why was I always so obsessed with having work?

Well, because I'd always worked. I worked to get out of high school early. Then I couldn't wait to jump into the entrepreneurial working world, and once I landed in television, I never took a breath. I defined myself by the work I was doing. Even my role as a mother morphed into jobs for Beech-Nut Baby Food, Hasbro, and parenting books.

Habits are formed over years, and I had certainly formed the habit of working. But it was more than a habit; it was an ethic. I was always pushing, driving for the next exciting project. And for the last twenty years, it had been *Good Morning America*.

As all the chatter about what I would do next continued, my William Morris agent, Jim Griffin, called to tell me that he was in discussions with ABC about possibly finding another role for me at the network. "Since you're still under contract," he said, with perhaps a bit too much enthusiasm, "I suggested that they move you to *20/20*."

I was so blinded by my upset at ABC for pulling the rug out from under me that I was almost flabbergasted that he thought I would entertain staying at ABC and trusting them. "And you think they'll do that? Really? You think I can trust them at this point?"

Jim was quiet for a minute. This wasn't the Joan Lunden he was used to dealing with. In fact, he had never heard this side of me—obviously hurt and angry and nursing some self-doubt. He put a little sugar in his voice.

"Come on, Joan. They have to keep paying you for another thirty months. It makes all the sense in the world."

And it did. It absolutely did.

In retrospect, I can see that because of my disappointment and anger, I simply couldn't use the rational part of my brain.

Jim dropped his voice into an almost conspiratorial whisper. "I've also had some discussions with NBC. They're designing a third hour of the *Today* show to run from nine to ten a.m."

On paper, that was perfect. A new opportunity. A chance to stay in the game. So why wasn't my heart racing with possibility?

What was going on? Was it my upset in the moment or my sheer exhaustion from all the years of the early-morning schedule that was clouding my judgment? The process of writing this book made me dig deep on this point. Jeff and I talked about it, since he'd been with me through it all. He was quick to point out that for three decades—from Sacramento to around the world to Mexico City to New York—I had never taken a pause, ever. Even my maternity leaves were laughably short. He helped me see that my lackluster reponse to these possible opportunities was likely a message from my body and my subconscious. They were telling me: *Take a moment. Take a victory lap. Take a nap, for God's sake!*

I was no longer on "Lunden time," which was different from the time everyone who lived on normal schedules was on. Truth be told, I had a hard time tearing myself out of bed before noon for months. At one point I went to my doctor, who bluntly told me, "Well, you've been severely sleep-deprived for two decades. What did you expect?"

I didn't realize it then, but my body was throwing me a lifeline. It had shut down my ambition long enough for me to start healing.

I wish I could go back and shake that version of me, tell her

WHEN A DOOR CLOSES...

to snap out of it and recognize a lifeline when it's thrown. But now, with distance and compassion, I can see what was really going on. My body had taken over where my willpower left off.

Looking back with clearer eyes, I can see what an opportunity that NBC show might have been. A third hour of the *Today* show. A chance to stay in early-morning television. It could have been one of the great media coups of the decade.

But I wasn't ready. Not because I lacked ambition but because I had run on ambition alone for too long.

I've always tried to live without regrets—and while I wouldn't rewrite the decision, I would rewrite the way I judged myself for it. If I've learned anything, it's that knowing when to step forward is important—but so is knowing when to stop, listen, and heal.

Chapter 38

BECOMING BRAVE AND BOLD

*Bravery is being the only one
who knows you're afraid.*

—Franklin P. Jones, American humorist

As 1997 was drawing to a close, I was crisscrossing the country shooting exciting episodes of *Behind Closed Doors*. It was actually those specials that helped propel me out of this frustrating period of my life. Not only did the program give our viewers unprecedented looks inside extraordinary professions but each episode gave me a chance to show up in a big, bold way—giving me permission to take risks, stretch, and start over.

On our very first show for ABC, I opened from the deck of the USS *Eisenhower* aircraft carrier in the middle of the Atlantic Ocean.

I'd been allowed to take a heart-pounding flight in the rear seat of an F/A-18 Hornet, landing on the deck of the carrier as it made its way through the Atlantic, and then later being catapulted off the ship!

Also on that first show, I shadowed basketball phenom Shaquille O'Neal, who at the time was a star player for the Orlando Magic. We jumped on his private jet to make a quick trip from Orlando to New York City for a game against the Knicks at Madison Square Garden. The seven-foot-one superstar was so playful on that plane ride; it reminded me that while he was making millions, he was still only in his twenties.

And, finally, I got the first look inside the Betty Ford Center. No press had ever been allowed behind those closed doors, but I'd always had a good relationship with President Ford, and he convinced his wife that I would tell her story with respect. This wasn't an assignment pitched by a *GMA* booker—it was an interview granted because of trust I had earned over the years.

While serving as first lady, Betty Ford secretly battled alcoholism and a dependence on prescription medication. After she left the White House in 1977, her addiction worsened. Eventually, her family staged an intervention, and she entered treatment. She went public with her struggles in 1978, making her one of the first prominent women to openly discuss addiction. Following her successful treatment, she became a passionate advocate for addiction recovery and founded the Betty Ford Center in Rancho Mirage, California, now one of the leading treatment facilities in the country.

Betty Ford insisted that I experience the program before documenting it. We agreed I would be "admitted" to the center like anyone else—my bags were searched, my mouthwash was confiscated (I had never thought about its alcohol content). I had a roommate, did daily housekeeping chores, and went to private and group counseling sessions with no camera crew.

My days as a patient were eye-opening. I began to understand that addiction—whether to alcohol or drugs—isn't about weak willpower or moral failing. It's a chronic, relapsing brain disease that can affect anyone, often rendering them powerless to stop even when they understand the consequences.

The most heartbreaking moment came on family day. Patients' families visited their loved ones in treatment, and the emotional charge in the room was immediate. I felt the effects—the animosity and the frustration—addiction had on these families and their relationships. While the person in recovery often felt eager to share their progress, their families weren't always ready to hear it. Some couldn't believe change was possible, let alone forgive the pain that had already been inflicted. Watching those exchanges—some hopeful, others deeply strained—was devastating.

When Betty Ford and the president sat for an interview, they candidly discussed living in the White House, hiding alcoholism from the public, and the difficult time when her family confronted her. Their honesty and united front was powerful. It reminded me that healing doesn't come from pretending everything is perfect—it comes from facing difficult truths.

On another show I deployed with a Special Forces SWAT team, participating in the ultimate adrenaline rush, a "helo extraction." This is where a harness is hooked around your waist and a helicopter swoops in overhead, drops a line that you connect to, lifts you into the sky, and then whisks you several miles away as you're literally dangling from the rope like a rag doll.

And you'd better not have a fear of heights when jumping from a plane at thirteen thousand feet with the Golden Knights US Army Parachute Team!

I should explain myself at this point: I wasn't a totally irresponsible mother of three taking dangerous chances. I was always in the hands of elite experts. In this case, I was attached to a Golden Knight as we tumbled out the door of the plane and free-fell through the sky until we deployed our parachute and then glided to the ground (where I stuck a perfect landing, I might add).

If I had to pick a favorite assignment, it was tagging along with the legendary Navy SEAL Team Six on a training mission aboard the nuclear submarine USS *Key West*. I deployed with those badass boys out of the sub's hatch in the dead of night, under a moonlit sky, descending the side of the sub—which I'd estimate to have been at least a three-story drop into the cold, dark ocean—in a Zodiac inflatable boat. We then headed to our "fight zone" on the island of Vieques (off Puerto Rico). Once in position, we exchanged fire with another training squad for two hours. It was, in a word, exhilarating. Well, maybe two words: exhilarating *and* terrifying.

Oh yeah, this show had always been just the right vehicle for becoming brave and bold.

For years I've been asked how I had the nerve to take on these stories. I think I had a secret weapon in my producer, Eric Schotz, who had an unwavering belief in me and my ability to take on just about anything. His faith in me sparked a faith in myself that allowed me to never question whether I could rise to the occasion and train with our elite armed forces. All it took was a glance from him and a flash of his boyish grin that said, *You got this, girl.* And so I did.

With each of these adventures, I derived strength and self-confidence.

Admittedly, there were occasions when I'd leave my house with yet another military uniform packed in my suitcase and ask myself: *Why am I taking on another daunting challenge? What am I trying to prove? Am I just a thrill seeker?*

Maybe I was trying to prove to the men in my work environment, who for years had underestimated me, that I could succeed at a high level in these elite male worlds. Or was I just trying to prove to myself that I was becoming even more brave and bold?

Probably both—though I imagine the former had a little something to do with it.

Not to get too psychoanalytical, but why did I seem to be attracted to stories that involved flying when I'd lost my dad in a flying accident? I've been asked this question by other people, but now I was asking myself. While I was only thirteen when my father was killed in our family plane, I'd gotten to know him well enough to know that he would never have wanted me to have a fear of flying. On the contrary—I'm quite sure that he would have wanted me to be adventurous and to explore the world. And so I did.

As it would turn out, it wasn't one of these adrenaline-producing adventures, which Jeff fondly called my "stupid human tricks," that would provide me the perfect comeback story after leaving *GMA*; it came in the form of feathers, sequins, and fishnets—and an invitation to become a Las Vegas showgirl.

Eric called one day and said, "We have an amazing opportunity, Joan, for you to strut your stuff in a tiny, jeweled showgirl outfit amid a hundred professional dancers."

Without even pausing for a breath, I answered, "I'll do it, of course."

There was silence on the other end of the line, and then Eric said, "Really? You're serious? You do understand what I'm asking—that you perform in a live Vegas stage show—and again, it's with feathers, rhinestones, and not much else."

"I totally get it," I said. "Who ever gets to do something like that?"

Now, admittedly, the idea of dancing around a stage in a showgirl costume did trigger all sorts of immediate insecurities. I hadn't worked out much since leaving *GMA*, as I was suffering from a herniated cervical disc picked up while taking nine g's flying with the Thunderbirds in an F-16. But that aside, I was forty-eight at the time. Was I nuts?

I didn't stop to answer that question; I saw this as a chance to present myself to the public in a completely different light, doing something gutsy and glamorous—a chance to say to America, "In case you were wondering what I'm doing now, no need to worry about me. I'm dancing with the Bally's Jubilee Showgirls on a Las Vegas stage!"

Forget the tired argument that being a showgirl is only about objectification. In fact, it's about commanding the room and stepping onto that stage and holding every eye, not as a passive object but as a force. Showgirls don't shrink. They don't apologize. They own the space, their bodies, and the way the audience responds to them. And I was about to learn just how much power that held.

I also knew that going behind the scenes and in front of the footlights as a showgirl was just the right carrot to dangle before me to get me back into peak physical shape. I called in additional support from my fitness trainer Barbara Brandt. Barbara had helped me transform my life, my body, and my health as I turned forty, though now she truly had her work cut out for her. But she was perfect for this job because, in addition to being a fitness trainer, she had a dance background.

As I explained to her what I'd signed up to do, she was silent for a moment and then said, "You have no idea what you just said yes to. Dancing with showgirls is incredibly difficult. We have to get started immediately."

I got to her house as quickly as I could. We began with balancing a book on my head as I walked up and down stairs . . . for an hour. Bally's had sent a video of the stage show, so Barbara and I watched the showgirls strut and dip, and then I got busy learning how to do it.

After my first five-hour training session, I called my producer, Eric, and must have sounded like a madwoman. "You have no idea how hard this is!" After some silence he sheepishly said, "Uh-oh; are you going to back out?"

"Are you kidding? You know I wouldn't do that. I'm just sharing. I'm in. I'm totally in."

I just had to train harder.

I had come to understand that with most of my *Behind Closed Doors* programs, the degree of risk-taking is often deceiving. The risk seems enormous when I'm jumping out of a plane at thirteen thousand feet with the Golden Knights or landing on an aircraft carrier in an F/A-18. But it was actually very small, because I was with the best experts in the world, and they were at the controls.

This time, the risk was mine alone. There was no elite pilot or tactical trainer guiding me across the stage. No safety net, no retakes. This wasn't about technical precision—it was about vulnerability. And for me, that was a different kind of danger altogether.

Once in Las Vegas, Jeff and I sat in the audience at Bally's to watch the spectacular Jubilee performance. Beautiful, tall, leggy dancers, dripping with rhinestones and feathers and wearing very little else, paraded before us. I was in awe, feeling more inadequate by the minute. Little did I know that in the true spirit of Las Vegas, my production crew had the odds at ten to one that I'd never go through with it.

The hardest thing to change is your perception of yourself— but that was what was required of me. In addition to learning the steps, my main focus had to be on changing the way I saw myself.

Day one was my costume fitting. They handed me my tiny costume, fishnets, and high heels. As I stood there blinking at my reflection, I thought, *This may be the most ridiculous thing I've ever done—and I've been hoisted into the sky by a helicopter.* I wasn't jumping out of a plane or firing a weapon, but this was its own kind of challenge. The experience pulled me out of my comfort zone and dropped me into someone else's world. Only this time, the world was sequined.

Next, I took to the stage in my black leotard. That's the day I learned the famous "showgirl stance" and the "showgirl dip." Imagine standing in three-inch high heels with your right leg crossed in front of your left. All your body weight is on your back left foot. Now, lift the heel of that front right foot and point your toe until your calf hurts. Don't forget to tighten your stomach muscles, keep your chest up, your shoulders down and back, your arms out to your sides, and your head up—and, of course, smile. Now dip. That means bend and straighten your standing leg. Then do it about fifty more times to the beat of the music.

For one performance I was to wear a sheer red floor-length cape trimmed in red boa that trailed several feet behind me. When I put it on, I felt so glamorous . . . and sexy. The real Jubilee dancer wore it over her bare skin with a few rhinestones strategically placed on her naked body to match her rhinestone G-string. I added a nude beige leotard under the cape for obvious reasons. When I'd watched the routine two days earlier, I couldn't imagine that it would be so difficult. It looked like it was just a lot of graceful walking around the stage.

How could I flunk walking, something I'd been doing all my life?

Then I heard the commanding voice of the legendary leader

of the Jubilee dancers, Fluff LeCoque. "This is actually your most difficult number, Joan. In your other number you can dazzle them with dance steps, but in this one, it's just you and your sensuality out there on the stage. When the curtain rises and the drums sound, you will stand there and ask them to look at you . . . and you will do it with your body."

I was listening to Fluff as she gave me direction, which is what I do for a living working in TV. It was terrifying direction, yes, but as a performer, I was able to hear it without jumping off the stage.

This wasn't about choreography. It was about presence. I'd spent a lifetime being measured, composed, careful. Now I was being asked to take up space—deliberately and unapologetically.

When I tried it, I thought about the essence of being a child—that "Mommy, look at me" kind of energy when you did a cartwheel or a handstand. That innocence, that freedom, is something we lose when we grow up. We begin to think, *I hope no one's watching.* But that is completely counterproductive to being a showgirl. I would have to reprogram myself to think like that child inside. I would have to engage my feminine power.

Not the kind of power that wins arguments or makes headlines but the quieter, more magnetic kind. The kind that comes from owning your body, your presence, your joy.

I fell asleep that night with such determination that the dance steps raced through my mind. When I awoke on Monday morning, the day of the performance, I had the added challenge of knowing the press had arrived in Vegas to catch my act. The tabloids had gotten wind of my harebrained showgirl idea and they wanted pictures—and, of course, a chance to ask how I was doing since departing from *Good Morning America*. Oh, and they also wanted to know if my younger boyfriend was here with me. Yep, that about covers it.

To avoid an evening audience full of press and camera lights, we scheduled an afternoon press conference. I spent forty-five minutes onstage, in full costume, posing for photos for the *Globe*, the *Enquirer*, the *Star*, *ET*, *Access Hollywood*, and *People* magazine. I knew enough to be appropriately worried that the press might attack me simply for attempting this. I was well aware of the risk I was taking. One awkward move on stage and they could turn my best efforts into an opportunity for ridicule. They took their photos, I answered their questions, and whether it was my positive attitude or my enthusiasm, they were surprisingly nice to me.

I flashed back to all my dancing lessons as a young girl and the opportunities I had gotten to perform and be showcased in front of crowds. They had taught me stage presence and given me a chance to build my self-confidence. Only in retrospect can I see how formative those experiences were—how they allowed me to challenge myself and experience the feeling of success. I can still hear my mom telling me, "Remember to smile at the crowds, Joni. A smile makes a woman even more beautiful."

Then there was my dance instructor, Shari Lou Casey, who would chime in, "But don't let the crowds distract you, Joni. Keep focused on your routine. Your mom is right—always be smiling—but also stay focused, *always*."

Now here I was, about to test that stage presence and focused confidence in a Las Vegas show. Of course, the stakes were much higher now.

A few hours later it was time for the dress rehearsal onstage with the entire cast. I did as I had been taught, stretching out my legs as far as I possibly could so that they would propel me across the stage. A normal step would never have gotten me to my mark in time, and that was crucial; right behind me, twenty dancers were bolting forward, kicking their long legs where I had just been. If I didn't get out of the way in time, I would get knocked right off the stage. I imagined the embarrassment of landing in someone's lap in the audience, a mental image that was enough to keep me stretching and stepping out in time to the music.

For the disco number, my dance partner and I were loaded onto a massive hydraulic lift three stories below the stage at the dressing-room level. The unique elevator would then slowly rise until we were level with the stage and could step out and join the other dancers.

Finally it was showtime.

I stepped onto the elevator lift in my fishnet stockings, three-inch silver heels, my very skimpy outfit, a twenty-five-pound feather backpack, fifteen pounds of arm jewelry, and a pair of huge rhinestone earrings. An inch-thick rhinestone choker encircled my neck, long black gloves covered my arms, my hair was pulled back so tight that my head throbbed, a crown of jewels draped my face, and two pairs of thick false eyelashes weighed heavily on my eyelids.

The elevator lift hummed beneath my feet, and as we rose past each floor, I felt the same jolt I had felt on the deck of the aircraft carrier or in the moment before skydiving: *You're doing this. Right now. For real.*

By the time I reached the stage, I wasn't Joan Lunden playing dress-up. I wasn't a journalist stepping into someone else's shoes. I was a showgirl. And showgirls don't doubt. They don't hesitate. They step into the light and own it.

It had been announced that Joan Lunden would be performing with the showgirls at the evening performance. The moment my foot hit the stage, I felt the weight of hundreds of eyes, a packed theater waiting, expecting. But instead of shrinking, I expanded with the sheer thrill of knowing that for the next few minutes, I held their full attention. *Okay, the crew just lost their bet; the odds are now in my favor.*

Once onstage, I saw a woman with this big smile on her face, elbowing her husband as she watched me move. I flashed her a "Can you believe this?" smile, but then quickly brought my attention back to the steps and the music. I didn't want to lose my place and get behind.

Watching the tape of that show recently, I saw during those first moments the fear that flickered behind my smile. For a few seconds, I hated seeing that. But then I realized that fear *wasn't* weakness. It was the evidence. The proof that I'd stepped up. That I'd said yes. That I'd dared.

And that, perhaps, was the greatest transformation of all.

Dancing on stage with those showgirls, I realized that bravery doesn't always come with a helmet or a harness. Sometimes it shows up in aching feet, stiff hips, and the choice to say yes to something that makes absolutely no sense on paper—but makes perfect sense to your spirit.

Sometimes the boldest thing you can do is not to fall from the sky but to walk—gracefully, if you can—into a brand-new version of yourself.

After the show, my producers met me backstage with congratulatory hugs. Eric looked at me with a grin and said, "The cliff divers just called from Acapulco. Grab your bikini. The tide's in."

Note to self: When *Dancing with the Stars* calls decades later to be on their program, remember the Las Vegas stage experience so you can wisely say, "Thanks, but no thanks."

Behind Closed Doors *promo:*
Vegas Showgirl and Secret Service

Chapter 39

THE UNEXPECTED WEIGHT OF OPPORTUNITY

*Accept what is, let go of what was,
and have faith in what will be.*

—Sonia Ricotti,
The Law of Attraction Plain and Simple (2008)

I couldn't have been happier to close the door on 1997 and look at 1998 as a "New Year, New You" opportunity. I was still shooting episodes of *Behind Closed Doors* and putting the finishing touches on my upcoming book about dealing with change, *Joan Lunden's A Bend in the Road Is Not the End of the Road*, when I got an exciting call.

Kevin Huvane and Lee Gabler of the Creative Artists Agency (CAA) wanted to meet. OMG—these were two of the most powerful agents in the industry, who represented the biggest stars in Hollywood and music. And they had a big idea for me—a national afternoon talk show that I would host.

I didn't waste time. The next day, my attorney, Marc, and I met them for lunch at the Peninsula Hotel on Fifth Avenue in Manhattan. Over salads and iced teas, Kevin cut right to the chase: "Joan, we're always on the lookout for *that next big afternoon show*, and there's been a lot of buzz around you lately. America loves you. We think *you* should be the next big talk show host."

Because that's how they talk.

I smiled. "It does seem like a natural next step." Then I said hesitantly, "But . . . there's an awful lot of competition in the afternoon time period."

Kevin and Lee weren't concerned in the slightest. "Joan, you'll have an audience that adores you. Women at home will love the chance to get to know you better than they did on *GMA*. You're a natural for this time slot."

Gulp.

It wasn't my ability to host that worried me—I knew I could do a great job. My concern was simple: Could I pull in enough viewers to make it a success?

"Help me understand," I said carefully. "You guys are the experts. Is there really room for another talk show? I mean, the afternoon lineup is already packed: Oprah, Leeza, Rosie, Sally Jessy Raphael, Ricki Lake, Jenny Jones, Montel, Maury, Geraldo, Springer—so many shows, and only so many time slots."

Marc chimed in. "I think that's what's held Joan back—afternoon TV is just so crowded right now."

As they debated which hosts would survive and who was on their way out, I had a hard time keeping my head in the conversation. Something was off.

This wasn't like me. Where was my Bally's showgirl energy? What was going on here? I had always been the glass-half-full girl,

THE UNEXPECTED WEIGHT OF OPPORTUNITY

the say-yes-and-jump-into-the-deep-end girl. But now? My gut wasn't leaping. It was twisting. I could feel my grip tightening around my iced tea, condensation pooling between my fingers as I forced a smile.

Kevin leaned in, reading my hesitation. "Look, Joan, I won't lie—everyone's fighting for margins in this space. But you bring something different: that warm, relatable mom factor that connects with women, but also the respected journalist whom guests will trust. There's no one else quite like you."

I looked at these two men—two of the most powerful agents in entertainment, who had flown to New York just to persuade me to do this. They believed I could pull it off.

Before I could respond, they laid out their final pitch: "Telepictures is fully on board. They're ready to start selling *The Joan Lunden Show* to affiliates across the country. Everything is in place. All you have to do is say yes."

All I had to do was say yes. Hadn't that been my motto my entire life? Just say yes and figure it out later? I went with it and answered enthusiastically, "Gentlemen, it's a fabulous idea, and I really appreciate your confidence in me. So let's do this!"

Everyone shook hands, exchanged hugs, and picked up their briefcases.

As we stepped onto Fifth Avenue, a memory hit me like a slap: That snide reporter from my last day on *GMA* asking, "How will you ever top this job?" I hadn't been able to shake that remark, and I suddenly realized why. That tiny seed of doubt had taken root. But this move could prove him wrong, couldn't it? Yet here I was, standing at the biggest career decision of my life, and instead of feeling confident, I was conflicted.

Agreeing to the talk show meant big changes. First, I had to leave my longtime agent, Jim Griffin, at William Morris—a relationship I'd had for twenty years. I'm the most conflict-averse person ever, so the thought of that meeting made my stomach churn. Marc, ever the confidante, reassured me on the elevator ride up. "Let me do the talking," he said. "You just thank him, say this was an opportunity you couldn't pass up, and leave it at that. He's going to be mad. Be prepared. But once you've said that line, sit back and I'll handle him from there."

And that's exactly what happened. Jim was really mad, and Marc was as diplomatic as he could be, while I was as apologetic as I could be. I did this with a great deal of trepidation, even though I was upset with him for his part—whatever that was—in my *GMA* job ending. And maybe he had nothing to do with my demise; maybe I just needed someone to blame instead of myself.

With that done, we moved forward. Telepictures rented office space in New York. We hired Emmy-winning TV veteran Nancy Alspaugh to produce the show. It was happening.

So why wasn't I excited? I couldn't understand my lack of enthusiasm—until I started writing this book and realized my judgment may have been clouded by emotional muscle memory. Back in 1990, I had reluctantly agreed to host another talk show, *Everyday*, produced by my then-husband.

When he first pressed me to do it, I protested, "I host *GMA* every morning; I need another daily TV show like I need a hole in my head." But in the end, I caved. And I paid a price—total exhaustion, too much time away from my kids, and a lot of resentment for being put in that untenable position.

What made that hosting experience so exhausting? The show had a live studio audience, a live band, an opening monologue, and

THE UNEXPECTED WEIGHT OF OPPORTUNITY

a different cohost to contend with every week, making it especially demanding for the host. Every morning when I finished *GMA*, my car would take me through the Lincoln Tunnel to Hoboken, New Jersey, to another studio to start all over again. A new script, more interviews, wardrobe, and orchestrating the interplay with my various cohosts, who included Chita Rivera and Joan Collins. Amid that controlled chaos, I was a reluctant participant trying to placate my former spouse.

The intense exhaustion from the double schedule not only impacted my well-being but made me constantly worried that it would upset the producers of my "real job" at *GMA*. That experience at *Everyday* ended up being the final straw in that marriage. It was also what my brain remembered about hosting a talk show; scientific research has shown that our bodies "keep score."[1] As I've put the pieces of the puzzle together, I've come to realize how often that unpleasant memory must have played in the back of my mind for me to repeatedly ask myself, *Do I really want to do this every day . . . like the* Everyday *show?*

That brutal experience left a scar I hadn't realized was still tender. No one had to tell me to hesitate—I could feel it in my bones and the very fiber of my being. My body had stored the exhaustion, the resentment, and the burnout, even if my brain had convinced itself I'd moved on. *Don't do this again.* The thought wasn't logical; it was instinctual. And for the first time in my life, I was listening to that hesitant voice.

And in the end, I didn't have to do it again. Telepictures had been developing a talk show with Queen Latifah as well, which they had already sold to more than 50 percent of the syndicated

---

[1] If you're not familiar with this perennial bestseller, pick up a copy of *The Body Keeps the Score: Brain, Mind, and Body in the Healing of Trauma* by Bessel van der Kolk, MD.

marketplace. Trying to sell both shows to the available time slots wasn't adding up. They had to make a business decision, so before 1998 ended, *The Joan Lunden Show* was history.

And you know what? I was relieved. I remember exhaling and thinking, *Thank God that didn't happen; the competition in the afternoon time slot would have been exhausting.* Then again, I was feeling the weight of everyone in the industry and the public waiting with bated breath for me to pop up on a *live daily show* somewhere. And I was expecting that too. It didn't seem to register with anyone that I was still hosting a series of prime-time specials, *Behind Closed Doors*. But I get it; that show aired only twice a year.

I couldn't shake how I saw myself. My identity was "host of a live daily show." While I wasn't saying it out loud, I started entertaining the possibility that there might be something else out there, that my life could unfold differently. But how?

Chapter 40

REINVENTION NEVER RETIRES

*If your dreams do not scare you,
they are not big enough.*

—Ellen Johnson Sirleaf,
first female head of state in Africa

While I was having a hard time navigating change myself, I was writing a book about doing just that. My literary agent had often said, "You'll always write about that which you want to know about."

That book, *Joan Lunden's A Bend in the Road Is Not the End of the Road*, was published with the subtitle *10 Positive Principles for Dealing with Change*. And since books don't sell themselves, I was thrilled when motivational and peak performance coach Tony Robbins heard about it and asked me to join his two-year nationwide "Unleash Your Greatness" Tour.

My role would be to kick off all twenty-six events for audiences of up to twenty-four thousand people as the first morning speaker. (I'll likely always be doing wake-up duty in one way or another!)

Given the focus of *A Bend in the Road*, it was natural that my topic for the tour was "Navigating Change."

The problem is, even after all those years performing in front of a TV camera with Charlie, I'd yet to become confident commanding a live stage by myself. I know—it surprises people to hear that I was uncomfortable with public speaking after twenty-odd years of working on TV, where millions watched me every day. How could I be nervous in front of a few thousand people? *Well, I never saw the TV audience!*

But I had researched the topic of navigating change. I'd written a book about it. Why was this so hard? As it turns out, writing about something and bringing it to life for forty-five minutes in front of thousands of people require two different skills.

Performing in front of a live audience had always made my neck and chest red and blotchy and dried my mouth to the humidity level of Death Valley, so I had simply avoided it. To succeed on this tour, I would have to do some Jedi mind tricks on myself, and Tony knew them all. I could go on about deep knee bends, adrenaline flow, and the need for hydration, but it was a simple backstage interaction with him that helped me turn the corner.

I arrived at the arena tense and rattled from a particularly annoying press issue, and Tony immediately picked up on it. "You okay today?" he asked.

The truth? I wasn't. I was letting outside noise shape my mood—letting someone else's narrative steer my own. I hesitated, unsure of how much to share.

Tony didn't push. He simply said, "You know, if change in your own life is getting the best of you, you can always just go out there and talk to the audience about it. They love that."

It was such a simple suggestion, but it hit me like a bolt of lightning. A surge of resolve replaced my doubt.

REINVENTION NEVER RETIRES

As I stepped onstage, I began delivering my prepared opening lines, but the words felt like they belonged to the page, not to me there on that stage. And then—without planning it, without analyzing it—I veered off course. I ignored the teleprompter, my own script rolling forward without me.

My assistant, Jill, who was sitting beside the teleprompter operator, told me she panicked. *What in the world is Joan doing?*

For a split second, I panicked too. My heart pounded. I had abandoned the script—the thing that had always made me feel safe when giving speeches.

But then something incredible happened.

I made eye contact with the audience—and held it. They were with me. Engaged. Reacting not to carefully crafted sentences but to me. I was speaking directly, honestly, about the anxiety that change can bring. About how reinvention—while exciting—can also be terrifying.

The fear cracked apart like ice breaking during a spring thaw. *Hey, I've got this.*

And in that moment, I found it—my real voice. This was the path forward—not just to speak but to connect. To share my story so that others could see themselves in it, and maybe feel a little braver about their own.

It took two years of baptism by fire, but by the end, I wasn't just surviving onstage—I was thriving. The thing I had feared most had become one of the greatest reinventions of my career.

Fear doesn't always mean stop. Sometimes, it's pointing you toward your next transformation. Moments of reinvention are almost always accompanied by self-doubt and trepidation over what will come on the other side. But the other side is the place where you'll find new skills, confidence, and—ultimately—possibilities.

Thanks to Tony, I learned that the road is always ahead, never behind.

That sense of discovery didn't end when I stepped off the stage; it became a compass, guiding me through a new chapter of life filled with purpose-driven work. One of the projects I'm most proud of is the documentary *America's Invisible Children*, which tackles the growing crisis of children and youth experiencing homelessness.

I almost didn't take it.

One day, an agent forwarded an email with a brief note: *You can take a look at the request below, but it pays so little that I'm sure it's a pass.*

Then I clicked on the link.

The producers had sent a short video trailer of the children they'd been following. And I was horrified. Kids living in cars; sleeping on floors; eating breakfast in gas stations. For a few moments, I just stared at the screen. Something inside me tightened. I knew instantly that this was not a project to pass on.

Until that moment, I'd always associated unstable housing with adults—people who, for any number of reasons, had ended up on the streets or in shelters. But children? Young kids without a bed, a routine, a sense of safety? That caught me off guard. I'd had a privileged childhood. Even after my father's death, my mother created stability for us. I had childhood friends with fewer material comforts than I did, but I didn't know anyone who lived out of a backpack in a motel or had to worry about where they would sleep next week.

Working on the documentary confronted me with a kind of raw, daily chaos I had never witnessed up close—kids bouncing from one relative's home to another while society attempted, and often failed, to keep them in school. There was no clean storyline, no neat resolution. Just children—vulnerable, resilient, exhausted—trying to survive while the world looked away.

REINVENTION NEVER RETIRES

I felt impassioned that their stories needed to be told, and I knew I could help tell them.

When *America's Invisible Children* won the Emmy for Best Daytime TV Special, I felt a flash of pride—but it didn't last. The project had left something heavier inside me—a pit in my stomach; a sense that not much had changed. In fact, we were seeing deeper cuts to the very programs meant to help kids like these.

What I didn't know at the time—but understand now—is that childhood poverty and housing instability aren't rare. They're just invisible to many of us. We don't see the families living in their cars because they can't meet the first and last month's rent. These children are often clean, polite, and doing their best in school. They don't all "look" homeless, which is precisely why they're so often overlooked.

And yet they're everywhere.

That realization changed me. It made me see how easy it is to live in a bubble of security, assuming that if something isn't visible, it isn't happening. It made me question how we define success in our society. *America's Invisible Children* was more than a special; it was a call to consciousness. And though I moved on to other projects, I've never stopped thinking about those kids. Their faces come back to me in quiet moments—especially when I see headlines today about cuts to food assistance, affordable housing, or school support programs. I always wonder: Where are those kids now?

I've heard many times that "one person can make a difference," and I've come to believe it. Every time I leave an event—whether it's a fundraising luncheon or a senior caregiving forum—I feel it again: that quiet rush of fulfillment.

Where does it come from?

It's the knowing—knowing that I got to shine a light on something that mattered. That my voice, my presence, my willingness to speak up may have made a difference. Whether it was hosting campaigns for the American Heart Association on women's cardiac health, partnering with Amgen on consumer campaigns for lifesaving cancer drugs, or speaking on caregiving and successful aging, I've chosen projects that mattered: campaigns that informed, partnerships that empowered, and roles that stretched me in unexpected ways. And then one of the most surprising opportunities of all came from a college campus.

Of all the roles I imagined for myself after leaving network television, becoming a professor wasn't on the list. But then Lehigh University—Jeff's alma mater—came calling. They invited me to become an adjunct professor in their newly opened College of Health, teaching a course called Population Health and the Media.

As a young girl, I had played teacher for hours in my bedroom, creating a classroom full of imaginary students. I gave them all names, assigned homework (which, according to my mother, I sometimes did for them), and graded their work. And now, all these years later, I found myself standing in front of thirty-eight real students—students with their own names, their own ideas, and, thankfully, their own ability to complete their assignments.

I must say, I've spoken before huge audiences in my career, but these young college students were by far my toughest audience ever. Most audiences I speak to are filled with longtime early-morning fans, eager to smile, nod, and engage. Not these kids. They were too young to have watched me on TV, unless perhaps they'd caught one of my commercials for senior living. Winning them over wasn't going to be automatic.

My goal wasn't just to teach facts. Rather than relying on traditional lectures, I leaned into my television background and turned my class into a live interview series, bringing in top experts in public health, media, and policy to engage with the students.

REINVENTION NEVER RETIRES

Some of the speakers included:

- Dr. Julie Gerberding, first female director of the Centers for Disease Control (CDC) and current CEO of the National Institutes of Health Foundation, on her career, running the CDC, and the challenge of managing public health

- Bill McKibben, author and environmental activist, on the impact that climate change will have on public health

- Charlie Dent, former US congressman, explaining how public health policy is shaped in Washington

My lifelong passion to educate was initially fulfilled through journalism—but it didn't end there. It led me to write books, to speak publicly, and, ultimately, to teach at Lehigh University. My goal was to immerse students in a dynamic learning environment where they could feel the passion these experts brought to their work—and, hopefully, be inspired to pursue careers in public health or journalism themselves.

My guiding principle as a professor came from a quote by Plutarch that has stayed with me for decades: "Education is not the filling of a pail, but the lighting of a fire."

Ironically, as I stepped away from teaching, I realized that the fire I'd tried to light in my undergraduate students had also ignited something in me. The experience helped me more fully appreciate the arc of my career from daily television host to health and wellness advocate, and affirmed that saying yes to reinvention had been the right path all along.

BECOMING BRAVE AND BOLD

My first TV appearance after leaving *Good Morning America* was on my primetime show *Behind Closed Doors*, dancing on a Las Vegas stage as a showgirl at Bally's Jubilee. (Just like Taylor Swift . . . well, kind of.)

BEHIND CLOSED DOORS WAS THE PERFECT RX TO EMERGE STRONG AND BOLD

Suited up, ready to learn to drive a 70-ton M1A2 Abrams tank. Left: At the Quantico training facility for the Secret Service. I'm pictured here with a few of my new buddies who put me through an intense protection course.

All ready for takeoff! We'll be heading toward the White House through restricted airspace in a Sikorsky Patriot helicopter.

Just another day at the beach—with the US Navy SEALs on the Caribbean island of Vieques learning to handle an M16 rifle. We had launched from the USS *Key West* nuclear attack sub in the dead of night to practice "taking this beach." Oh yeah, I was feeling pretty badass with these iconic warriors.

Relaxing after a long day of filming with Sir Richard Branson on Necker Island, his luxurious private island retreat in the British Virgin Islands.

I felt like the Stay Puft Marshmallow Man from *Ghostbusters* in my "high-altitude" space suit I needed to wear in order to fly at 70,000 feet, effectively at the edge of space. Left: With basketball giant Shaquille O'Neal —literally, at 7'1"—when he played for the Orlando Magic. He was already a massive super-star, yet still a twenty-two-year-old kid at heart. We even had his favorite pinball machines delivered to his hotel room so he could "unwind" before our interview.

FINDING MY TRUE LIFE PARTNER

Jeff with me on our wedding day, April 18, 2000.

Right; I was forty-five when I met Jeff, and here we are celebrating my 75th birthday.

Jeff and I love our summers on Long Lake in Maine.

Above left: He had me at hello! This picture was taken just a few months after we met in November of 1996.   Above right: When your partner in marriage is also your best friend, you are very lucky. I'm lucky.

ARRIVAL OF TWINS

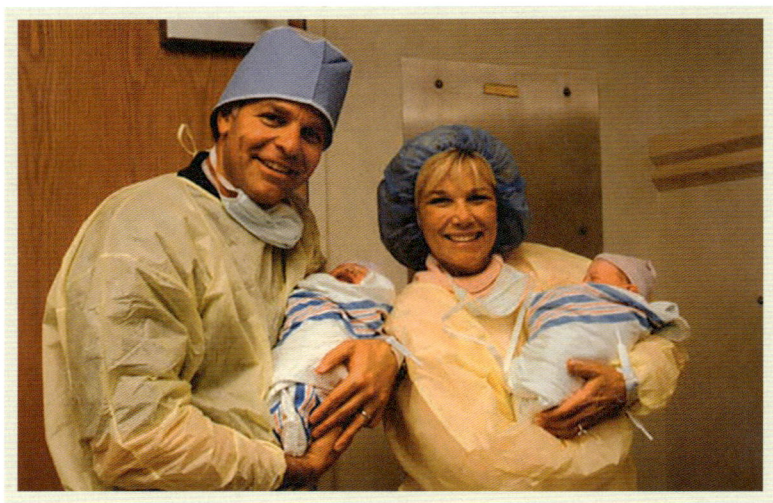

In the hospital with newborn twins! Kate and Max were born in June 2003, and a second set of twins, Kim and Jack, were born 20 months later!

Sarah and Lindsay joined us at the hospital when Kate and Max were born and were instantly fabulous big sisters.

Grandparents Janey and Donny Konigsberg with newborns Kate and Max.

Barbara Walters and me with newborns Kate and Max (2003).

Below: In 2003, our surrogate, Debra Bolig, flew in for the sit-down interview with Barbara Walters for a story she did about our surrogacy experience for *20/20*.

Bottom left: Torie Sutterfield has been with our family since the twins were infants and is truly like a member of our family.

Bottom right: I'm not exaggerating when I say "I've always felt like it kept me young."

A CANCER BATTLE THAT BECAME A CRUSADE

Just when you think everything in life is perfect… on April 5, 2014, I was diagnosed with breast cancer. *GMA*'s Robin Roberts advised me to preempt the inevitable hair loss and shave my head. She said it would make me feel more in charge of my cancer treatment. As weird as it may sound, Robin was right!

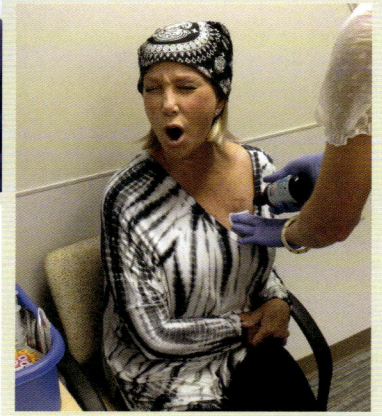

I started aggressive chemo immediately after my diagnosis. I'm thankful that I had wonderful doctors, but I also feel that the chemo nurses—who are there to help me feel brave and strong when I certainly didn't feel brave and strong—are unsung heroes.

The morning I sat down with Robin Roberts on *Good Morning America* to share my diagnosis with my "early morning friends," I found it difficult to get the words out: "I have cancer." However a few hours later, I had my first infusion of chemotherapy, and it became very real.

By turning my cancer battle into advocacy to help inform and inspire other women facing breast cancer, I felt I was carrying on the legacy of my dad, a cancer surgeon who had saved so many lives. Right: Wig on . . . game on . . . and happy to join an Amgen cancer awareness campaign. I even got to work with Patrick Dempsey, aka, Dr. McDreamy. I know, tough job, but someone's got to do it.

It's not easy to impress teenage boys, but I succeeded with my sons, Max and Jack, when the WWE gave me their Warrior Award in 2016 for championing the cause of breast cancer.

TURNING MY PASSIONS INTO ADVOCACY

Speaking at the Breast Cancer Research Foundation.

Above: In 2023, speaking about the sweeping changes in media and politics that have shaped public opinion of journalists at the National Association of Secretaries of State.

Left: In 2024, delivering the keynote at the Omaha Town Hall speaker series.

As an advocate for families, I testified before Congress in January 2020 in support of the Paid Family and Medical Leave Act urging that paid leave also extend to those caring for aging or ill relatives.

Right: My advocacy for senior care and successful aging grew out of caring for my own mother. In August 2013, just as Camp Reveille came to a close, I got the call that Mom was failing. I flew immediately to her side, and she passed away a few days later on August 24.

As a health advocate, I launched my women's wellness camp, Camp Reveille, in Maine in 2007. For the next ten summers, several hundred women joined me for fitness, friendship, and plenty of s'mores.

MY LIFE TODAY. . . A LIFE FILLED WITH LOVE & LAUGHTER

Summers in Maine at Camp Takajo on Long Lake—
our family's happy place for generations.

Nothing like a family trip to Disney World with JoJo, as my grandkids call me.
I hosted the Disney parades for fifteen years, so I'm still close with
Mickey and all my Disney friends.

With my five fabulous girls, how lucky am I? Right: Our life today, with the twins in college. Here, with Jeff and our son Jack where he is a student at the University of Michigan.

Left: Three generations all glammed up at a Taylor Swift concert with my daughter Lindsay and her daughter Parker making Parker's birthday wish come true.

Lindsay had a rockin' 40th birthday party. Here I'm channeling the '90s with my birthday girl and Sarah.

THEN . . . AND NOW

THEN: In 1990, my older daughters, Jamie and Lindsay, applauded little Sarah for winning a ribbon in a horse show. NOW: With my three older daughters, Sarah, Jamie, and Lindsay, who are my confidantes, my cheerleaders, and my protectors.

THEN: A summer day in 2015 at camp in Maine surrounded by twins: Kate, Max, Jack, and Kim.

NOW: Jeff and me with our twins Jack, Kim, Max, and Kate in August 2025.

THEN: With seven children, it is always a feat to have every single one of us smiling at the annual family photo session (2008).

NOW: With four grandchildren added to the mix, the family photo sessions have gotten a little more chaotic but always filled with so much joy (2024).

MY DREAM TEAM... I COUDN'T HAVE DONE IT WITHOUT THEM

The magnificent makeup artist and hair stylist Emir Pehilj, who always keeps me looking stage/camera ready.

In addition to being best friends for life, Laura Morton has been my coauthor, my video producer, and now my publisher. She has also been the ultimate collaborator, advising me, pushing me, and protecting me.

Left: Tamela Rich was a dream cowriter, quick with the perfect adjective and a master at setting a scene.

Best lunch bunch ever... Deb Bierman, Elise Silvestri, me, Lindsay Weinberg, Jill Siegerman, and Nicole Scaramuzzo O'Neill.

Chapter 41

LOVE, MOTHERHOOD, AND THE FREEDOM OF AGELESS LIVING

*And so . . . she decided to start
living the life she'd imagined. . . .*

—Kobi Yamada, *Compendium, Inc.* (circa 2007)

I had just landed at JFK and found my driver, David, at the curb. When I got into the car, he said, "Welcome back, Miss Lunden; I hope everything went well on your trip. I got a call from my dispatcher, who said that I'm supposed to take you right to Emilio's Restaurant in Harrison, New York to meet Mr. Konigsberg and your daughters."

Now, this was a Saturday, and if you have kids, you know how preposterous it is to ask teenage girls to have dinner with you on a Saturday night instead of going out with their friends. However, Jeff and I had dated for three and a half years and the girls were really fond of him—not to mention that Jeff was a very persuasive guy.

When I arrived at the restaurant, they were already there and seated at a table. Jeff stood and pulled my chair out, and the girls said they'd gone ahead and ordered appetizers and a Caesar salad for me; they knew that was a safe bet. As Lindsay related a story about something that was going on at her high school, a bevy of waiters surrounded our table, and in unison they set our plates down. Then, with a dramatic flourish, the waiter next to me pulled the silver dome from my plate to expose a small open box with a dazzling emerald cut diamond ring. I looked at it in complete shock, and then looked around the table at everyone's huge smiles. To make it official, Jeff gave me his most irresistible smile and said, "Will you marry me?"

It took me a second to catch up to the reality of the moment and say, "Yes, of course, yes!"

Jeff looked around at all of us and said, "The reason I wanted to have your girls with us here tonight is because, while I'm proposing to you, in a sense I'm also proposing to them, since we'll all be in this life together."

The girls gushed at that, and everyone started talking at once. They almost missed what I said next. "A week from Tuesday." Seriously, I really said that.

After years of dealing with the tabloids, I figured the only way to have a private wedding that wasn't exploited by them was to plan it quietly before they could even find out. Instead of sending invitations by mail, we called guests a few days prior to the Tuesday-evening ceremony, which we held at the country club Jeff's family belonged to. The tabloids often attempt to get their snoops hired as valets or waiters, so I engaged an outside security company to help ensure the event stayed private. The wedding went off without a hitch on April 18, 2000.

I opened my vows with, "You had me at hello."

Jeff and I had talked about marriage and children all throughout our three and a half years of dating. Ironically, while I watched Jeff oversee the care of hundreds of young boys every summer at Camp Takajo, he had never been married or had children of his own. He had come from a big, close-knit family, however, and I knew he was anxious to be a parent one day. And I was intrigued by the opportunity to raise children again—this time without the degree of work and travel that my *GMA* job had demanded of me.

Of course, that would mean being pregnant again. But hey, I figured that would be a piece of cake; I'd already had three kids, right? Yeah, but that was when I was younger.

I was now in my late forties, and after several rounds of in vitro failed, Jeff said, "This shouldn't be a 'pregnancy challenge' for you." With that, he and I decided to explore surrogacy. After a great deal of research, we chose to work with the California-based Center for Surrogate Parenting, which would match us with a woman who was willing to carry a child for us. They took care of every detail, from psychological and legal issues to financial arrangements.

Three years after saying "I do," Jeff and I welcomed our twins, Kate and Max. Everyone had an opinion about my decision to have children in my fifties—and as you can imagine, not all of those opinions were positive or kind. For decades men have married younger women and had children while in their sixties, seventies, and beyond, and the public barely even blinks. It's become normal; think Robert De Niro, Al Pacino, Mick Jagger, and Billy Joel. But when women marry younger men or have children later in life, it's open season for scrutiny and ridicule.

Nevertheless, Jeff and I were loving our life and enjoying

parenting together. We remained in touch with our surrogate, and one day Jeff asked her, "Would you be willing to carry for us once again?" Twenty months after Kate and Max were born, we welcomed Kim and Jack to our family. Yep—twins again!

* * * * *

Raising kids later in life has brought a different kind of joy. My earlier years were a blur of deadlines, diaper bags, and dance recitals. With the twins, I had the gift of time—and a front-row seat to the little moments I once had to catch up on by phone. It's a privilege I don't take for granted.

It's obviously a very individual decision and it isn't for everyone; but I felt that I was fit and healthy, and by now you should know that I'm not one to be daunted by much. I do hope, though, as we see more women have children later in life, that people will get used to it—and get over it.

During the twins' infancy and toddlerhood, our home became a crazy, hectic household filled with lots of giggles and diapers . . . *lots* of diapers. Their births also brought my older daughters back home more than one might expect as they entered adulthood. Our house was a *fun* house, and they reveled in the chaos just as much as we did.

Shortly after Kim and Jack were born, we threw a party at our home to celebrate. When our friends arrived, Kate and Max, now toddlers, were running around the place like little banshees, and the new set of twins were snuggled together sound asleep in a double stroller. Several of my type-A girlfriends took in the scene and said, "I'm exhausted just looking at this." A few hours before the party began, however, as the French caterers were arriving, several of the women on their staff looked at the same scene and exclaimed, "Oh my goodness, with these babies in your life, you will never grow old." It fascinated me how two sets of people could see the same moment so differently—one as exhausting, the other as exhilarating. It confirmed what I had long believed: In life, so much of what we experience comes down to attitude.

Kate, Max, Kim, and Jack are all young adults now—each finishing college and preparing to launch into the world in their own way. They are just starting to decide exactly where they'll land, and that's more than okay. I think of how many times I changed course in my own life—and how television news wasn't even on my radar until it suddenly was.

Kate, the oldest, is starting a master's degree in social work. She has a remarkable gift for reading people and offering insight that feels both wise and grounded; she's the one her friends turn to when they need a sounding board. Max, who's likely headed to law school, didn't technically choose government and law as his major; I may or may not have checked that box while helping him fill out his freshman orientation survey. Thankfully, he ended up loving his coursework. Sometimes moms really do know best.

Kim, who's studying to become a teacher, has an extraordinary ability to connect with young children. I've watched her in action as a camp counselor at Takajo since she was sixteen, and it's clear that she was born to do this; she's patient, intuitive, and full of heart. And Jack, my Michigan man, is gravitating toward business and sports management. He's driven and purposeful, and has a mind for sports statistics that rivals that of an ESPN anchor—traits that will serve him well wherever he goes.

It's been a joy to watch all four of them grow through their college years as they learned how to live independently, make (mostly) good decisions, and, yes, finally do their own laundry. I'm deeply proud of the people they're becoming: socially conscious, thoughtful, independent thinkers—and, above all, genuinely kind human beings.

My three older daughters, Jamie, Lindsay, and Sarah, all grew into strong, intelligent, and secure women who've established interesting lives and careers. I couldn't be more proud of the adults these three girls have become. Over the years, as they've navigated their own challenges, they've told me how much they drew on my example and learned by watching me juggle, prioritize, and sacrifice. All three of my older girls have amazing work ethics (I wonder where those came from) and are smart, creative, entrepeneurial, and successful.

Jamie, following a twenty-year career as a senior-level corporate PR and marketing executive, is an entrepreneurial force. She's now a global wellness influencer and a personal development coach. She hosts the popular podcast *Gratitudeology* and is a national speaker and author.

Lindsay, after eleven years of running Joan Lunden Productions, followed her creative talents (I also don't know where those came from) to a career as a Play-Doh artist creating unique artwork using the colorful children's modeling compound. She now does commissioned pieces and custom work with big brands such as Netflix and Nickelodeon.

Sarah, after more than a decade working in reality and daytime TV, is now head of content at Yes Collective, a creative agency for celebrities and high-profile clients. She develops, oversees, and writes creative campaigns and helps bring large-scale experiential events to life.

Jamie and Lindsay have children of their own now, and I

LOVE, MOTHERHOOD, AND THE FREEDOM OF AGELESS LIVING

marvel at what great mommies they are; I tell them that all the time. I'm JoJo now to Jamie's boys, Mason and Asher, and to Lindsay's daughter, Parker, and son, Leo.

And if I were a betting person, I'd say my odds are pretty good that between my seven kids and four grandkids, one of them will surely be there to take care of me in my old age—which I have definitely not reached.

These days I remain in the fast lane much of the time. My current life as a half–empty nester with college kids allows me to comfortably continue to crisscross the country, spearheading various campaigns and keynoting events. I am noticing one annoying change, though: It seems as if during every press interview I do, no matter what project I'm promoting, a question about age always comes up.

Really? What's the deal?

I guess it's just the way our Western society is wired; women will likely always have to deal with the subject. My own perspective on aging was turned on its head forever during a trip I took to Morocco with my daughters some years ago. We spent an unforgettable week traveling from the bustling streets of Casablanca to the ancient cities of Rabat and Marrakesh before experiencing a magical night in the Sahara. We slept in elaborately decorated tents and rode camels at dawn to watch the sun rise over the endless dunes. It was breathtaking—one of those once-in-a-lifetime experiences we'll never forget.

But the thing that stuck with me the most happened on the drive back to Casablanca.

Our guide spotted some sheepherders and pulled over to the side of the road. While we got out to take pictures, he struck up a conversation with them. Then he turned to us and asked, "Would you like to see how they live?"

Without hesitation, the sheepherders invited us into their tent—their home on the move. We followed them with no idea what to expect. As we made our way to the large structure, our guide told us that the small group who lived in the tent was a nomadic tribe that moved their herd with the seasons, picking up their belongings and taking them all with them as they moved through the desert and the surrounding mountains.

As we entered their tent home, we were greeted by an older woman who seemed to be the matriarch of the family. Her skin was weathered from the desert sun and wind, making it difficult to tell her age. Through our guide, who also served as our translator, I asked the woman about her life as a nomad. I then gingerly asked, "Do you mind if I ask you how old you are?" The weathered woman looked at me as though she didn't know what I was talking about. I repeated my question through the translator, and she said that she had no idea whatsoever.

We were all stunned that this woman had absolutely no concept of her age. But how could she, without clocks or calendars? She lived according to sunrises and sunsets and the changing seasons.

So, how old was she? Did it matter? Obviously, it didn't. So why, then, does age matter so much to us in the Western world?

That exchange in the Moroccan desert was an eye-opening moment that had a profound effect on me and changed my view of age forever.

When I returned home to this Hallmark way of living that's measured in birthdays, I began to question why we described our current fitness, our health, our strength, our abilities, and even our sexual appeal in terms of our age. "Oh, I can't possibly think of doing that; I'm too old." Really? Says who?

LOVE, MOTHERHOOD, AND THE FREEDOM OF AGELESS LIVING

I wonder what that woman out in the Moroccan desert would say to that. She didn't doubt whether she could do anything—because she had never received a birthday card that said she was *over the hill.*

 *Joan announces birth of twins on* **GMA.**

Chapter 42

FROM PATIENT TO ADVOCATE

*You have been assigned this mountain
to show others that it can be moved.*

—Mel Robbins

You have cancer.

Those are the words no one ever wants to hear, but on June 5, 2014, they became my reality. That morning, I drove to the radiology lab for my annual mammogram, saying a little prayer for a clean bill of health, as many women do. With no family history of cancer, I'd assumed I was immune. I was wrong.

This was the first time since I'd begun getting mammograms that I'd added an ancillary test, a breast tissue ultrasound. I always try to ease my tension by chatting up the technicians, and I bet I'm not alone in this. I can only imagine the odd conversations they must have as they handle strangers' breasts. But in the ultrasound, as the technician probed my right breast, her banter faltered. She kept returning to the same spot, taking multiple images.

This can't be good, I thought.

She then said that the radiologist would be in shortly to take a look.

My stomach tightened as I recalled the reason I'd asked for an ultrasound in the first place. I'd had an interview with breast cancer expert Dr. Susan Love for a story I was doing for *Health Corner*, a show I hosted on Lifetime TV. I'd shared with her that I would often be called back in for "more pictures." Dr. Love nodded gravely as she listened, then explained that since both tumors and dense breast tissue show up as white on a mammogram, finding tumors in breasts with dense tissue can be like looking for a snowball in a snowstorm.

As I waited for my radiologist, Dr. Calamari, my thoughts battled it out. *Oh, it's probably nothing. No, it's gotta be something! Something bad!*

Dr. Calamari entered the examination room and said she just wanted to have a look for herself. I appreciate that she didn't pretend not to be concerned. I watched the grainy screen as she circled my right breast with the ultrasound probe, returning again and again to the same area. Her face gave away her suspicions, so I finally asked, "Do you see something?"

Then came those dreaded words: "I believe I see a tumor, Joan. I need to do a needle biopsy, but I'm afraid you might have breast cancer."

After the biopsy, I was diagnosed with stage 2 triple-negative breast cancer. My cancer surgeon, Dr. Barbara Ward, explained that TNBC, as it's known, was an aggressive form of cancer and that the treatment required months of chemotherapy, radiation, and surgery. About an inch away from that tumor was a stage 1 DCIS tumor. (DCIS, or ductal carcinoma in situ, is a noninvasive, early form of breast cancer where abnormal cells develop in the lining of breast ducts but have not spread to surrounding tissue.) This would also need to be removed.

In the days following my diagnosis, even through the fog of shock, I felt something else stirring within me: a strange clarity. For years, I'd quietly hoped that somehow, in some meaningful way, I might follow in the footsteps of my father, the cancer surgeon. And here it was—not the path I would have chosen, but a surprising inheritance all the same.

I realized that my cancer battle would not be only a personal journey; advocating for other women battling cancer would become my new mission, and in taking on that mantle, I would be able to carry on my dad's legacy. Frankly, I've never been given a more important assignment.

If I hadn't interviewed Dr. Love, I could easily have walked out of that radiology lab after a clean mammogram thinking everything was fine, never knowing I had a fast-growing tumor in my right breast. Without that interview I wouldn't have known to ask for an ultrasound. I shudder to think where my story might have been eighteen to twenty-four months later if I hadn't had that ancillary test. Yes, even a journalist who interviewed medical experts could be completely wrong about something so important.

I detailed my breast cancer journey in my 2015 book *Had I Known*, so what I have to say here isn't even the half of it. If anything about my story makes you think you might need to talk to your doctor, please don't delay.

I knew I had to tell the public. After decades of building trust with viewers, I understood that people would eventually find out—and I wanted to be the one to share my story on my own terms. So I reached out to my friend Robin Roberts, who'd been hosting *GMA* since 2005. She had faced her own cancer battle with openness and grace, and she immediately stepped into a mentoring role and offered two pieces of advice that stayed with me: "Get ahead of it before the press does," she said, and later, "Shave your head before your hair starts falling out. That way, you're in control—not the cancer."

Robin also helped orchestrate my quiet arrival at the *Good Morning America* studio. She knew that if word got out, the crew would rally around me, which could turn into an emotional avalanche. To keep things calm, the producer left my name off the guest list, and I slipped into the building just moments before the segment.

When the commercial break ended, Robin looked straight into the camera and said, "We are joined this morning by one of our favorite family members here at *GMA*, Joan Lunden." Then she turned to me and asked what I wanted to share.

I could barely speak. My throat tightened. It was surreal and nerve-wracking to utter the words out loud: "I have breast cancer."

With that first big announcement, it was time to take Robin's other advice and shave my head. But first, I needed to find a wig at Bitz-n-Pieces, the specialty salon that my oncologist had recommended. I had never seen anything like the vast array of styles, textures, and colors on display in the salon. Without divulging the names of his other clients, owner Barry Hendrickson let me know that he had provided wigs for many TV and film stars—some in my position, and others because they needed a wig for a role they were playing. I was fitted for a wig that very same day and wore it out of the salon over my own hair. Later, I went to get a mani-pedi with my longtime friend and former assistant Elise to see if she would notice. I knew I had pulled it off when someone who'd known me for thirty years didn't look twice.

When it was time to shave my head, I didn't overthink it. I

FROM PATIENT TO ADVOCATE

grabbed my car keys, drove to a local hair salon, and told them what I needed. The woman at the counter froze in shock, but a tall, dark man with kind eyes walked to the front of the salon, took me by the hand, and led me back to his station. "I'll take care of it, don't worry," he said.

The shaver buzzed to life, and I squirmed as it came closer to my head—specifically my ear, where the sound was amplified. Just before he pressed the shaver to the nape of my neck, I said, "Stop. I need my phone. I need to capture this on video."

Three months into my treatment, *People* magazine asked to do a cover shoot along with an update on my cancer battle. I'd had a great rapport with the magazine over the years and agreed, although I had some misgivings about whether I should allow them to feature me on the cover with my now completely bald head.

The day the *People* magazine photo crew came to my house, we decided to shoot the cover three ways: one with my wig, one with a chic scarf tied around my head, and one with nothing covering my head. During the photographing of the first two options, all I could think about was whether a startling picture of a bald me on the cover of the magazine would inspire anyone. While I'd lived in the public eye for most of my life, I still didn't want to do anything that would bring criticism when I was going through aggressive chemotherapy.

When the moment came to take off the wig and look into the camera, everyone left the room but me and the photographer. I kept telling myself I needed to dig down deep into my soul and put a smile on my face that said "I am strong, and I will beat this."

After the session was finished, the crew and I sat in my living room as the photographer clicked through all the photos on his laptop. When we came to the bald photos, there was a collective gasp. We all saw it: a smile and a twinkle in my eye that spoke to the viewer more than the bald head. There was really no decision to be made. That was the cover shot.

A few days before the beginning of Breast Cancer Awareness Month in October, the *Today* show asked if I would come on the program to give their audience an update on the progress of my treatment and to unveil my upcoming *People* magazine cover. After my appearances on *GMA*, *People*, and the *Today* show, I was flooded with messages from women who'd had the same misconception I once had—that no family history meant no risk. I learned that less than 15 percent of women who were diagnosed with breast cancer have a family history. That realization, and an offer by the *Today* show's producers to be a special correspondent for breast cancer awareness, propelled me into advocacy.

I became a spokesperson, speaking at breast cancer luncheons and Pink 5Ks and appearing on television to raise awareness about dense breast tissue and early cancer detection. I wanted women to know that they could walk out of a mammogram with a false sense of security, and that additional screening could save their lives.

The publication of *Had I Known* not only sent me jetting across the country to speak and do book signings but also led to a request to help lobby the FDA and Congress to pass a bill that would require mandatory mammogram reporting for patients. This would ensure that every woman who went for a mammogram would obtain the full report. Why is this essential information? Because nearly 50 percent of American women have dense breast tissue, which can mask cancer in a mammogram. Acting on this knowledge can save their lives. Without this legislation, only the referring physician received the full report.

The right to this lifesaving information was obvious to me, so I began making trips to Washington, DC, to lobby for a bill called

FROM PATIENT TO ADVOCATE

the Mandatory Mammogram Reporting Act. Surprisingly—and frustratingly—after several years of lobbying and even testifying before the FDA, we couldn't even get all the female members of Congress to sign on. Even though the bill didn't require funding, the next obvious domino to fall if the bill passed would be to push for insurance companies to cover follow-up tests. Members of Congress didn't want to tangle with the insurance lobby, which was more experienced and better funded than our effort. But, while it took a lot longer than we'd hoped, the bill finally passed.

Years later, I would see how far the message had traveled. My good friend and the coauthor of *Had I Known*, Laura Morton, went for her annual mammogram as we were finishing the book, and for the first time in her life, she saw a big pink sign in the waiting area that read: "When your mammography is performed, aside from checking for any changes or abnormalities, we are checking how dense your breast tissue is. If you are 75% dense, a screening ultrasound will be recommended. Please feel free to ask questions."

Laura snapped a picture with her phone and sent it to me with a caption that read, "I call this a small win."

During her screening, she told the technician that she wanted to know if she had dense breasts. The technician sighed and said, "Oh yeah, you and every other woman, ever since Joan Lunden was bald on the cover of *People* magazine."

That moment made us both laugh—but it also made something clear: The message had landed.

Not long after receiving a clean result from that mammogram, Laura found a small lump in her left breast. Because she had walked beside me through my journey, she knew immediately that something felt off. She acted quickly. The news wasn't what she'd hoped for: In addition to stage 1 DCIS, she tested positive for the BRCA1 gene. Women with BRCA1 mutation face a significantly higher risk of developing breast cancer, with lifetime risks ranging from fifty-five percent to upward of seventy percent. BRCA1 mutations are also strongly associated with increased risk of ovarian cancer (estimated between thirty-nine percent to forty-six percent over a lifetime). These mutations may also increase risk for developing more aggressive forms of cancer, such as triple-negative breast cancer. BRCA1 mutations may also increase the risk of prostate cancer, pancreatic cancer, and melanoma in men as well as women. BRCA1 mutations are inherited from parent to child.

But early action made all the difference. Laura later told me, "If I hadn't written that book with you, I wouldn't have pushed so hard for answers. I might have waited. And things could've turned out very differently."

As for me, I'm happy to tell you that after sixteen rounds of chemo, six weeks of radiation, and surgery, I'm now cancer free. You never know how strong you are until being strong is the only choice you have.

My team of doctors told me one of the major reasons I did so well with all the chemo and radiation was my good health as I was going into the battle. I'm so grateful that as I turned forty years old, I took charge of my health and dramatically changed how I approached my fitness.

Physical health was only one component in my cancer battle, however. The positive attitude that has served me all throughout my life and career also helped me fight like a warrior. Healthy aging today means being proactive in our health management, knowing our family history, doing self-exams so we know what our normal is, and being vigilant about our screenings. If you're getting mammograms and don't know your breast density, call and find out. When you're asked who else you want the report sent to, tell them to send it to *you*.

I believe that information empowers each of us to be more fully in charge of our health and, more important, to stay ahead of disease, so that if we're diagnosed we have a better chance at a good prognosis. This is why it's so important to me as a breast cancer survivor to be an advocate and to share what I've learned.

As all survivors know, the battle never feels truly over. Breast cancer leaves its mark not just on the body but also on the mind and heart. There are no scans for emotional scars, but they remain.

On my last day of treatment, I came a bit unglued. Tears rolled down my cheeks as I told my oncologist, "People on social media keep asking how I'm dealing with the fear of recurrence. I hadn't even thought about that until they brought it up."

He smiled gently, took my hands in his, and said, "You need to follow the wisdom of the great philosopher Wile E. Coyote." I looked at him, puzzled. He continued, "Remember? He would race off a cliff, and then stay suspended in midair. He was never in trouble—until he looked down. Keep your head up. Expect to keep going strong. Expect a good ending to your story."

That's exactly how I'm choosing to live.

Looking back now, I see my cancer journey not just as a personal trial but as a calling. It gave me a mission larger than myself. I didn't follow in my father's footsteps the way I'd once imagined I would—but I did follow him. By turning my diagnosis into advocacy, I found a surprising inheritance after all.

People *magazine on Joan's breast cancer diagnosis*

Chapter 43

THEN THERE WAS ONE

*There is no influence so powerful
as that of the mother.*

—Sarah Josepha Hale, editor and author

I had spent years preparing for this moment—traveling back and forth between New York and California, making sure Mom had the best care, and soaking up as much time with her as I could. One day, she was the woman who taught me how to walk in heels; the next, I was guiding her gently across the room, steadying her steps. But I took care of her the way she had once taken care of me. And when I was with her, I made sure she still felt like herself—my glamorous, unstoppable, full-of-life mom. The day she turned down a shopping trip, I knew something had shifted. Shopping was a part of who she was. So, of course, I went shopping for her. She smiled at each new piece, delighting in every package. If she was performing, she did it flawlessly—as she had done everything in life.

When it was evident that her cognitive abilities no longer served her, I found a wonderful final home, Ashley Manor, a small residential facility serving three other seniors, where I knew she was well cared for by James Ashley and his staff. Those of us with aging parents want them to be more than cared for; we want them to be happy, and Mom certainly seemed happy.

As the summer of 2013 drew to a close, James called me to say he had hospice on its way, and he didn't expect Mom to last more than a couple of days. Jeff and I went straight to the airport. We landed in Sacramento and checked in on Mom, then went to the funeral home to begin making plans. Jeff seemed unusually subdued and asked to go back to the hotel to rest. Within hours he was in the emergency room under the care of one of Dad's now-middle-aged protégés. Somehow, somewhere, Jeff had been exposed to spinal meningitis, of all things.

The next two days were a blur as he was treated and Mom retreated. I went from the ICU to Mom's bedside, making her funeral arrangements in between. On that note, I was guided by a stack of worn yellow legal pad pages—Mom's handwritten instructions for her funeral. She had planned it down to the last detail, even titling it her "Bon Voyage Party." It was classic Glady—no sadness; just a grand sendoff, exactly the way she wanted.

As I shuttled back and forth, I missed her final breath by mere moments. That was hard to accept, but I know this about her—she would have wanted to make her exit on her own terms. She had never been one for long, drawn-out goodbyes.

Jeff thankfully made a recovery just in time to attend her service at the East Lawn Memorial Park chapel. Now, you might think there wouldn't be more than a handful of mourners for a woman who'd lived for ninety-four years, but you'd be wrong. We counted nearly two hundred people she had touched directly, including my longtime friend Michele Dillingham, whom you may remember as having illustrated the Joni Lisa Charm and Modeling School curriculum. Since I lived back east, I was so grateful that she had visited Mom week in and week out through the years.

There were also dozens of people who wanted to honor her memory as Dad's beloved partner. Many had been patients of Dad's; one mourner had been delivered by him. Another had been a coinvestor with Dad in the Phoenix Field airport.

And then, of course, there was Mom's longtime hairdresser, Jo Avila, her accomplice in achieving her life's goal to "dye 'til you die."

Just as James Ashley had lovingly cared for Mom, he conducted the funeral service with that same spirit. When it was time for her eulogy, I stood at the lectern:

> We are here today to celebrate the life of Glady Blunden, otherwise known as Glitzy Glady. I remember when I threw Mom a seventy-fifth birthday party; one of the guests said she was like a shooting star—that whenever Glady entered a room, she lit it up with her effusive smile and charismatic personality, and that when she left, her energy lingered like a trail in the sky.
>
> For me, she was my own personal guru of positive thinking and living your dreams. Mom always told me to "look at life through my rose-colored glasses." My friends joke that I was raised by Gandhi, because I'm always pulling out another "Positive Gladyism"—like:
>
> - The word impossible isn't in our dictionary.

- When you fight with your mate, never tell your mother or best friend—you'll make up, but they'll remember what a jerk he was.

And, my personal favorite:

- Tan fat is better than white fat.

Glady always saw the glass as half full, and her positive outlook was contagious. She lived an amazingly full and wonderful life—not void of adversity or sadness but bounding with energy and enthusiasm while she was here.

Mom once told me that as a young girl, she would get all dressed up when it came time for family dinner, and her gruff, no-nonsense father would look at her and ask, "Who are you trying to impress, farm girl?" And she would always reply, "Me. I'm trying to impress upon myself that my life can be better than this."

She wasn't afraid of hard work. She waitressed her way through training and became a comptometer operator—one of the few women in a field typically dominated by men. She was sharp, ambitious, and always determined to build a better life for herself.

Then, one fateful night, she went to dinner with a new friend—and that friend made a big mistake. She introduced Mom to her date, a handsome doctor named Erle Blunden, who fell for Glady. Soon they were inseparable. But before he would propose, he had one condition: she had to get her pilot's license so she could be his copilot in life. So, of course, she did!

She was living a charmed life—until January

THEN THERE WAS ONE

1964, when my dad's plane went down in a storm over Malibu Canyon. Just like that, she was a widow with two young kids. And while I was a fiercely independent teenager who challenged her every step of the way, she never wavered. She had an amazing capacity to forgive and forget. The most important lesson she taught me was the art of letting go. No grudges, no anger—just moving forward and asking, "Okay, what's next?"

I made sure Glady B was all gussied up for her Bon Voyage party—white St. John knit, gold trim, gold shoes, and her favorite gold Chanel bag. But there was one little problem—I couldn't find any underwear; after all, Mom had been in the "Depends Years" for some time. One of her caregivers saved the day when she ran to her room and came back with a brand-new pair of hot-pink bikini briefs. So, when I handed them over to the funeral director, I felt the need to explain. "When Glady B goes through the Pearly Gates and Dr. Blunden sees those pink bikini briefs, she's going to have some explaining to do." And you know exactly what she'll say: "Swear to God, I don't know where these came from!"

Heaven will never be the same now that Glitzy Glady's there.

As I stepped away from the podium, I felt the weight of finality settle in. But grief is never just about one moment; it lingers, surfacing in the most unexpected places, and at the most unexpected times. I thought about the many ways Glady had shaped me—her unshakable optimism and her ability to see the glass as half full, even in the darkest of times.

I can't tell you how often I've had a question while writing this book and instinctively reached for the phone to call Mom—only to remember I couldn't do that anymore. I imagine all of you who have lost a parent know that feeling: that split second when you forget they're gone, when the instinct to share something with them that's still so deeply ingrained in your being takes over.

Losing my mom didn't just mean losing a parent—it meant losing my last immediate family member. My dad was gone. My only brother, Jeff, had passed. My grandparents had long since left us. Suddenly, I was the last one standing. That kind of loneliness is hard to describe. It hits you in moments you don't expect, like when you're standing in line at the grocery store and you realize there's no one left who remembers what you looked like at five years old.

That aloneness has been made much easier by the fact that I married a man with a big, loving, deeply connected family that embraces togetherness in a way that's both heartwarming and, at times, overwhelming. In Jeff's world, birthdays aren't just celebrations; they're full-scale *events*, with a group text chain that could rival that of the planning committee for a royal wedding. Holidays are a team sport, and family vacations involve logistics fit for an army. For someone who spent much of my life in a small, tight-knit but relatively independent family, stepping into Jeff's was a learning curve. But oh, what a gift it has been.

Jeff didn't realize when he married me that he was getting a hopeless romantic who relishes people coming together to celebrate life. But in that way, I am my mother's daughter. As a little girl, I remember Mom saying, "Half the fun of doing anything is sharing it with others." And she was right. Friends and family help us savor our successes, comfort us in our struggles, and provide a mirror for us to learn more about ourselves.

THEN THERE WAS ONE

Mom showed me that in how she raised me. And when I had to step into the role of parenting my parent, I saw firsthand just how difficult—and deeply necessary—that role is. After a lifetime as her child, I had to become her advocate, her protector, her voice. Caregiving is exhausting. It's emotional. It's complicated. We're suddenly expected to navigate health care, finances, and difficult decisions without a road map.

Caring for my mother wasn't just an emotional journey, it was an education. I quickly realized how unprepared most of us are for this role. That's why I became a spokesperson for A Place for Mom, coauthored with Amy Newmark *Chicken Soup for the Soul: Family Caregivers*, and eventually found myself speaking to audiences across the country on the topic. Because no one should have to figure this out alone. And in time, I took my experience to the halls of Congress to testify before the House Ways and Means Committee about expanding the Family and Medical Leave Act to include senior care. Because caregiving isn't just something we do at the start of life—it happens at the end too.

In my own way, I carry on Glady's legacy. She was my first teacher, my first cheerleader, my first role model. She taught me to let go of what I couldn't change and to move forward. Even now, I still hear her voice telling me to put on my rose-colored glasses. To savor the moment. To celebrate life instead of mourning what's lost.

And I do. Because Glitzy Glady wouldn't have it any other way.

 *Congressional testimony*

Chapter 44

SPEAKING OF LEGACY

*The only person you are destined
to become is the person you decide to be.*
—Ralph Waldo Emerson,
Essays on Self-Reliance and Individualism

As my flight lifted off the runway at JFK one bright May morning, I felt lighter than air. At the other end of this journey, I would stand on stage at Loma Linda University's School of Medicine, delivering the commencement address. But I wasn't just a speaker—I was a daughter, honoring the man who had shaped my life in ways I was still discovering.

The occasion? The seventy-fifth anniversary of my father's earning his medical degree from Loma Linda. I swirled my sparkling water with lime, staring out at the clouds. What would Dad say if he knew I was giving this speech?

I was being granted the ultimate gift: an opportunity to honor my father, whose influence had shaped me long after he was gone.

Some speakers thrive under pressure, harnessing the power of procrastination to craft their speeches at the last minute, but that's never been my style. Without realizing it, I had actually begun preparing this commencement speech years earlier, during a visit to my hometown of Sacramento. I had gone there to interview some of my dad's colleagues, hoping to bridge the gap between the legend he had become in my mind and the man who had once tackled the everyday challenges of life, just like the rest of us. As a journalist, I'd interviewed countless doctors, researchers, and clinicians, but I was especially curious to understand what it was like to practice medicine in the 1950s and early '60s—an era I had known only through stories. The two doctors I reached out to, Dr. Marvin Klein and Dr. James Reece, were gracious enough to accept my request and allow me to videotape our interviews.

I started with Dr. Klein, whom you may remember from the early chapters of this book. I often pictured him in my mind's eye wearing ski attire in Squaw Valley, where he and his family often vacationed with ours. He was now retired and his health was beginning to fail him, so he was casually dressed in a sweater and joggers. His specialty was gynecology. In fact, he'd been my doctor for many years, and he had always referred his patients to Dad if they needed surgery. Dr. Klein was also Dad's business partner in the Country Club Medical Center and the Bel Air Hospital.

Dr. Klein lived alone now that his wife, Helen, had passed away, and I couldn't help but wonder how he was faring by himself. I set up my video camera in their family room so that he could settle into his leather recliner and be comfortable. Dr. Klein was a gregarious guy—he'd always been the life of the party—and I wasn't surprised when he launched into a story without any prompting from me.

"I remember one of my patients who had developed a serious

vascular condition that meant she might lose her leg. That wasn't even the worst of it. She could just as likely die if she didn't have surgery. But back then we didn't have many specialists, and there were no vascular surgeons in Sacramento. I felt horrible. She wasn't that old, and I was so worried I was going to lose her."

His grimace told me that he was remembering the helpless feeling of this woman in her forties who would possibly die because she needed surgery that he couldn't find for her.

"I turned to your dad to see if he could possibly help her, and he said, 'Don't worry, I'll learn how to do the surgery she needs.' And damned if he didn't do it."

The weight of that sentence settled over me.

Dr. Klein's face broke into a grin as he continued. "Your dad called a cardiovascular surgeon down in Houston, Texas, a Dr. DeBakey, and asked if he could fly down to Baylor University Hospital and learn this surgical technique. DeBakey agreed, and next thing I know, your dad got in his plane, spent a week at Baylor, and learned the technique. It was unbelievable. That's the kind of amazing guy your dad was."

I later learned that Dr. Michael DeBakey became world-renowned for inventing a critical component of the heart-lung machine that made open-heart surgery possible.

This was what I'd been hoping for when I'd scheduled these interviews, and on hearing this story I was filled with pride in Dad, but I wasn't surprised he'd taken the bull by the horns.

"He performed that surgery," Dr. Klein continued, "like he'd been doing it for years. And that woman? She walked out of that hospital. Lived a full life."

I just sat there in awe.

Next on my journey down memory lane was Dr. James Reece,

an internist who had shared an office with my father for many years. Like Dad, he was a Seventh-Day Adventist and a Loma Linda School of Medicine graduate. When I arrived, his wife, Carolyn, greeted me at the door. She looked remarkably like the elegant blonde I remembered—just fifty years older. "Oh, Joni, dear, it's been so long," she said, wrapping me in a hug. "We're so happy you've come to talk about your father. He was such a special man."

We settled into the same living room I remembered from childhood. Carolyn brought in a tray of cucumber sandwiches and mint iced tea as I set up my camera. Dr. Reece beamed. "Where do I even begin telling you about your dad?" He spoke first about their education at Loma Linda and its mission of service. "Your father moved to Fair Oaks right out of med school and opened a family practice. There weren't many doctors here then, so he started recruiting others. After a few years, that let him transition to general surgery—his real passion and talent."

Carolyn added, "Your father was a missionary at heart. It didn't matter if someone couldn't pay—he always treated them." Dr. Reece recalled how Dad made five-dollar house calls, then chuckled. "And if he thought someone couldn't afford their prescription, he'd quietly tuck a ten-dollar bill under it on the bedside table. That was just the kind of doctor he was."

They shared story after story—of house calls, patients who became friends, and the way my father's care extended far beyond medicine. "Joni," Dr. Reece said, "many of your dad's patients helped build your house at the airport. If someone insisted on repaying him, he'd find a project they could work on once they recovered. And they loved it. We all loved your dad."

I never would have known these stories had I not gone back home and interviewed the doctors who had worked side by side with

SPEAKING OF LEGACY

Dad. And after listening to them speak about the legacy he'd left, it was now clearer to me how he had inspired my childhood dream, which has stuck with me throughout my life.

* * * *

Two years later, strolling across the campus of Loma Linda, I retraced my father's steps as Dr. Richard Hart, the university president, led me through the manicured grounds. We stopped at a walkway embedded with plaques (like stars on the Hollywood Walk of Fame), each honoring a distinguished alumnus who had impacted medicine. Dr. Hart gestured toward one: Dr. Erle Blunden. I knelt and traced my fingers over his name, feeling an unexpected rush of emotion. This was where he had once walked, studied, dreamed.

Rachelle Bussell, senior vice president of advancement, was also on the tour. She broke in a bit sheepishly, saying, "And if I may, Dr. Hart, I think it's only fair that we also show Joan the one for her father's older sister, Dr. Dulcie Anderson, who started her studies here first and paved the way for her little brother. She was one of the first women to get a medical degree from Loma Linda, and went on to become an anesthesiologist."

My Auntie Dulcie had always been a bit of a mystery to me when I was a child, since we never lived close enough to visit her on the East Coast. But I reveled in pride for the woman who was breaking glass ceilings before that was even a concept.

As I stood between their two plaques, I let it sink in: The Blunden legacy in medicine wasn't just my father's.

"Now," Dr. Hart said with a twinkle in his eye, "I have something special to show you." We entered a massive building: the James M. Slater, MD, Proton Treatment & Research Center, the first of its kind to be based at a hospital. Inside, I was awestruck. Before me stood a multistory machine with an enormous articulating arm, like something out of *Star Wars*.

"What . . . *is* this?" I asked.

It was the most complex piece of medical machinery ever built. Proton therapy, the newest type of radiation treatment, can destroy cancer cells using high-energy proton beams with unprecedented precision, something that's especially valuable when operating near the brain, spine, or eyes.

"This," Rachelle whispered, "is what radiation therapy is becoming."

As I stood there, overwhelmed by the scale of it all, I thought of my father. He had been a surgeon—but more than that, he was a problem solver. He didn't wait for innovation; he built it. That's when I recalled a story Dr. Klein told me. We'd been talking about fishing in Mexico when he stopped mid-sentence, sat up in his recliner, and said, "Wait—I have to tell you something brilliant your dad did." He described a patient with severe varicose veins. "Your dad agreed to do the difficult surgery—but here's the wild part: He made his own vein-stripping tools. In his workshop. At your house."

I remembered that workshop beside the hangar, but I never knew he'd used it to develop medical devices!

If Dad had been with me that day, standing in the Proton Center, I think he would have marveled at how far medical technology had come in treating patients who were battling cancer. In his day, the only tool they'd had available was surgery.

* * * * *

SPEAKING OF LEGACY

The School of Medicine's commencement was held the following morning at 8:30. Sitting on the dais at Loma Linda's University Mall with the faculty, I had a sweeping view of the open-air setting, which was designed to inspire both reverence and celebration. In front of me, rows of neatly arranged white chairs stretched across the manicured lawn, occupied by soon-to-be doctors in traditional black academic regalia. Beyond them, family and friends sat attentively, shaded by the tall trees that lined the mall, their branches swaying gently in the breeze.

I recalled a large black-and-white picture, a bit faded from age, of my dad's graduating class from medical school. I remember trying to pick him out, which at first was difficult because back then he had a thick head of shining black hair. During my life, his cropped hair had become salt-and-pepper. As I sat listening to Dr. Roger Hadley, the dean of the School of Medicine, proudly talk about the merits of this graduating class, which represented thirty-eight different countries, I found my mind flashing between the scene before me and the black-and-white image of my dad when he was the age of this audience, sitting with his colleagues and listening to their commencement speaker.

After Dr. Hart's introduction, I stepped up to the podium in my long black-and-white commencement robe and my cap adorned with the traditional gold tassel. The proceedings were streamed on the university's website for those international students who couldn't be present, and they expected upward of four thousand people to be watching.

> Loma Linda is where my father discovered his passion—healing others. This is where he was taught to treat all patients regardless of their ability to pay. This is where he

had it impressed on him to get involved in his community and work to provide care to all who need it. This is where he learned that the goal is not to leave the learning behind but to continue learning for the rest of your life. This is where he learned never to rest on his laurels but to always challenge his mind and to discover new ways to treat his sick patients.

You will leave here today with that same foundation that my father took with him to the small community of Fair Oaks, California, and all the people who lived there. As he walked off this campus, he began to create his legacy of service. There was never any bravado or boasting; just a calm sense of purpose and an appreciation for his gifts as a surgeon.

You are all here today because you have a gift. Your talent and knowledge as a doctor can have a tremendous impact on this world of ours. That talent, along with a compassion for people and a passion for your mission, can guide you to create your own legacy.

My father would have wanted me to be passionate about cures that needed to be found, about injustices that needed attention, and about fellow humans who simply needed a helping hand. He taught me that each one of us can make a difference, and that together we have tremendous power to create new laws, back needed research, open new medical institutions, and bring about social change. This world needs leaders, it needs risk-takers; and what it needs more than anything is people who ground their decisions in values and integrity, and who have a sense that community is as important as self. . . .

SPEAKING OF LEGACY

As I stepped away from the podium, the sun was rising higher, casting long shadows across the campus where Dad had once walked. I took a slow, satisfied breath, thinking about how my father had quietly shaped my path—not through expectation but through example. He never told me to become a doctor, but he showed me how to care. He never pushed me to follow his footsteps, but somehow, I had done so in my own way.

Thanks, Dad.

Chapter 45

SURFACING WITH INTENTION

When your soul gets quiet, your purpose gets loud.
—Anonymous

Sitting on the dock of our home on Long Lake in Naples, Maine, I watched a pair of loons pop up from the still morning waters, only to disappear again for what seemed like an eternity.

How did they do it? I googled it. Loons can hold their breath for up to five minutes. So I sat and waited. As I leaned into the quiet, soaking in the sun, listening to the rustle of pine trees and the soft lap of water on the shore, I could hear, faintly, the sound of little boys laughing and playing at Jeff's summer camp just a few hundred yards away.

It occurred to me that this kind of immersion in nature, this rare kind of stillness, had profoundly impacted my health, my happiness, and my sense of self. I'll admit that sitting still didn't come easily. I'm hardwired to go, go, go—and, let's be honest, so is the culture I came up in. For years, busyness was my badge of honor, and even now I bristle when someone asks how I'm enjoying retirement. I'm not retired; I've just shifted focus. I've learned that reinvention isn't always about *doing* more—it's about *seeing* more. These days, I'm learning to appreciate not just what I've accomplished but also the gift of being able to sit quietly and luxuriate in the stillness of an early morning. To listen. To breathe. To love the life I've built and to embrace the chapter I'm in with pride and gratitude—for the man by my side, and for my seven incredible children who are out there thriving in the world. I used to think slowing down meant stepping back. Now I see it for what it truly is: showing up in a different, more present way.

Here on this dock, watching the loons surface and vanish again, I found myself reflecting on everything that had unfolded since I left the early-morning grind of network television. Ironically, nothing had really slowed down. In fact, I'd reinvented myself more times than I could count. But something had changed; *I* had changed.

The photos on my office walls serve as daily reminders of what an extraordinary ride it's been. Perhaps it's this chapter of life—my seventies—that allows me to see those images through a new lens, one shaded with gratitude and even a little awe. When I stopped hosting a daily network morning show, I stumbled around until I reimagined what my career—and my purpose—could be.

One of my most fulfilling reinventions didn't happen on camera or behind a podium. It happened right here, in the quiet stillness of Long Lake, where I discovered the power of pressing pause.

Nothing compares to waking up on Long Lake, slipping out from under my comforter, and walking barefoot to the dock with a hot cup of coffee. The early-morning light reflects off the water like glass, calm and undisturbed before the boats and water-skiers arrive. I started coming here after Jeff and I became a couple. He had purchased Camp Takajo from its founder at just twenty-seven and poured his heart into its mission: helping boys develop independence and self-reliance.

After watching his campers grow and transform in the outdoors, I had an idea—why not create something similar for women? A space where they could step out of their routines, reconnect with themselves, and leave stronger than they came.

That's how Camp Reveille was born.

I teamed up with my fitness trainer, Beth Bielat, and together we built a program that blended traditional camp activities—archery, waterskiing, wall climbing, and campfires—with wellness seminars, spa treatments, and creative workshops like pottery and jewelry making. I'll never forget the cardboard boat race, where participants built boats out of cardboard, duct tape, and heavy-duty plastic. One year, a mother-daughter team led the pack—until their boat tipped just before the finish line, sending them both into the lake laughing.

At a boys' camp like Takajo, reveille is played on a bugle at sunrise—a brassy, energetic tune that cuts through the morning quiet and summons campers to breakfast. It's essentially a wake-up call. And for many of the women who came to our camp, that's exactly what it became. Some arrived solo and left with lifelong friends. Others came with daughters or mothers, using the weekend as a time to bond. They lived in the same "camp bunks" just like the boys did, held flashlights under their chins, and talked late into the night. I watched them show up stressed and worn out and leave lighter, stronger, recharged.

That's when I realized something: Healing doesn't happen only in hospitals. It happens around campfires, in honest conversations, and in shared laughter that feels like medicine.

The first time Jeff saw me delivering flowers, floor mats, and soft toilet paper to the bunk bathrooms, he shook his head and laughed. "Flowers and potpourri? What have I unleashed?" What he saw me unleash was something extraordinary. Camp Reveille gave hundreds of women a chance to hit pause, breathe deeply, and return to their lives with renewed strength and clarity.

That same impulse—to help people find resilience, reinvention, and purpose—has always guided my work. Whether through journalism, advocacy, public speaking, or projects like Camp Reveille, I've tried to shine a light where it matters. And even as my path has evolved, the mission has stayed the same: to make a difference.

Which brings me back to the loons.

When they dive beneath the surface, they don't disappear; that's where they feed, gather strength, and prepare for their next appearance. And when I stepped away from the public eye, it may have seemed as though I had vanished, but I was nourishing myself, taking stock, and preparing for what came next.

My mantra—*Just say yes*—has given me an extraordinary life. But it took what felt like a setback to understand the importance of being open to new paths that allowed me to find a new sense of purpose—one that had always been there, but that I'd never fully explored.

I used to live at a full sprint—chasing deadlines, defying limits, revving my engine to its highest gear. That drive carried me through some extraordinary life chapters. But now I've learned that strength doesn't always roar. Sometimes it floats. Sometimes it sits still on a quiet dock. Like the loons, I've discovered the power of going deep—not to retreat but to restore. Reinvention isn't about leaving the past behind. It's about surfacing with intention, about taking everything you've learned and using it to rise again—with a little more perspective.

SURFACING WITH INTENTION

So, like the loons, you never know where—or when—you or I might pop up next.

If you've read this book because you're at your own turning point—facing change, challenge, or uncertainty—I hope it's offered something more than stories. I hope it's given you your own road map for reinvention, a reminder that you're not alone and that it's never too late to shift course, to find new purpose, to rise in a new way.

The truth is, life never stops asking us to become.

And I, for one, am still becoming.

FOR YOUR VIEWING PLEASURE

I've loved sharing my life and career with you—it's been an amazing adventure. If you'd like more, I've posted full-length videos of some of the fascinating stories I've covered. Each is labeled so you can choose what interests you. Thanks for being part of the journey!

Joan takes to the Las Vegas stage with the Bally's Jubilee Dancers.

Joan skydives with the US Army Parachute team, the Golden Knights.

Joan on a training mission with the US Navy SEALs on a nuclear submarine.

FOR YOUR VIEWING PLEASURE

 *Joan trains with the Special Forces, culminating in a helo extraction.*

 *Joan tags along with Shaquille O'Neal as he plays with Orlando Magic.*

 *Joan flies in an F-18 and lands on the USS* Eisenhower *aircraft carrier.*

 *Joan flies with the United States Air Force Thunderbirds.*

 *Joan interviews Prince Charles (now King Charles).*

 *Joan on the Larry King show discussing surrogacy.*

 *Joan talks about motherhood with Robin Roberts on* GMA.

FOR YOUR VIEWING PLEASURE

Prevention Magazine *interviews Joan about life after 60.*

Joan on the David Letterman Show, *as she signs off of GMA.*

Joan on the Ellen DeGeneres Show.

Joan on the Rosie O'Donnell Show.

Joan on The Tonight Show *with Jay Leno.*

Joan and daughter Jamie Hess speak about gratitude on the Today *show.*

Joan tries her hand at stand-up comedy at Catch a Rising Star Comedy Club.

FOR YOUR VIEWING PLEASURE

Joan discusses breast cancer with fellow survivor Robin Roberts on GMA.

Promo reel for Joan as keynote speaker.

Joan Lunden speaking reel.

ACKNOWLEDGMENTS

I've been working on this book for a number of years. I knew it would be written, but something always seemed to get in the way. I put it away twice—first when I was diagnosed with breast cancer in order to write about that chapter of my life in *Had I Known*, and then again when I felt the urge to write my previous book, *Why Did I Come Into This Room?*. It reminded me of my college days when I would put aside the most difficult essay and get the easy ones out of the way so I could really buckle down on the toughie.

But oh my, once I got started reflecting on my life—the exciting journey, the challenges, the opportunities, the missed opportunities, and the many, many reinventions—everything simply poured out of my memories and onto the page.

There are a number of wonderful friends and collegues who've helped this book—my eleventh—come to life. My longtime friend Laura Morton has been a coauthor on several books with me—in fact, we started this writing thing together with our first book, *Healthy Cooking with Joan Lunden*, in 1996, followed by *Healthy Living with Joan Lunden* and *Had I Known*, in which I shared my breast cancer journey. Whenever I work with Laura I'm always confident that we'll end up with something we're proud of. Since working

ACKNOWLEDGMENTS

with me on that first book, she's authored more than sixty others, twenty-two of which are *New York Times* bestsellers, and has now become a publisher. I'm excited to be one of the first books published under her new imprint, Lasega Books.

After I'd written an initial manuscript and given it to Laura, she said, "This is Joan Lunden reporting on Joan Lunden's life. It's understandable that that's the way you'd approach it, since you've spent your life doing just that—reporting. However, I think your readers want you to take them into your life; they'll want a memoir." And with that, she teamed me with Tamela Rich, who is a wonderful editor. But I got much more than I bargained for; what I got was a master-level course in memoir writing. After hundreds of Zoom sessions with Tamela, the book was transformed in a way that I never could have imagined. Laura had connected me with the most incredible writing partner, and there are barely words to express my gratitude for her expertise and guidance. I know Tamela accepted the job simply to help edit, but then she dove in—and I mean *all* in—and took an amazing journey with me in the telling of my life story.

On each of my last few books, once the writing was complete, I've turned the manuscript over to the very capable hands of Hope Innelli, our line editor. Thank you, Hope, for your diligence, understanding of my voice, and commitment to excellence. Once again, it was Laura who connected us, and she sang your praises—and you certainly have lived up to them.

Laura also introduced me to Adam Mitchell, who has worked diligently on editing the videos that are used throughout this book and creating the QR codes, not to mention obtaining the rights to all of the photos used. He is a jack-of-all-trades. I seriously don't think there is anything I could ask him to do that he wont figure out. I owe him a debt of gratitude for not just the extensive work that he's done

ACKNOWLEDGMENTS

for me, but for his patience and relentless pursuit of the answer to any and all of my needs.

When I published my last book, Laura introduced me to Jonathan Merkh, a wonderful publisher and the founder of Forefront Books. Laura's imprint, Lasega Books, is a part of Forefront, and I want to thank everyone at both entities who helped bring this book to life.

At Forefront Books, thank you to Jennifer Gingerich, VP and editorial director; Bruce Gore, for your wonderful cover design, Mary Susan Oleson, for the beautiful interior design; Landon Dickerson for running production; and Benjamin Holmes, for copyediting the manuscript.

My thanks also to Simon & Schuster; I greatly appreciate all the work that everyone at S&S has done to bring everything together to print, distribute, and support this book.

I also want to thank the talented Gus Butera for graciously allowing me to use his photograph of me for the cover of the book. It's one of my favorites. And, of course, what is a great photograph without a great makeup artist and hairstylist? I've been fortunate to have the brilliant Emir Pehilj in my life to travel the country with me and always make sure that I'm camera ready. He's really much more than that; he's also a dear friend and a delight to have on the road with me after all these years.

As it's said, there is no such thing as a self-made man—or woman—and I would not have had my great career without the many mentors in my life: Bill DeBlonk, Paul Thompson, Harry Geise, Jed Johnson, Phil Nye, Woody Fraser, Chickie Silver, Jim Griffin, George Merlis, Susan Winston, Squire Rushnell, Elton Rule, David Hartman, and of course, Charlie Gibson. I also want to extend my thanks to my long-time attorney, Marc Chamlin, and

ACKNOWLEDGMENTS

my accountant, Richard Koenigsberg, for their critically important advice throughout my career. They have all given me their vote of confidence, and have been generous in their support and guidance all along this incredible journey and I am eternally thankful for each and every one of them.

A special thanks to Simone Swink, *Good Morning America* executive producer, for her support in the launch of this book.

A special thanks to Michele Mustacchio and Camille Collett, Disney Entertainment photo editors, for securing all the memorable photos from over my years at ABC.

I've also been incredibly fortunate to have worked with a wonderful group of bright and capable women throughout my career who have remained in my life. In fact, some are my best friends to this day. They've all been generous with their time and assistance in helping me track down many of the details of my life and career.

When I first began working for *Good Morning America* as a correspondent, I had a young college student, Elise Silvestri, as an intern. As I took my seat in the anchor chair in September 1980, she was graduating, and she became my first assistant. Neither of us knew exactly what was in store—topped with the fact that I had a new baby with me at work—but we learned together. For almost five decades Elise has continued to work with me on various shows. She's still at the helm of my current work, booking me to speak, host, and moderate panels at events around the country.

Debbie Bierman followed Elise in 1983, and she was with me for more than eight years. Her tenure saw the births of Lindsay and Sarah and, finally, the ending of my marriage, so she had a lot to contend with—not just show scripts and wardrobe but magazines and tabloids.

When Debbie left to raise her children in 1992, she found my

ACKNOWLEDGMENTS

next assistant, Samantha Berg, who was with me during my newly divorced and out-on-the-town days. I wrangled her into dancing on my exercise video and bungee jumping off a twenty-six-story bridge while on location in Queenstown, New Zealand. She too had to wrangle the press during those sometimes precarious dating years.

When Samantha became engaged and moved away from New York in 1995, she found my next assistant, Jill Seigerman, who was with me for the next eight years. Jill saw me through my last years at *GMA*, during my daring exploits on *Behind Closed Doors*, and my subsequent career reinventions, as well as my meeting my life partner, Jeff, marrying, and having twins. So, once again, Jill had her hands full with my many new ventures and my new family life.

It occurred to me during the writing of this book that each of my assistants over the years has essentially worked for a different Joan Lunden: the network newbie/new mom; the overwhelmed working mom with three little ones and a really big job; the newly divorced and newly single working mom; and, finally, the wiser and calmer woman who found happiness and redefined her career and life.

In 2008, Lindsay Weinberg took over as vice president and business manager of Joan Lunden Productions. For the next eleven years Lindsay was my right hand—my trusted business confidante—and she also happens to be one of my daughters. A talented writer and producer, she was a tireless worker and a loyal protector of me and my Joan Lunden brand. It's an amazing gift in life when one of your children joins you in your life passion.

For the past six years, Nicole Scaramuzzo O'Neill has been my trusted executive assistant. She left briefly to have a baby, but now that Mackenzie is a toddler, Nicole is working with me once again. She has been a godsend on this project, helping with research, photos, and videos.

ACKNOWLEDGMENTS

I've saved the best—my family—for last. For the past few years, they've been very patient and understanding as I split my attention between them and this book. My older daughters, Jamie, Lindsay, and Sarah, are my best friends, my cheerleaders, and also my voices of reason, who are always willing to tell me "Mom, you can't say that" or "Mom, you can't wear that!"

My younger four—Kate, Max, Kim, and Jack—were also understanding as long as I still made myself available to help edit their college essays. I'm eager for them to read this book, although it seems a bit strange that they'll learn so much about me and my life right along with you.

And, finally, to the love of my life, my husband, Jeff—the person who knows me best, who's seen every version of me and still stayed; thanks for always keeping me grounded. Sorry, sweetie, for all the nights I stayed up until the wee hours with my writing—including when I brought my laptop to bed while you were trying to sleep.

You have made my life so wonderful. I love you.